Building a Solid Personal Finance Foundation in Your 20s and 30s

You're finished with school and entering the workforce. You want to make sure you create a firm foundation for your personal finances. Keep the following in mind when you start:

>> **Get a checkup:** Just as you benefit from a health checkup, be sure to get a checkup on your finances to ensure you're making the most of your money and your financial decisions.

>> **Determine what you need with transaction and savings accounts and evaluate which banks and other financial firms offer accounts that best meet your needs.** Be on guard for high fees that erode your savings.

>> **Celebrate the savings habit.** The earlier in life you're able to save money regularly, the smaller the portion of your income you'll need to save to accomplish a given goal. Scrutinize your current spending so you know where your money is going and you can identify what to do about it.

>> **Be on the lookout for spending reduction opportunities.** Regularly saving money, especially on a modest income, is challenging. I present many ideas for reducing your spending, but ultimately, how you cut your spending is a matter of personal preference.

>> **Understand good and bad debt.** Debt can be a useful tool to enable the purchase of real estate or other valuable assets. Avoid consumer debt, such as on credit cards and auto loans. Consumer debt tends to be costly, and the interest isn't tax-deductible.

Managing Finances and Daily Living in Your Young-Adult Years

Getting a paycheck and having a job requires more responsibility. Be sure to consider these important points when you're encountering finances in your 20s and 30s:

» **Know and manage your credit score.** Your *credit score* is a number that quantifies for lenders how likely you are to repay debts. Periodically access your credit reports, which you can do for free, and understand the steps you can take, as needed, to boost your credit score. Also take steps to protect your identity.

» **Consider all options before deciding to rent or buy.** Renting and sharing living space can be both economical and fun if you avoid the pitfalls. Buying and owning may make sense if you see yourself staying put for an extended period of time.

» **Communicate with your partner about money.** Money is often a source of friction in relationships. Thinking about money and planning how to manage it upfront with loved ones is usually time well spent.

Protecting Yourself and Your Income

Insurance plays a significant role in protecting your interests, including your health, your income, your property, and so on. Make sure you insure the following:

» **Your health:** Though you may feel that you're not likely to need it, having health insurance is wise. With a properly designed plan, you can contain the cost and get needed coverage.

» **Your income:** Even if you have no dependents, you surely depend on your income, so you should have long-term disability insurance. And if you have dependents, you may need life insurance, too.

» **Your possessions:** Insurance on your car, home, and other valuable possessions protects those assets from loss and damage and protects you from lawsuits. Beware, though, of small-stuff policies that aren't worth buying.

Praise for Eric Tyson

"Eric Tyson is doing something important — namely, helping people at all income levels to take control of their financial futures. This book is a natural outgrowth of Tyson's vision that he has nurtured for years. Like Henry Ford, he wants to make something that was previously accessible only to the wealthy accessible to middle-income Americans."

— James C. Collins, coauthor of the national bestseller *Built to Last*; former lecturer in business, Stanford Graduate School of Business

"*Personal Finance For Dummies* is the perfect book for people who feel guilty about inadequately managing their money but are intimidated by all of the publications out there. It's a painless way to learn how to take control."

— National Public Radio's *Sound Money*

"Eric Tyson . . . seems the perfect writer for a *For Dummies* book. He doesn't tell you what to do or consider doing without explaining the whys and hows — and the booby traps to avoid — in plain English. . . . It will lead you through the thickets of your own finances as painlessly as I can imagine."

— *Chicago Tribune*

"This book provides easy-to-understand personal financial information and advice for those without great wealth or knowledge in this area. Practitioners like Eric Tyson, who care about the well-being of middle-income people, are rare in today's society."

— Joel Hyatt, founder of Hyatt Legal Services, one of the nation's largest general-practice personal legal service firms

More Bestselling *For Dummies* Titles by Eric Tyson

Investing For Dummies

A *Wall Street Journal* bestseller, this book walks you through how to build wealth in stocks, real estate, and small business as well as other investments. Also check out *Investing in Your 20s and 30s For Dummies*.

Mutual Funds For Dummies

This best-selling guide is now updated to include current fund and portfolio recommendations. Using the practical tips and techniques, you'll design a mutual fund investment plan suited to your income, lifestyle, and risk preferences.

Home Buying Kit For Dummies

America's #1 real-estate book includes coverage of online resources in addition to sound financial advice from Eric Tyson and frontline real-estate insights from industry veteran Ray Brown. Also available from America's best-selling real-estate team of Tyson and Brown: *House Selling For Dummies* and *Mortgages For Dummies* with Robert Griswold.

Real Estate Investing For Dummies

Real estate is a proven wealth-building investment, but many people don't know how to go about making and managing rental property investments. Real-estate and property management expert Robert Griswold and Eric Tyson cover the gamut of property investment options, strategies, and techniques.

Small Business For Dummies

Take control of your future, and make the leap from employee to entrepreneur with this enterprising guide. From drafting a business plan to managing costs, you'll profit from expert advice and real-world examples that cover every aspect of building your own business. Also check out Tyson's *Small Business Taxes For Dummies*.

Personal Finance in Your 20s & 30s

for
dummies®
A Wiley Brand

Personal Finance in Your 20s & 30s

3rd Edition

by Eric Tyson, MBA

Author of *Investing For Dummies* and *Mutual Funds For Dummies*

A Wiley Brand

Personal Finance in Your 20s & 30s For Dummies®, 3rd Edition

Published by: **John Wiley & Sons, Inc.,** 111 River Street, Hoboken, NJ 07030-5774, www.wiley.com

Copyright © 2021 by John Wiley & Sons, Inc., Hoboken, New Jersey

Published simultaneously in Canada

For general information on our other products and services, please contact our Customer Care Department within the U.S. at 877-762-2974, outside the U.S. at 317-572-3993, or fax 317-572-4002. For technical support, please visit https://hub.wiley.com/community/support/dummies.

Wiley publishes in a variety of print and electronic formats and by print-on-demand. Some material included with standard print versions of this book may not be included in e-books or in print-on-demand. If this book refers to media such as a CD or DVD that is not included in the version you purchased, you may download this material at http://booksupport.wiley.com. For more information about Wiley products, visit www.wiley.com.

Library of Congress Control Number: 2021936959

ISBN 978-1-119-80543-4 (pbk); ISBN 978-1-119-80544-1 (ebk); ISBN 978-1-119-80545-8 (ebk)

Manufactured in the United States of America

SKY10037985_110722

Contents at a Glance

Table of Contents

Introduction

Your 20s and 30s are such an exciting time. During this period you're experiencing some dramatic changes in your life, exploring new endeavors, making your way in the world, trying new things, and meeting new people, while hopefully staying in touch with old friends and your family.

But as with anything else in life, your young-adult years can pose challenges as well. Some young people suffered layoffs and reduced employment incomes during the 2008 financial crisis and its aftermath and then again with the 2020 COVID-19 pandemic. Maybe you've experienced a failed relationship and a broken heart. You've likely had to deal with a difficult boss (or two) or a job (or two) you don't like — or perhaps you're in danger of losing your job.

And then there are the money issues. Most of you are out of the nest and out from under your parents' wings, and your 20s are when you experience firsthand earning your own money and paying your own expenses. This isn't true for all twenty-somethings, of course, because some young people still live at home or have some financial dependence on their folks — maybe that's why *they* bought you this book! No matter your living situation, your young adult years can be a challenging time, but this friendly guide can help make those years smoother and more rewarding financially.

About This Book

Based on my experiences teaching courses, counseling clients, writing articles and books, and corresponding with friends, family, and people through my website, I've discovered how important having healthy and strong personal finances is. With that in mind, I wrote this book to help you begin to lay a strong financial foundation. Your early adult years are the best time to start.

I've worked with and taught people from all financial situations, so I know the financial concerns and questions of real folks just like you. Believe it or not, I first became interested in money matters when, as a middle-school student, my father was laid off and received some retirement money. I worked with my dad as he made investing decisions with the money. A couple of years later, I won my high school's science fair with a project on what influences the stock market.

In my 20s, I worked hard to keep my living expenses low and save money so I could leave my job and pursue my entrepreneurial ideas. I accomplished that goal in my late 20s. My goal in writing this book is to give you lots of tools and information to help you get your personal finances in order so you, too, can achieve your goals and dreams.

I also wrote this book to protect you, to watch your back. Hucksters out to separate you from your hard-earned money know an easy mark when they see one, and being young and, therefore, less experienced makes you a target. You're also at increased risk of "being taken" because your generation spends so much time online where the rules and agenda of many sites and apps are murky or worse. The information and advice in this book can help you identify and steer around common pitfalls and bad deals before you suffer the consequences.

Foolish Assumptions

No matter what your current situation is — whether you're entering the job market right after school, graduating college with or without student loans, living with your parents, or living on your own — I thought of you as I wrote this book. I made some assumptions about you:

>> You want expert advice about important financial topics — such as getting a financial checkup, budgeting, paying off some debt, boosting your credit score, and investing — and you want answers quickly.

>> Or perhaps you want a crash course in personal finance and are looking for a book you can read cover to cover to help solidify major financial concepts and get you thinking about your finances in a holistic fashion.

>> Or maybe you're just tired of feeling financially frazzled and want to get better organized and on top of your money matters.

This book is basic enough to help a novice get his or her arms around thorny financial issues. But readers who are a bit more advanced in financial matters will be challenged, as well, to think about their finances in a new way and identify areas for improvement.

Icons Used in This Book

The icons in this book help you find information you need:

TIP

This target flags strategy recommendations for making the most of your money.

REMEMBER

This icon points out information that you definitely want to remember.

WARNING

This icon marks things to avoid and points out common mistakes people make when managing their finances.

INVESTIGATE

This icon tells you when you should consider doing some additional research. Don't worry — I explain what to look for and what to look out for.

Beyond the Book

To view this book's Cheat Sheet, simply go to www.dummies.com and enter "Personal Finance in Your 20s and 30s For Dummies Cheat Sheet" in the Search box. There you'll get quick tips on understanding financial basics, managing day-to-day finances, and growing your money through basic investing.

Where to Go from Here

This book is organized so you can go wherever you want to find complete information. Want advice on minimizing your taxes, for example? Go to Part 2 for that. You can use the table of contents to find broad categories of information or the index to look up more specific topics.

If you're not sure where to go, you may want to start with Part 1. It gives you all the basic info you need to assess your financial situation and points to places where you can find more detailed information for improving it.

1

Getting Started with Personal Finance

Evaluate your net worth, savings rate, credit health, investment portfolio, and insurance coverage.

Develop a savings mindset, as well as budgeting and saving strategies.

Conquer consumer debt and recognize the best uses for loans and the types of debt to avoid.

Get and understand your credit report and credit score. Use your credit report and other tools to prevent identity theft.

Chapter **1**

Your Financial Checkup

Where did your childhood years go? Was it that long ago that you were concerned with what exams you had coming up, what you might be doing over your summer break, and what kind of job you were interested in and qualified to do?

As a young adult, you wonder where you are going to live, how much a decent apartment will cost, and how much you will actually have left over after taxes and those other pesky deductions that are taken from your paycheck. How much will it cost to buy a home that you'll really want? What are the best ways to save and invest your money?

And then life throws you a curveball like the COVID-19 government-mandated shutdowns which turned plenty of young people's lives upside down in a way that few saw coming. Or perhaps an aging parent or other relative needs some help. How can you handle these situations personally and financially?

Those are some pretty big questions that even people 20 and 30 years older than you struggle to answer. You're wise to be thinking about these topics now. In this chapter, I help you start to answer those questions by showing you how to evaluate your net worth (addressing any debt, such as student loans, credit cards, or auto or other consumer loans). I also help you assess your savings rate, credit health, investment portfolio, and insurance coverage so you can develop and implement a winning plan tailored to your situation.

Calculating Your Financial Worth

Having a sense of what you own (your *assets*) and what you owe (your *liabilities*) is important because it provides some measure of your financial security and your ability to accomplish financial goals such as buying a desired car, buying a home, traveling, starting a business, or retiring someday.

In this section, I define net worth and then walk you through the relatively simple calculations of determining your own personal net worth.

Defining net worth

Your *net worth* is quite simply your *financial assets* (for example, checking, savings, and investment accounts) minus your *financial liabilities* (debts such as student loans and credit-card debt). In the following sections, I walk you through how to perform these calculations.

REMEMBER

When I discuss your monetary *net worth*, I'm not talking about personal possessions. Your car, clothing, television, computer, and other personal items all have some value, of course. If you needed to sell them, you could get something for them. But the reality is that you're unlikely to accumulate personal items with the expectation of later selling them to finance such personal goals as buying a home, starting a business, retiring, and so forth. After all, personal property declines rapidly in value after purchase and use.

Figuring what you own: Financial assets

To calculate your financial assets, access your checking/savings, and investment account records, including retirement accounts and any other documentation that can help you. You may have only one or two accounts, and that's fine. The COVID-19 pandemic has proven the absolute need for emergency fund savings. Add up all the values of these accounts to find out what you own.

It's common for most young adults to be in the early stages of accumulating assets. This book helps you change and improve upon that.

In addition to excluding personal property and possessions because folks don't generally sell those to accomplish their personal and financial goals, I would also probably exclude your home as an asset if you happen to own one. (You can include it if you expect to downsize or to rent in retirement and live off of some of your home's equity.) Include investment real estate — that is, real estate that you own and rent out.

VALUING SOCIAL SECURITY AND PENSIONS

Now or in the years ahead, you may accumulate some retirement benefits based on your years of work. You may do so through the federal government's Social Security program and/or through an employer's pension plan.

When you work and earn money, your employer (or you if you're self-employed) pays taxes into Social Security, which earns you future Social Security retirement income benefits. Under current laws, which of course may change, you're eligible to receive full Social Security benefits at age 67. (You may collect a benefit reduced by 30 percent if you begin receiving your Social Security payments at age 62.)

In surveys, most young adults say that they're more likely to believe in things like UFOs than in actually getting money out of Social Security! Although being skeptical and questioning things is useful, such deep cynicism about Social Security isn't well founded. Those who are eligible to receive benefits (generally, folks who've paid Social Security taxes above relatively low threshold amounts over at least ten years in total) should get them. As a young adult, it's important for you to also know that some Social Security benefits, such as disability and survivorship benefits for your children under 18, are a part of your Social Security insurance coverage.

Some employers provide a retirement benefit known as a pension that's paid to you in retirement based on your years of service (employment) with the organization. Your employer puts aside money above and beyond your salary compensation into a separate account to fund your future pension payments. Pension plans are more common in public-sector organizations (governments, schools, and so on) and larger companies, especially those with labor unions. Pension plans are generally insured/guaranteed by government agency entities.

Now, I do have one exception to something that isn't generally thought of as a financial asset, which you may or may not want to include in this category. Some people have valuable collections of particular items, be they collectible coins, sports memorabilia, or whatever. You can count such collections as assets, but remember that they're only real assets if you'd be willing to sell them and use the proceeds toward one of your goals.

Determining what you owe: Financial liabilities

Most people accumulate debts and loans during periods in life when their expenditures exceed their income. I did that when I went through college. You may have student loans, an auto loan, credit-card debts, or a medical or pet debt. Access any statements that document your loans and debts and figure out the grand total of what you owe.

Netting the difference

After you total your financial assets and your financial liabilities, you can subtract the latter from the former to arrive at your *net worth*:

financial assets – financial liabilities = net worth

Don't worry if you have a small or negative net worth (where you have more debt than assets). There's no point wringing your hands over the results — you can't change history. And, it doesn't matter how you compare with your peers even if we can accurately define exactly who your peers are. *This isn't a competition or test.*

But you can change the direction of your finances in the future and boost your net worth surprisingly fast to work toward accomplishing your personal goals. First, you have to figure your savings rate and how to increase it, which I discuss next.

Grasping the Importance of Your Savings Rate

To accomplish important personal and financial goals such as building an emergency fund, buying a home, starting a business, traveling, and someday retiring, most folks need to save money. Some exceptions do exist, such as those folks who have trust funds or inherit significant-enough sums that they don't need to save money from their work earnings. But the vast majority of people must save in order to accomplish their goals.

You can't effectively save for a long-term goal if you don't know what your savings rate is. When I worked as a financial counselor and taught adult-education money-management courses (which I now do online), I was struck by how few people knew the rate at which they were saving money. Most people can tell you how much they earned from their work over the past year, but few folks really know what portion of their employment income they were able to save. That's because to have an accurate idea of this percentage, you really need to do some analysis and calculations. The math isn't that complicated, but it does require some time and effort, especially if you haven't been tracking your spending or net worth over the past year. In the following sections, I explain a couple of different ways to calculate your savings rate over the past year.

Calculating your income and outgo

The first way to determine your savings rate is to tally your employment income and expenses over the past year. By subtracting your total expenses, including taxes, from the past year from your employment income, you can arrive at *net savings*.

The *employment income* part of the equation is simple for most folks — it's simply the total amount of your paychecks from work. (If you have work from side or gig jobs you do outside of your regular job, be sure to count that too.) But unless you systematically track your spending, that piece of the puzzle is a lot more work to figure. I walk you through how to compile your spending in Chapter 5.

Assessing the change in your net worth

If you don't want to be bothered with the time-consuming task of tabulating your spending over the past year, here's an alternative method for arriving at your savings rate that may be quicker for you. Follow these few easy steps, and fill in the blanks in Table 1-1.

1. **Calculate your net worth.**

   Refer to the earlier section "Netting the difference" for an explanation of how to do so.

2. **Calculate your net worth from one year ago.**

   You can determine your year-ago net worth by tallying your financial assets (savings and investments) from one year ago and subtracting your financial liabilities (loans and debts) from one year ago. Don't count your home as an asset or your mortgage as a liability. Your concern here is financial assets.

3. **Correct for any changes in value of investments you owned the past year.**

   Suppose that your net worth today is $15,000, whereas one year ago it was $10,000. You might conclude from the change in your net worth that you've saved $5,000 ($15,000 – $10,000), but that figure may not be correct, and here's why. A year ago when you had a net worth of $10,000, you presumably had savings and investments, and those would have changed in value over the past year. Suppose you made some good investments and they produced $1,000 in returns (from interest, dividends, appreciation, and so on) over the past 12 months. Though you're happy to have made $1,000 on your investments, that money isn't new savings and shouldn't be counted in your savings-rate calculations. So you really saved $4,000 ($5,000 – $1,000).

Conversely, if your net worth was reduced over the past year by declines in the value of your investments, you should add back that figure when determining your savings rate. If your investments declined by $1,500 in value over the past year, you really saved $6,500 ($5,000 + $1,500). Table 1-1 walks you through this part of the analysis.

TABLE 1-1   ## Your Savings Rate over the Past Year

Calculate your net worth now and one year ago

Today	One Year Ago
Savings & investments $_____	Savings & invest-ments $_____
– Loans & debts $_____	– Loans & debts $_____
= Net worth today $_____	= Net worth a year ago $_____
Correct for changes in value of investments you owned the past year	
Net worth today	$_____ _____
– Net worth a year ago	$_____ _____
– Appreciation of investments (over past year)	$_____ _____
+ Depreciation of investments (over past year)	$_____ _____
= Savings amount	$_____ _____
Annual gross income	$_____ _____
Savings rate (savings amount divided by your annual gross income)	_____ _____ %

REMEMBER

If you have debt that you've been paying down over the past year, you can count the principal payment reduction on that debt as savings. For example, suppose a year ago you owed $5,000 on an auto loan. Now, a year later, you owe just $4,500. You can count that $500 reduction in what you owe as new savings.

Understanding and Improving Your Credit Score

If you expect to someday apply for a loan of any type and get a competitively low interest rate, you should understand your credit report and credit score and how to improve each. A *credit report* is basically your credit history, while a *credit score* is a three-digit score based on the information in your personal credit report. This section highlights what you need to know about your credit score and reports, including how to obtain and improve them. Chapter 4 provides more insight into managing your credit report and credit score.

Deciphering how lenders use credit reports and scores

Most people borrow money at various times in their life, whether it's to buy a home (or other real estate), to finance a small business, pay for educational expenses, or for other purposes. When you want to borrow money, lenders examine your credit report and your credit score(s) to determine how responsible you've been with credit and to help them decide whether they should lend you money (and if so, how much to charge you based on your creditworthiness habits).

Specifically, lenders examine your history of credit usage in your credit report. This information tells the lender when each of your accounts was opened, what the recent balance is, your track record of making payments on time, and whether you've defaulted on any loans. A credit report also tells a prospective lender where else you've been applying for credit most recently.

Lenders use your credit score to help them predict the likelihood that you'll default on repaying your borrowings. The higher your credit score the better, because a high credit score means that you have a lower likelihood of defaulting on a loan. Thus, more lenders will be willing to extend you credit and charge you lower rates for that credit. It's important for you to know your credit score because a high credit score puts you in a negotiating position to ask for better rates. Lenders are in the moneymaking business and many don't automatically give you the best rate for which you qualify.

The most widely used credit score is the FICO score, which was developed by the FICO company (formerly known as Fair, Isaac and Company). FICO scores range from a low of 300 to a high of 850. Most scores fall in the 600s and 700s, and the median is around 720. You generally qualify for the best lending rates if your credit score is in the mid-700s or higher.

Obtaining your credit reports and fixing errors

You want to get your hands on your credit report so you know what lenders are reviewing. You're entitled to receive a free copy of your credit report (which does *not* contain your credit score) every 12 months from each of the three credit bureaus — Equifax, Experian, and TransUnion. If you visit www.annualcreditreport.com, you can view and print copies of your credit report from each of the three credit agencies. (Alternatively, you can call 877-322-8228 and request that your reports be mailed to you.) You could also order your credit report from a different bureau every four months.

When you obtain your reports, inspect them for possible mistakes. Credit-reporting bureaus and the creditors who report credit information to these bureaus make plenty of errors.

If your problems are fixable, there's no need to hire someone to do so for you — you can fix them yourself, but you will likely have to make some phone calls or submit a dispute online via email or by writing a letter or two.

Some credit-report errors arise from other people's negative information getting on your credit report. This can happen if you have a common name, have moved a lot, or for other reasons. If the problematic information on your report appears not to be yours, tell that particular credit bureau and explain that you need more information because you don't recognize the creditor.

Creditors are the source of some reporting mistakes as well. For example, perhaps a bill you paid off is still incorrectly being reported as a balance you owe. If that's the case with your report, write or call the creditor to get the incorrect information fixed. Phoning first usually works best. (The credit bureau should be able to tell you how to reach the creditor if you don't know how.) If necessary, follow up with an email (preferred because it leaves a trail) or letter. You can also dispute errors online directly with the credit reporting agency.

TIP

Whether you speak with a credit bureau or an actual lender, make notes of your conversations. If representatives say that they can fix the problem, retain their contact information, and follow up with them if they don't deliver the promised results. If you're ensnared in bureaucratic red tape, escalate the situation by speaking with a department manager. By law, bureaus are required to respond to a request to fix a credit error within 30 days. And if you file a dispute and the creditor doesn't respond, the credit bureau must then remove the derogatory item.

You and a creditor may not see eye to eye on a problem, and the creditor may refuse to budge. If that's the case, credit bureaus are required by law to allow you to add a 100-word explanation to your credit file. Just remember that if you go this route, be factual in your write-up and steer clear of broad attacks on the creditor (such as "their customer service sucks"). You'll find sample 100-word statements online and a place to enter your statement on each bureau's website. Or, you can mail your statement to the bureau.

Avoid "credit-repair" firms that claim to be able to fix your credit report problems. In the worst cases I've seen, these firms charge outrageous amounts of money and don't come close to fulfilling their marketing hype. If you have legitimate glitches on your credit report, credit-repair firms can't make the glitches disappear. As I explain earlier in this section, you can easily fix errors on your own without the charge.

Getting your credit score

Many folks are disappointed to find that their credit reports lack their credit score. The reason for this is quite simple: The 2003 law mandating that the three credit agencies provide a free credit report annually to each U.S. citizen who requests a copy did *not* mandate that they provide the credit score. Thus, if you want to obtain your credit score, it's generally going to cost you.

One circumstance allows you to get one of your credit scores for free, but unfortunately, you can only do so when you're turned down for a loan. Current law allows you to obtain a free copy of the credit score a lender used in making a negative decision regarding your desired loan.

For recommended websites to use to obtain your credit score as well as those to avoid, please see Chapter 4.

Improving your credit reports and score

Take an interest in improving your credit standing and score rather than throwing money away to buy your credit score or paying for some ongoing monitoring service to which you may not pay attention. Working to boost your credit rating is especially worthwhile if you know that your credit report contains detrimental information or if your score is lower than 740.

TIP

Here are the most important actions that you can take to boost your attractiveness to lenders:

>> **Check your credit reports for accuracy.** Correct any errors, and be especially sure to get accounts removed if they aren't yours and they show late payments or have gone to collection. Refer to the earlier section "Obtaining your credit reports and fixing errors" for more information.

>> **Pay all your bills on time.** To ensure on-time payments, sign up for automatic bill payment, which most companies encourage customers to use. This enables companies to automatically deduct (typically monthly) what you owe from your checking account or to charge that amount to your credit card so you don't have to remember to pay the bill. (This also prevents you from being charged interest or late fees when you make a payment after the due date.) On-time payments carry the most weight when calculating your credit score.

>> **Be loyal if it doesn't cost you.** The older the age of loan accounts you have open, the better for your credit rating. Closing old accounts and opening a bunch of new ones generally lowers your credit score, so don't jump at a new credit-card offer unless it's really going to save you money. Examples would include if you're carrying credit-card debt at a high interest rate and want to transfer that balance to a lower-rate card or a card that provides you with rewards/benefits greatly in excess of any costs. Ask your current credit-card provider to match a lower rate you find elsewhere.

>> **Limit your total debt and number of debt accounts.** The more loans, especially consumer loans (credit cards, auto loans, and so on), that you hold and the higher the balances, the lower your credit score will be. Work to pay down consumer revolving debt, such as on an auto loan and credit cards. See Chapter 5 for more information.

Comprehending Your Investment Options

If you're like most folks in their 20s or 30s, you may not have saved as much as you would have liked during your early working years. That's fine for now, because together, we address that in this book. Regardless of how much (or how little) you have invested in banks, mutual funds, or other types of accounts, you want to invest your money in the wisest way possible and have it grow over time without exposing it to extraordinary risks.

In this section, I provide some background to help you understand how to best focus your efforts to become a more knowledgeable and successful investor. (In Part 3, I delve into all the important details of investing.)

>> **Investment options:** Making the best investments without understanding your range of options and the strengths and weaknesses of each is difficult. Do you understand the investments that you currently own, including their potential returns and risks? If you invest in or plan to invest in individual stocks, do you understand how to evaluate a stock, including reviewing the company's balance sheet, income statement, competitive position, price-earnings ratio versus its peer group, and so on?

Last but not least are issues that come up if you work with a financial advisor for investment advice. Do you understand what that person is recommending that you do, are you comfortable with those actions and that advisor, and is that person compensated in a way that minimizes potential conflicts of interest in the strategies and investments he or she recommends? See Chapter 18 for advice on hiring professionals.

>> **Tax considerations:** For many working people, taxes are either the number-one or -two largest expense categories. For starters, do you know what marginal income tax bracket (combined federal and state) you're in, and do you factor that in when selecting investments? For money outside of retirement accounts, do you understand how these investments produce income and gains and whether these types of investments make the most sense given your tax situation?

>> **Short-term money:** *Short-term money* includes money you'd use in an emergency or for a major purchase within the next few years. Do you have enough money set aside for short-term emergencies, and is that money in an investment where it doesn't fluctuate in value? Is the money that you're going to need for a major expenditure in the next few years invested in a conservative, low-volatility investment?

>> **Long-term money:** *Long-term money* includes money set aside for longer-term use such as for retirement. Do you have your money in different, diversified investments that aren't dependent on one or a few securities or one type of investment (that is, bonds, stocks, real estate, and so on)? Is the money that you've earmarked for longer-term purposes (more than five years) invested to produce returns that are greater than the rate of inflation?

Examining Insurance Coverage

Just about everyone dislikes spending money on insurance. Who enjoys thinking about risks and possible catastrophes and then shopping for insurance that you hope will pay some of the bills should said catastrophes strike? Therein lie some major reasons why most people don't have all the coverage they really need and don't get the best value when they do buy insurance. But folks who've suffered a major loss understand the security provided by a good policy.

In Part 4, I discuss everything you need to know about insurance, including what policies you do and don't need. Here are the major points to consider as you review your insurance knowledge:

>> **Smart shopping:** Do you know when it makes sense to buy insurance through companies that sell directly to the public (bypassing agents) — and when it doesn't? Do you shop around for the best price on your insurance policies at least every couple of years? Do you know whether your insurance companies have good track records when it comes to paying claims and keeping customers satisfied?

>> **Coverage understanding:** Do you understand the individual coverages, protection types, and amounts of each insurance policy you have? Does your current insurance protection make sense given your current personal and financial situation (as opposed to your situation when you bought the policies)?

>> **Income protection:** If you wouldn't be able to make it financially without your employment income, do you have adequate long-term disability insurance coverage? If you have family members who are dependent on your continued working income, do you have adequate life-insurance coverage to replace your income should you die?

>> **Liability protection:** Do you carry enough liability insurance on your home, car (including umbrella/excess liability), and business to protect all your assets?

Identifying Common Financial Mistakes Young Adults Make

Your financial checkup is complete if you've been working along with me since the beginning of this chapter. The results should help you best understand where you can get the biggest return on your time invested elsewhere in the book.

One motivation for reading the rest of the book is to reduce your chances of making common mistakes. Your 20s and 30s are decades where lack of financial knowledge is exposed and reflected in the beginning of costly money mistakes such as

>> **Spending excessively and accumulating consumer debt:** Too many young adults leave home being experts in spending without having learned much about living within their means and saving and investing. Many things may tempt you — the never-ending stream of gadgets and electronics, cars, restaurants, bars, nightclubs, new clothing, concerts, sporting events, and so on. Check out Chapter 5 for information about reducing your spending on items you don't need.

>> **Defaulting on student loans or other debts:** This problem is often the consequence of the preceding problem of spending too much and accumulating too much debt. Being overwhelmed with debt, which may be exacerbated by a job loss or unexpected expenses, can cause folks to fall behind on their student loan or other debt payments. Given the ridiculously high cost of college these days, the amount of student debt that some young graduates have accumulated is also ridiculously large! See Chapter 3 for information on paying down debts.

>> **Experiencing failed relationships that damage your credit rating and financial health:** You know what they say about love being blind sometimes, right? Well, one of the things many 20- and 30-somethings don't think about when in a relationship is how the things they're doing are going to work out or not work out should the relationship fail. Sharing bank accounts and bill paying may not present glaring problems when everything is going well, but you can quickly end up with a tarnished credit report should your love boat run aground. See Chapter 8 for info about relationships and money.

>> **Falling behind on tax payments and violating tax laws:** Filing your annual tax return and making quarterly tax payments if you're self-employed aren't enjoyable tasks. In fact, you may find these chores downright intimidating and stressful. But if you fail to complete them correctly, or complete them at all, you could get socked with hefty interest and penalty charges and possibly do some jail time in the worst cases. Check out Chapter 6 for a complete discussion of paying taxes.

>> **Making poor investments:** You work hard to earn money and then to save it. So you should do your homework to ensure that you invest it well. Don't rush into making an investment you don't understand, because you have a lot to lose. There are plenty of slick-talking salesmen who will sell you an investment that helps to line their pockets but not yours. You also don't want your money sitting around for years on end in a low-interest bank account, which is what often happens to folks who don't know how to invest. Go to Chapter 10 for more in-depth information about investing your money.

>> **Neglecting to secure proper insurance coverage:** Most young people don't spend a lot of time thinking about risks. After all, most young adults are healthy and energetic. So things like health insurance or disability insurance seem unnecessary and for older folks. The good news is that insurance costs less when you're younger because you're less likely to suffer a major illness or disability than someone decades older than you. See the chapters in Part 4 for all the details about insurance.

>> **Being taken and duped by biased and/or shoddy advice:** Many companies and people have something to sell. Some of what they're selling is good stuff, much is mediocre, and some is downright awful. You don't need to pay high commissions or end up in the wrong type of investments or insurance. Check out Chapter 18 for what you need to know about dealing with professionals.

Chapter **2**

Budgeting, Goal Setting, and Valuing Saving

U nless you're the offspring of wealthy parents or grandparents who have left you a sizable sum of money, you need to save money to accomplish your personal and financial goals. Early in your working years, saving money can be a challenge, of course, especially since you're likely not earning a super-high income.

When you're first starting out, your salary is probably somewhat low, and after fixed expenses (such as rent/mortgage, food, insurance, cell-phone service, and other payments that you can't easily get rid of), you may not have much money left for "fun" discretionary spending, let alone additional savings. Remember, though, that when it comes to building wealth, it doesn't matter what you make — it's what you spend and, therefore, are able to save. Many wealthy people didn't get rich based exclusively on their big salaries, but through disciplined savings and wise investing over time.

In this chapter, I discuss smart budgeting strategies and the tremendous and surprising long-term value that comes from regular saving and investing.

Developing a Savings Mindset

People typically learn their financial habits, both good and not so good, at a young age. During childhood, most people are exposed to messages and lessons about money, both at home with their parents and siblings and also in the world at large, such as at school; with their friends; and through society and media, including social media. In fact, social media presents a challenge to the savings mindset and has taken center stage in marketing to young adults on ways to spend their money.

The expression "You can't teach an old dog new tricks" has some validity, at least for our four-legged friends, but even then, the expression actually requires some modification to be accurate. It should be, "It's hard to teach an old dog new tricks, but how hard it is depends on the dog."

My experiences have shown me the same to be true for people and their financial habits and decision making. For most people, spending money is easier and more enjoyable than earning and saving it. Of course, you can and should spend money, but there's a world of difference between spending money carelessly and spending money wisely.

I show you how to save money, even if you haven't been a good saver before. And even if you do think you're pretty good at saving, I have some tips and tricks so you can get even better at saving more and spending less:

>> **Live within your means.** Spending too much is a relative problem. If you spend $40,000 per year and your income is $50,000 annually, you should be in good shape and will be able to save a decent chunk of your income. But if your income is only $35,000 per year and you spend $40,000 annually, you'll be accumulating debt or spending from your investments to finance your lifestyle.

TIP

How much you can safely spend while working toward your financial goals depends on what your goals are and where you are financially. At a minimum, you should be saving at least 5 percent of your gross annual income (*pretax* — that is, before taxes are deducted from your paycheck), and ideally, you should save at least 10 percent.

>> **Search for the best values.** The expression "You get what you pay for" is an excuse for being a lazy shopper. The truth is that you can find high quality and low cost in the same product. Conversely, paying a high price is no guarantee that you're getting high quality. When you evaluate the cost of a product or service, think in terms of total, long-term costs. Buying a cheaper product only to spend a lot of additional money servicing and repairing it is no bargain. Research options and comparison shop to understand what's important to

you. Don't waste money on bells and whistles that you don't need and may not ever use. Is that $700 (or $1,000) smartphone significantly better than the best $200 or $300 smartphones?

>> **Don't assume brand names are the best.** Be suspicious of companies that spend gobs on image-oriented advertising. Branding is often used to charge premium prices. Blind taste tests have demonstrated that consumers can't readily discern quality differences between high- and low-cost brands with many products. Question the importance of the name and image of the products you buy. Companies spend a lot of money creating and cultivating an image, which has no impact on how their products taste or perform.

TIP

When you're grocery shopping, consider the store or house brand. Most of the time the ingredients are the same as the brand-name product (and may even be made by that same manufacturer). You don't need to shell out money to pay for the name, as store/house brands are typically much less costly than the well-known brands in a given category.

>> **Get your refunds.** Have you ever bought a product or service and not gotten what was promised? What did you do about it? Most people do nothing and let the company off the hook. Ask for your money back or at least a partial refund.

TIP

If you don't get satisfaction from a frontline employee, request to speak with a supervisor. Most larger companies have websites through which you can submit complaints. Reputable companies that stand behind their products and services will offer partial refunds or gift cards good toward a future purchase. If all else fails and you bought the item with your credit or debit card, dispute the charge with the credit-card company. You generally have up to 60 days to dispute and get your money back.

>> **Trim your spending fat.** What you spend your money on is sometimes a matter of habit rather than a matter of what you really want or value. When was the last time you comparison priced and shopped for the most common things that you buy? See Chapter 5 for lots of tips for reducing your spending.

>> **Turn your back on consumer credit (for example, credit-card debt, auto loans).** Borrowing money to buy consumer items that depreciate (such as cars and electronics) is hazardous to your long-term financial health. Buy only what you can afford today. If you'll be forced to carry a debt on credit cards or an auto loan for many months or years, you can't really afford what you're buying on credit today (see Chapter 19 for the details on saving on cars). Not only does consumer debt enable you to spend more than you can afford today, but the interest rate on that consumer debt is generally high, and it isn't tax-deductible.

REMEMBER

If you spend too much and spend unwisely, you put pressure on your income and your future need to continue working, perhaps at a job that you don't really enjoy. Savings dwindle, debts may accumulate, and you won't be able to achieve your personal and financial goals. Living within your means and continually growing your savings can give you more freedom, choices, and comfort with taking some risks (for example, changing careers, leaving your job to raise children, joining a start-up or starting your own company, and so on) that you may not otherwise feel as comfortable taking.

What It's Worth: Valuing Savings over Time

Without a doubt, the amazing financial success stories get the headlines. You hear about company founders who make millions — sometimes billions — of dollars. Early investors in stocks such as Apple, Google, and Facebook have made gargantuan returns. Who wouldn't want to make a return of 100 times, 200 times, or more on his investment?

REMEMBER

However, expecting to make such gargantuan returns is a recipe for disappointment and problems. (In Chapter 10, I discuss how to use the best investments in stocks, real estate, and small business to earn generous long-term returns.) The vast, vast majority of folks I've worked with and seen accumulate long-term wealth have done well because they regularly save money and they invest in somewhat riskier assets that produce expected long-term returns well above the rate of inflation, as the following sections discuss.

The power of continual savings

Continually saving money on a regular basis can generate amazingly large returns.

For example, suppose you haven't been able to save money because your spending equals your income. Further suppose you earn (after taxes) an extra $1,000 this year at a side job and you decide to save that money. In future years, you decide it's not worth the bother to do the extra work, so you're unable to save the money.

Now, compare that situation to one where you reduce your spending so you can save $1,000 per year every year from your employment earnings. In both cases, assume that you put the money in a savings account and earn 3 percent annually (which has actually been about the long-term average over the generations). Historically, such a return is achievable from bonds. Table 2-1 shows an example.

TABLE 2-1

Nest Egg Growth

Amount Saved	Nest Egg after 40 Years
One-time $1,000 saved	$3,260
$1,000 saved annually	$75,400

That's quite a stunning difference, huh? And that's just putting away the small amount of $1,000 annually and earning a modest 3 percent per year (and you can do better than that as I highlight in the next section). If you can put away $5,000 or $10,000 annually, then simply multiply the figures by 5 or 10.

The rewards of earning a (slightly) higher annual return on your investment

When you save money, you want to try and get higher returns. Bonds, stocks, and other investment vehicles (check out Chapter 10) typically produce much better long-term average returns than a savings account or a certificate of deposit (CD), which usually offers a measly 3 percent annual return over the long term (or much less in recent years). The trade-off with the stocks, bonds, and such is that you must be able to withstand shorter-term declines in those investments' values.

If you put together a diversified portfolio of mostly stocks and a lesser number of bonds, for example, you should be able to earn about 8 percent per year, on average, over the long term. You won't, of course, earn that amount every year — some years it will be less and some years it will be more. The following table shows how much you'd have after 40 years if you got a 3 percent annual return versus an 8 percent annual return.

Investment	3% Annual Return over 40 Years	8% Annual Return over 40 Years
One-time $1,000 saved	$3,260	$21,720
$1,000 saved annually	$75,400	$259,060

When you combine regular saving with more-aggressive yet sensible investing, you end up with lots more money.

Saving $1,000 yearly and getting just an average 8 percent annual return results in a nest egg of $259,060 in 40 years compared to ending up with just $3,260 if you invest $1,000 one time at a 3 percent return over the same time period. And remember, if you can save more — such as $5,000 or $10,000 annually — you can multiply these numbers by 5 or 10.

With historic annual inflation running at about 3 percent, you're basically treading water if you're only earning a 3 percent investment return. In other words, your investments may be worth more, but the cost of other things will have increased as well, so the overall purchasing power of your money won't have increased. As I discuss in Chapter 10, the goal of long-term investors is to grow the purchasing power of their portfolio, and that's where investments (such as stocks and bonds) with expected higher returns play a part.

Budgeting and Boosting Your Savings

When most people hear the word *budgeting*, they think unpleasant thoughts, like those associated with dieting, and rightfully so. Who wants to count calories or dollars and pennies? But *budgeting* — planning your future spending — can help you move from knowing how much you spend on various things to reducing your spending.

The following process breaks down budgeting in simple steps:

1. Analyze how and where you're currently spending.

Chapter 5 explains how to conduct your spending analysis.

2. Calculate how much more you want to save each month.

Everyone has different goals. This book can help you develop yours and figure how much you should be saving to accomplish them.

3. Determine where to make cuts in your spending.

Where you decide to make reductions is a personal decision. While many people need to save more (and spend less) to accomplish their goals, it's possible you may not need to reduce your spending. In Chapter 5, I provide plenty of ideas for how and where to make reductions if you're among the many who want to save a greater portion of your current earnings.

Suppose you're currently not saving any of your monthly income and you want to save 10 percent for retirement. If you can save and invest through a tax-sheltered retirement account — such as a 401(k), 403(b), SEP-IRA, and so forth (see the section "Valuing retirement accounts and financial independence" later in this chapter) — then you don't actually need to cut your spending by 10 percent to reach a savings goal of 10 percent of your gross income.

When you contribute money to a tax-deductible retirement account, you generally reduce your federal and state income taxes. If you're a moderate-income earner paying approximately 30 percent in federal and state taxes on your *marginal income* (see Chapter 6), you actually need to reduce your spending by only 7 percent to save 10 percent. The other 3 percent of the savings comes from the lowering of your taxes. (The higher your tax bracket, the less you need to cut your spending to reach a particular savings goal.)

So to boost your savings rate to 10 percent, you simply need to go through your current spending, category by category, until you come up with enough proposed cuts to reduce your overall spending by 7 percent. Make your cuts in areas that are the least painful and in areas where you're getting the least value from your current level of spending.

REMEMBER

If you don't have access to a tax-deductible retirement account or you're saving for other goals in nonretirement accounts, budgeting still involves the same process of assessment and making reductions in various spending categories.

CONSIDERING ANOTHER BUDGETING METHOD

Another method of budgeting involves starting completely from scratch rather than examining your current expenses and making cuts from that starting point. Ask yourself how much you'd like to spend on different areas (such as rent, meals out, and so on). This is called *zero-based budgeting*.

The advantage of this approach is that it doesn't allow your current spending levels to constrain your thinking. Just because your current rent is $1,500 per month doesn't mean that it needs to remain there. When your current lease expires, you could change your housing arrangements and perhaps find a nice rental you can share with others. I did this in my early years after college, and doing so enabled me to keep my rent low and save more money.

You'll likely be amazed at the discrepancies between what you think you should be spending and what you actually are spending in certain categories. Take going out to eat, to bars, and to concerts, for example. You may think that spending $150 per month is reasonable and then discover that you've been averaging $250 per month in this category. Thus, you'd need to slash your spending here by 40 percent to get to your target.

Setting and Prioritizing Your Savings Goals

You probably have some financial goals. If you don't, you should begin thinking about some personal and financial goals you want to reach. Because everyone is unique, you surely have different goals than your parents, friends, neighbors, and siblings. Although goals may differ from person to person, accomplishing personal and financial goals almost always requires saving money. In this section, I discuss common financial goals and how to work toward them.

REMEMBER

Unless you earn a large income from your work or have a family inheritance to fall back on, your personal and financial desires probably outstrip your resources. Thus, you have to make choices.

Identifying common goals of accomplished savers

As a result of my experience counseling and teaching people about better personal financial management, I can share with you the common traits among folks who accomplish their goals. No matter how much money they made, the people I worked with who were the most successful were the ones who identified reasonable goals and worked toward them.

Among the common goals for young adults with whom I've worked are the following:

>> **Making major purchases:** You need to plan for major purchases. So if you have a future purchase in mind for a car, living-room furniture, the newest smartphone, vacations, and so on, you should save toward that.

>> **Owning a business:** Many people want to pursue the dream of starting and running their own business. The primary reason that most people continue just to dream is that they lack the money (and a specific plan) to leave their job. Although many businesses don't require gobs of start-up cash, almost all require that you withstand a substantial reduction in your income during the early years.

>> **Buying a home:** Renting and dealing with landlords can be a financial and emotional drag, so most folks aspire to buy and own their own home. Real estate has a pretty solid track record as a long-term investment. Sure, there are downturns just as there are in the stock market, but buying during such times may be good because real estate is more affordable then. (See Chapter 7 for more on housing.)

>> **Starting a family/educating kids:** Having children leads some parents to cut back on work, which requires planning for living on a reduced income and facing higher expenses. And, if you have kids or are planning to have kids, you may want to help them get a college education or other higher education. Unfortunately, that can cost a truckload of dough. Although you may never be in a position to cover all that cost, you'd probably like to be able to pay for a portion of it.

>> **Retiring:** *Retiring* is a catchall term for discontinuing full-time work, or perhaps not even working for pay at all. It can also mean achieving financial independence and feeling that you no longer have to work for the income. While your retirement may still be many years away, planning ahead for retirement is important. You may enjoy working and thus may not have given retirement much thought, but most people eventually do want to retire, and you want to be prepared. I address how to do that in the next section.

Valuing retirement accounts and financial independence

Where possible, focus on saving and investing in accounts that offer you tax advantages. Retirement accounts — such as a 401(k), 403(b), SEP-IRA, and so on — offer tax breaks to people of all economic means. So, start thinking of them as "tax reduction" accounts, rather than retirement accounts! In fact, lower-income and moderate-income earners have some additional tax breaks not available to higher-income earners (see my discussion of them later in this section).

Consider the following advantages to investing in retirement accounts:

>> **Contributions are generally tax-deductible.** By putting money in a retirement account, you not only plan wisely for your future but also get an immediate financial reward: lower income taxes. Paying less in income taxes now means more money is available for saving and investing. Retirement account contributions are generally not taxed at either the federal or state income-tax level until withdrawal (but they're still subject to Social Security and Medicare taxes when earned).

If you're paying, say, 30 percent between federal and state taxes (see Chapter 6 to determine your tax bracket and get more details on tax-reduction strategies), a $5,000 contribution to a retirement account immediately lowers your income taxes by $1,500.

>> **Returns on your investment compound over time without taxation.**
After you put money into a retirement account, any interest, dividends, and
appreciation (investment returns) add to your account without being taxed.
Of course, there's no such thing as a free lunch; these accounts don't generally
allow for complete tax avoidance. Yet you can get a really great lunch at a
discount: You get to defer income taxes on all the accumulating gains and
profits until you withdraw the money down the road. Thus, more money is
working for you over a longer period of time. (Health savings accounts, which
I discuss in Chapter 14, can offer complete tax avoidance. Also, though it
offers no upfront tax breaks, the Roth IRA, which I discuss in Chapter 6,
enables future tax-free withdrawals.)

>> **Lower-income earners can get a special tax credit.** In addition to the tax
breaks I discuss previously, U.S. tax laws also provide a special tax *credit*,
which is a percentage (ranging from 10 to 50 percent) of the first $2,000
contributed (or $4,000 on a joint return) to a retirement account. Unlike a
deduction, a tax credit directly reduces your tax bill by the amount of the
credit. The credit isn't available to those under the age of 18, full-time
students, or people who are claimed as dependents on someone else's
tax return.

Married couples filing jointly with adjusted gross incomes (AGIs) of less than
$66,000 and single taxpayers with an adjusted gross income of less than
$33,000 can earn this retirement saver's tax credit (claimed on Form 8880) for
retirement account contributions.

>> **Matching money may be available.** In some company retirement accounts,
companies match a portion of your own contributions. Thus, in addition to tax
breaks, you get free extra money (terms vary by company) courtesy of your
employer. But you have to contribute some of your own money to get the
matching money. If you don't, you're essentially throwing away money, which
you should never do!

Dealing with competing goals

Unless you enjoy paying higher taxes, you may wonder why you'd choose to save
money outside of retirement accounts, which shelter your money from taxation.
The reason is that some personal and financial goals aren't readily achieved by
saving in retirement accounts. Also, retirement accounts have caps on the amount
you can contribute annually and restrictions for accessing the account.

TIP

Because you're constrained by your financial resources, you need to prioritize your goals. Before funding your retirement accounts and racking up those tax breaks, you should consider your other goals, such as starting or buying a business or buying a home.

If you withdraw funds from traditional retirement accounts before age 59½, you not only have to pay income taxes on the withdrawals but also usually have to pay early withdrawal penalties — 10 percent of the withdrawn amount in federal tax, plus whatever your state charges. So if you're accumulating money for a down payment on a home or to start or buy a business, you probably should save that money outside of a retirement account so you get penalty-free access to the funds.

Saving When You're Strapped

You know that putting aside some money on a regular basis is important, but you may wonder how realistic it is, especially when you're burdened with a never-ending list of bills or are starting out on your own. And, those six-figure-per-year jobs haven't yet come your way! So what do you do? The first and most important thing is to work at paying down high-cost debt (see Chapter 3).

TIP

You can get into the habit of saving even when your income is low. Even if you can set aside just $25 or $50 of every paycheck, you're on the road. As you earn raises or bonuses, you can increase the amount you save. The bottom line: Put a little in savings on a regular basis. Develop the savings habit by making it automatic from your paycheck or an automatic draft from your bank or other transaction account into a savings or investment account.

TIP

You may consider getting a second job. You can put the money you make from this second job right into savings. Don't even touch it. If you decide to get a part-time job, make sure that it's something you enjoy so you don't end up dreading it. For example, perhaps you enjoyed playing sports growing up and you'd enjoy putting that knowledge to work as a youth sports referee or umpire. If you're strapped and barely making ends meet, you can also cut expenses. Chapter 5 has tips on reducing your spending.

Chapter **3**

Using Loans and Paying Down Debts

Borrowing money and taking on debt is like using a chainsaw. With proper training and safety precautions, a chainsaw can be a useful tool. In the hands of an insufficiently trained user or when used in the wrong situations, this otherwise helpful tool can do serious damage. The same can be said for borrowing money. Used sensibly, loans can help you accomplish important goals — such as furthering your education, buying real estate, or expanding your business — and boost your net worth over time. Unfortunately, taking on debt can also cause problems: living beyond your means, borrowing against your future earnings, and lowering your longer-term net worth. Too much debt and the wrong kind of high-cost debt can also cause personal stress.

In this chapter, I help you understand the best uses for loans and what debts to avoid. I also explain how to deal with and vanquish student-loan debt and how to conquer the all-too-common problem of consumer debt on credit cards, auto loans, and so on.

Eyeing the Causes of Generational Debt

For a number of years now, it has been argued that young adults are under pressures that lead them to go deeper into debt than prior generations. The reasons cited for this *generational debt* have typically included the following:

>> **High costs of college:** Annual increases in the costs of a college education have far outstripped the increases in general prices of other products and services. The price of some private colleges now is over $80,000 per year!

>> **Stagnating incomes and job prospects:** Most industries and companies compete in an increasingly global economy. And, the Internet has undermined and disrupted numerous retailers and other industries, causing incomes in those businesses to stagnate.

>> **High housing costs:** The 1990s and most of the 2000s saw rising housing prices, which priced many entry-level buyers out of their local markets.

>> **College campus credit-card promotions:** The availability and promotion of credit cards is a big problem. Credit cards are tempting to use during college when your income is minimal or nonexistent. Due to the high number of college students getting into unmanageable credit-card debt, the CARD Act of 2009 restricts card issuers from marketing within 1,000 feet of college campuses. But beware, they set up right across the street and bombard young adults at the age of 21 with all sorts of offers and solicitations. This practice and credit cards offering rewards are getting more young adults hooked on credit cards.

>> **Economic disruptions:** Plenty of young people had their jobs and economic lives take a hit during and in the aftermath of the 2008 financial crisis and the 2020 COVID-19 pandemic.

>> **More temptations to spend money:** Never before have so many temptations existed for spending money through so many outlets. In addition to the ubiquity of places to shop both nearby and online, people are bombarded with ads everywhere.

Most of these reasons for incurring generational debt are valid. In truth, however, this gloomy list isn't really fair and balanced. Here are some counter-arguments to the previous list:

>> Less costly higher-education options are increasing in number. Yes, there are plenty of high-priced four-year colleges, especially private ones. But they don't have a monopoly on the best higher-education options!

>> Unemployment hit a 50-year low just before the 2020 COVID-19 pandemic hit. And incomes were rising briskly, especially for those near or below the median income levels. (While the Internet and big tech companies have their downsides, it's easier now to research and find better values online, which enables smart consumers to get more bang for their bucks.)

>> Many metro areas have affordable housing, and more workers can work remotely. Increasing numbers of employers are actively trying to grow their employment away from high-cost cities such as New York, San Francisco, and the like.

>> College students don't need to have a credit card, which is the cause of students potentially running up debts they will be unable to quickly pay off. Debit cards, with a VISA or MasterCard logo, enable students to pay for items and then have the funds immediately deducted from their checking account, thus preventing them from spending money that they don't have.

>> Opportunities happen during periods of economic disruption. Recessions can harm plenty of people, but they also provide opportunities for those whose finances are in order and who have courage and plans!

>> You don't have to subject yourself to endless advertising nor succumb to its directives. There are plenty of ad blocking tools you can use when online or watching your favorite programs. You can also choose to consume more media that employs less ads.

REMEMBER

You may encounter some or all of these debt traps during your 20s and 30s. Remember that you'll always face things in life that you can and can't control. If you're aware of these land mines and can discern the difference between what you can't control and what you can constructively do to contain your spending and debt, then you're on the right track. If certain venues or situations or people tempt you to overreach, then avoid them. The rest of this chapter can help.

Making the Most of Loans

Not all debt is bad. In fact, some debt can help you better your life and improve your financial situation in the long run. Taking out a loan for the right reasons can make good financial sense because you're making an investment. Loans for your education, for buying or starting a small business, or for purchasing real estate can give you a return on your investment. Furthering your education, for example, can increase your income-earning ability. Borrowing to invest in a good piece of real estate or a small business should pay off over the years as well. Despite the potential, however, there's no guarantee that you'll earn a return above and beyond your loan's interest costs. Money may get spent and borrowed on the wrong type of education or an inferior real-estate property, for example.

WARNING

Borrowing and taking on debt for consumption — such as for buying a new car, new furniture, or electronics or for a costly vacation trip — is a bad financial move because such borrowing encourages living beyond your means. And the interest on this so-called consumer debt is generally not tax-deductible and carries a higher rate than the interest on mortgage debt. (Check out the section "Paying Off Consumer Debt" later in this chapter for tips on how to eliminate such costly loans.)

Dealing With Student-Loan Debt

Higher education can cost big bucks. And as you read this book, you may not be done with this too-often-costly process. Whether it's finishing a degree or returning to school for some continuing education, you may have education expenditures, perhaps significant ones, in your future.

And, whether all those education costs are behind you now or not, paying off student loans is probably in your future if you're like most young adults. So, this section will help you to pay off those loans in a manner that best fits with your overall financial situation and that minimizes costs.

Tracking your student loans and making timely payments

You may have multiple types of loans with different loan servicers. It's your responsibility to keep track of them, provide changes of address as necessary, and pay them on time. All your federal student loans can be found through the U.S. Department of Education's Federal Student Aid website (studentaid.gov/).

TIP

Signing up for automatic electronic payments can knock ¼ percent or more off of the interest rate on your student loans. And, autopayment on your loans will keep you current on those loans, benefit your credit score, and eliminate the chance of getting hit with late fees.

If you fall on hard times (for example, you get laid off from your job) and can't make a payment, communicate with your loan servicer and request a deferment. While your deferment request may be turned down if your circumstances are deemed not severe enough, you may qualify for *forbearance*, during which interest continues accumulating on your loans but you stop making payments for up to one year. The pandemic of 2020 caused government student loans to be paused, collections stopped, and interest waived until October 1, 2021. If you fail to get in touch and communicate with your loan servicer when you're having problems making payments, your credit report will show that you are deliquent on your loans and your credit score will suffer greatly (see Chapters 1 and 4 for more about credit scores).

Prioritizing the payback of student loans

How fast you pay back student loans should be a function of a number of factors. First, if you plan on doing more higher education and possibly applying for any type of financial aid, it generally makes sense to pay the minimum possible on your loans; the more debt you have outstanding, the better positioned you will be to see your future education bills reduced. You can see your repayment options on the website at `studentaid.gov/loan-simulator/`.

You should be aware of another quirky feature of federal student loans if you're contemplating working for certain nonprofit or public-sector employers. The Public Service Loan Forgiveness Program may help wipe out your remaining federal student debt after you've made ten years of repayments if you work for a qualifying employer such as the federal, state, or local government or a nonprofit organization covered under Section 501(c)(3) of the Internal Revenue Code, or if you're serving in a full-time AmeriCorps or Peace Corps position. See `studentaid.gov/manage-loans/forgiveness-cancellation/public-service` for more information.

When weighing which student loans to pay back faster, you should consider the interest rate on your loans. If you have extra cash and would like to pay back your loans faster, start with the ones with the highest interest rate. If the overall interest rates on your student loans are relatively low, don't miss out on the tax benefits you can earn by funding a retirement savings account, especially if that retirement account offers you free matching money from your employer.

TIP

If you're sure you are finished with your higher education and associated costs and are debating paying down your student loans faster than required versus investing your extra cash, do a comparison of the interest cost on your most costly loans versus the likely investment returns if you were to invest that money. (The rules governing the tax-deductible amount of your student-loan interest are covered in the next section.) If, for example, your student loan interest is 4 percent and you are reasonably confident that you can earn, say, 6 to 8 percent by investing your extra cash, you may want to go for the investment.

Using education tax breaks

Whether you are finished with your higher education or not, be sure you understand and maximize your use of the U.S. federal government tax benefits relating to those costs. Here's a summary of key provisions you should know about:

>> **Student-loan interest deduction:** You may take up to a $2,500 federal income-tax deduction for student-loan interest that you pay on IRS Form 1040 for college costs as long as your modified adjusted gross income (AGI) is less than or equal to $70,000 for single taxpayers or $140,000 for married couples filing jointly. (**Note:** Your deduction is phased out if your AGI is between $70,000 and $85,000 for single taxpayers or between $140,000 and $170,000 for married couples filing jointly.) Loans must be for qualified education expenses at an eligible higher-education institution such as a college, university, vocational or technical school, or other post-secondary educational institution eligible to participate in student-aid programs overseen by the U.S. Department of Education. The student must have taken out the loan during a period when they were enrolled at least half-time in a degree program.

>> **Tax-free investment earnings in special accounts:** Money invested in so-called section 529 plans is sheltered from taxation and is not taxed upon withdrawal as long as the money is used to pay for eligible education expenses. Subject to eligibility requirements, 529 plans allow you to sock away $250,000+. Please be aware, however, that funding such accounts may harm your potential financial aid.

>> **Tax credits:** The American Opportunity (AO) credit and Lifetime Learning (LL) credit provide tax relief to low- and moderate-income earners facing education costs. The AO credit may be up to $2,500 per student per year of undergraduate education, while the LL credit may be up to $2,000 per taxpayer. Each student may take only one of these credits per tax year, and they are subject to income limitations. And in a year in which a credit is taken, you may not withdraw money from a 529 plan or take a tax deduction for your college expenses.

A number of so-called miscellaneous education and career-related expenses are deductible on IRS Form 1040 Schedule A. These include

>> **Educational expenses:** You may be able to deduct the cost of tuition, books, and travel to and from classes if your education is related to your career. Specifically, you can deduct these expenses if your course work improves your work skills. Courses required by law or your employer to maintain your position are deductible if you pay for them. Continuing education classes for professionals may also be tax deductible. **Note:** Educational expenses that lead to your moving into a new field or career aren't deductible.

>> **Job searches and career counseling:** After you obtain your first job, you may deduct legitimate costs related to finding another job within your field. You can even deduct the cost of courses and trips for new job interviews — even if you don't change jobs. And if you hire a career counselor to help you, you can deduct that cost as well.

Weighing the costs and benefits of education expenditures

If you are considering more higher education, it is imperative to weigh what this education will actually enable you to do in the workforce. (These issues also should be contemplated if you have kids and will be making higher-education expenditures on their behalf.) Simply spending more on education may not be the answer.

Americans spend a lot of money on obtaining traditional college degrees. Yet, a good number of students fail to graduate with the education and training that they need to secure good, available jobs. A survey of those (especially young adults) currently unemployed and underemployed supports these concerns. There are good-quality job openings, but the young adults available to work lack the proper training and educational background to do those jobs.

Simply put, too much money is wasted on higher education that is failing to train young adults to qualify for the best available jobs.

Just as government programs encouraged and enabled excessive mortgage borrowing and contributed to a housing bubble in the late 2000s, the same is happening with higher education.

TIP

When considering an advanced or undergraduate degree, try as best you can to research the value of particular colleges and degree programs. There are numerous resources for doing this. My new book, *Paying For College For Dummies* (Wiley) includes lots of material on fast-growing and cheaper alternatives to traditional four-year colleges and which ones lead to great jobs and careers. And it also covers, of course, more traditional higher-education options.

Among other resources for rating and evaluating traditional higher-education options, those which I've reviewed and found useful are the following:

>> Kiplingers' "Best Value Colleges" considers numerous factors including student-to-faculty ratio, the test scores of incoming freshmen, four-year graduation rates, likelihood of graduating students with financial need, affordable sticker prices, generous financial aid and consistency of that during time at school, and low student debt at graduation. See www.kiplinger.com/college-rankings.

>> PayScale, the large online salary and benfits information collector, ranks colleges and majors on a return-on-investment basis over 20 years. Visit www. payscale.com/college-roi.

Making the most of student loans, grants, and other financial aid

If you're still in school or considering going back to school, a host of financial-aid programs, including a number of loan programs, allow you to borrow at reasonable interest rates. Most programs add a few percentage points to the current interest rates on three-month to one-year Treasury bills. Thus, current rates on educational loans for students are in the vicinity of rates charged on fixed-rate mortgages (parent loan rates are a little higher). The rates are also capped so the interest rate on your student loan can never exceed several percent more than the initial rate on the loan.

A number of loan programs, such as unsubsidized Stafford Loans and Parent Loans for Undergraduate Students (PLUS), are available even when your family is not deemed financially needy. Only subsidized Stafford Loans, on which the federal government pays the interest that accumulates while the student is still in school, are limited to students deemed financially needy.

WARNING

Most loan programs limit the amount that you can borrow per year, as well as the total you can borrow for a student's educational career. If you need more money than your limits allow, PLUS loans can fill the gap: Parents can borrow the full amount needed after other financial aid is factored in. The only obstacle is that you must go through a credit qualification process. Unlike privately funded college loans, you can't qualify for a federal loan if you have negative credit (recent bankruptcy, more than three debts over three months past due, and so on). For more information from the federal government about these student-loan programs, call the Federal Student Aid Information Center at 800-433-3243 or visit its website at studentaid.gov.

If you (or your parents) are homeowners, you may be able to borrow against the equity (market value less the outstanding mortgage loan) in your property. This option is useful because you can borrow against your home at a reasonable interest rate, and the interest is generally tax-deductible on up to $100,000 borrowed. Some company retirement plans — for example, 401(k)s — allow borrowing as well.

Parents are allowed to make penalty-free withdrawals from individual retirement accounts if the funds are used for college expenses. Although you won't be charged an early-withdrawal penalty, the IRS (and most states) will treat the amount withdrawn as taxable income. On top of that, the financial-aid office will look at your beefed-up income and assume that you don't need as much financial aid. Because of these negative ramifications, funding college costs in this fashion should only be done as an absolute last resort.

TIP

In addition to loans, a number of grant programs are available through schools, the government, and independent sources. You can apply for federal government grants via the Free Application for Federal Student Aid (FAFSA). Grants available through state government programs may require a separate application. Specific colleges and other private organizations (including employers, banks, credit unions, and community groups) also offer grants and scholarships.

One of the most important aspects of getting financial aid is choosing to apply, even if you're not sure whether you qualify. Many scholarships and grants don't require any extra work on your part — simply apply for financial aid through colleges. Other aid programs need seeking out — check directories and databases at your local library, your high-school counseling department, and college financial-aid offices. You can also contact local organizations, churches, employers, and so on. You have a better chance of getting scholarship money through these avenues.

Benefits for military people

Special student-loan benefits are available to those who serve in the U.S. military. If you have student loans and then join a branch of the U.S. military (except the Marines), up to one-third of the amount you borrowed or $1,500 per year of service, whichever is greater, may be forgiven. There's a reimbursement limit of up to $10,000 for the Air Force and $65,000 for the Army and Navy.

Numerous educational assistance programs are available for those who serve while in college or go to college after serving. See www.military.com/education/money-for-school for details by branch of the military, as there are many programs and they vary by branch.

Paying Off Consumer Debt

Assuming you aren't saving money, you accumulate *consumer debt* (credit-card debt, auto loan debts, and so on) when your expenses exceed your income. Therefore, it stands to reason that to pay off consumer debt, you need to decrease your spending (see Chapter 5) and/or increase your income. Slowing down the growth of your debt can also assist. The following sections help you jump-start the elimination of your consumer debt.

Kicking the credit-card habit

It's fine to use your credit cards as a convenient payment method — and possibly to earn benefits and rewards — if you pay your bill in full each month *and* don't spend more due to having the cards. I've used them my entire adult life and also have reward cards that provide me with free and discounted airline tickets and hotel stays.

However, with their wide acceptance by merchants and their ease of use, having credit cards can foster living beyond your means by extending credit. That's why I recommend that you cut up all your credit cards and call the card issuers to cancel your accounts if you have a habit of accumulating debt on credit cards.

You can manage your finances and expenditures without having a credit card. Now, if you can trust yourself to be responsible, keep one credit card only for new purchases that you know you can absolutely pay in full each month. But if you decide to keep one widely accepted credit card instead of getting rid of them all, be careful. You may be tempted to let debt accumulate and roll over for a month or two, starting up the whole horrible process of running up your consumer debt again. Even better than keeping one credit card is getting a debit card (see the next section).

TIP

If you're not going to take my advice to get rid of all your credit cards or secure a debit card (discussed in the next section), be sure to keep a lid on your credit card's *credit limit* (the maximum balance allowed on your card). You don't have to accept a higher limit just because your bank keeps raising your credit limit to reward you for being such a profitable customer. Call your credit-card service's toll-free phone number and lower your credit limit to a level you're comfortable with. Also ask your card-issuing bank not to automatically raise that limit in the future when you're deemed eligible for an increase.

Discovering debit cards: Convenience without credit temptation

Just because you get rid of your credit cards doesn't mean you have to always pay by check or cash. Enter the debit card, which offers you the convenience of making purchases with a piece of plastic without the temptation or ability to run up credit-card debt. A debit card looks just like a credit card with either the Visa or Mastercard logo. Debit cards have the following characteristics, which are different from credit cards:

>> **Deduction from your checking account:** As with checks, debit-card purchase amounts are deducted electronically from your checking account typically within one or two business days. By contrast, if you pay your credit-card bill in full and on time each month, your credit card gives you free use of the money you owe until it's time to pay the bill.

>> **Potential for overdrawing your checking account:** If you switch to a debit card and you keep your checking-account balance low and don't consistently track your account balance, you may need to start doing so. Otherwise, you may incur an overdraft (an attempt to withdraw more money than is available in your checking account) and unnecessary *overdraft fees* (fees charged when you overdraw your account). *Overdraft protection* may be worth considering, but beware of the temptation to use that as an ongoing, high-interest credit line on balances borrowed, similar to a credit card.

>> **Shorter window of time for making disputes:** Credit cards make it easier for you to dispute charges for problematic merchandise through the issuing bank. Most banks allow you to dispute charges for up to 60 days after purchase and will credit the disputed amount to your account, pending resolution. (Longer exceptions are allowed in some circumstances, for example when a contractor is doing work for you over a period of time.) Most debit cards offer a much shorter window, typically less than one week, for making disputes. (Despite widespread misperception, personal debit cards have identical fraud protection to personal credit cards.)

TIP

If you don't already have a debit card, ask your current bank whether it offers Visa or Mastercard debit cards. If your bank doesn't offer one, shop among the major banks in your area, which are likely to offer such debit cards. As debit cards come with checking accounts, do some comparison shopping between the different account features and fees. Check out Chapter 11 for more information about finding the right bank for you.

Also check out getting a Visa or Mastercard debit card with the asset-management accounts offered by investment firms. *Asset-management accounts* basically are accounts that combine your investments, such as stocks, bonds, and mutual funds, with a transaction account. Check out the investment firms that I recommend in Chapter 12 for brokerage services with competitive investment offerings and prices and asset management accounts. (*Note:* Unfortunately, Vanguard discontinued offering their asset management account but may reintroduce it in the future, so stay tuned.)

Lowering the interest rate on consumer debt

If you do have credit-card debt, you can slow its growth until you get it paid off by reducing the interest rate you're paying. Here are some strategies for doing that:

>> **Stop making new charges on cards that have outstanding balances while you're paying down your credit-card balance(s).** Many people don't realize that interest starts to accumulate immediately when they carry a balance. You have no grace period, the 20 or so days you normally have to pay your balance in full without incurring interest charges, if you carry a credit-card balance from month to month.

>> **Apply for a lower-rate credit card.** To qualify, you need a top-notch credit report and score (see Chapter 4), and not too much debt outstanding relative to your income. After you're approved for a new, lower-interest-rate card, simply transfer your outstanding balance from your higher-rate card.

INVESTIGATE

As you shop for a low-interest-rate credit card, be sure to check out all the terms and conditions of each card. Start by reviewing the uniform rates and terms of disclosure, which detail the myriad fees and conditions (especially how much your interest rate could increase for missed or late payments). Also understand how the future interest rate is determined on cards that charge variable interest rates. See my website, www.erictyson.com/, for an up-to-date list of good, low-rate cards.

Negotiating better rates from your current credit card

Rather than transferring your current credit-card balance onto a lower-interest-rate card (as mentioned in the preceding section), you can try to negotiate a better deal from your current credit-card company. Start by calling the bank that issued your current, high-interest-rate credit card and inform the bank that you want to cancel your card because you found a competitor that offers no annual fee and a lower interest rate. Your bank may choose to match the terms of the competitor rather than lose you as a customer. If it doesn't, get that application completed for a lower-rate card.

Be careful with this strategy, and consider just paying off or transferring the balance without actually canceling the higher-interest-rate credit card. Canceling the card, especially if it's one you've had for a number of years, may lower your credit score a bit, especially in the short term. Just be sure not to run up new charges on the card you're transferring the balance from.

Tapping investments to reduce consumer debt

If you have savings and investment balances available to pay off consumer debt, like high-interest credit-card debt and auto loans, consider doing so. Pay off the loans with the highest interest rates first.

Although your savings and investments may be earning decent returns, the interest you're paying on your consumer debts is likely higher. Paying off consumer loans on a credit card at, say, 12 percent is like finding an investment with a guaranteed return of 12 percent — tax-free. You'd actually need to find an investment that yielded even more — around 18 percent if you're in a moderate tax bracket — to net 12 percent after paying taxes in order to justify not paying off your 12 percent loans.

The higher your tax bracket (explained in Chapter 6), the higher the return you need on your investments to justify keeping high-interest consumer debt. This discussion refers to investments in nonretirement accounts. Unless your tax bracket drops because of an extended layoff from work or from going back to school, withdrawing money from retirement accounts is costly because of the requirement to pay current federal and state income taxes on the amount withdrawn, not to mention early withdrawal penalties.

REMEMBER

When using your savings to pay down consumer debts, leave yourself enough cash to be in a position to withstand an unexpected large expense or temporary loss of income.

Paying down balances

If you've been reading this chapter from the beginning, you know that I discuss numerous strategies for zapping your consumer debt. Now I take the discussion to a deeper level. How do you handle paying down multiple consumer-debt balances? It's really pretty simple *after* you implement the advice I give up until this point in the chapter.

After meeting the minimum required monthly payment terms for each loan, I strongly advocate that you channel extra payments toward paying down those loans with the highest interest rates first. The financial benefit of doing so should be obvious. If you have one loan at a 15 percent annual interest cost and another at an 8 percent annual interest cost, you'll be saving yourself a 7 percent annual interest cost by paying down the higher-cost loan faster.

I'm amazed at the wrong-headed advice I continue to see on this topic, especially on the Internet. One guru with no discernible training in the financial-planning/personal-finance field advises that you rank your debt payments by their total outstanding balances and that you channel extra payments to those with the lowest total balance owed. The "theory" behind this is that the psychological boost from paying down smaller debts completely will lead you to keep paying down your other debts.

In my real-world experience as a financial counselor, I've found folks to be intelligent and more responsive to the psychological rewards of saving money. And you best save money by paying down your highest-interest debts first.

Getting Help for Extreme Debt

More drastic action may be required if you have significant debts or simply are overwhelmed with what to do about it. In this section, I discuss getting help from a credit counseling agency and the last-resort option of bankruptcy.

Seeking counseling

If you're seriously in debt, you may consider a credit counselor. The ads for these agencies are everywhere. Although some of these organizations do a decent job, many are effectively funded by the fees that creditors pay them. Before you hire a credit counseling agency, make sure you do your research on the company.

INVESTIGATE

Put together a list of questions to ask to find a credit counseling agency that meets your needs. Here are some key questions you can ask:

>> **Do you offer debt-management programs?** In a debt-management program (DMP), a counseling agency puts you on a repayment plan with your creditors and gets paid a monthly fee for handling the payments. You should avoid agencies offering DMPs because of conflicts of interest. An agency can't offer objective advice about all your options for dealing with debt, including bankruptcy, if it has a financial incentive to put you on a DMP.

This creates a bias in their counsel to place debt-laden folks seeking their advice on their debt-management programs wherein the consumer agrees to pay a certain amount per month to the agency, which in turn parcels out the money to the various creditors. Agencies typically recommend that debtors go on a repayment plan that has the consumer pay, say, 3 percent of each outstanding loan balance to the agency, which in turn pays the money to creditors.

WARNING

Although credit counseling agencies' promotional materials and counselors highlight the drawbacks to bankruptcy, counselors are reluctant to discuss the negative impact of signing up for a debt payment plan.

>> **What are your fees, including setup and/or monthly fees?** Get a specific price quote and contract in writing. Avoid any credit counseling service that charges a high upfront fee before it provides any services. And watch out if the service tells you to stop paying your bills; it may take your money and run while your credit gets ruined.

>> **Are you licensed to offer your services in my state?** You should only work with an agency licensed to operate in your state.

>> **What are your counselors' qualifications?** Are they accredited or certified by an outside organization? If so, by whom? If not, how are they trained? Try to use an organization whose counselors are trained by a nonaffiliated party.

>> **What assurance do I have that information about me will be kept confidential and secure?** This information includes your address, phone number, and financial information. Reputable agencies provide clearly written privacy policies.

>> **How are your employees compensated?** Are they paid more if I sign up for certain services, if I pay a fee, or if I make a contribution to your organization? Employees who work on an incentive basis are less likely to have your best interests in mind than those who earn a straight salary that isn't influenced by your choices.

Considering bankruptcy

When the amount of your high-interest consumer debt relative to your annual income exceeds 25 percent, filing bankruptcy may be your best option. Like any tool, it has its pros and cons.

Bankruptcy's potential advantages include the following:

>> **Certain debts can be completely eliminated or discharged.** Debts that typically can be discharged include credit card, medical, auto, utilities, and rent. Eliminating your debt also allows you to start working toward your financial goals, such as saving to purchase a home or toward retirement. Depending on the amount of outstanding debt you have relative to your income, you may need a decade or more to pay it all off.

Debts that may not be canceled through bankruptcy generally include child support, alimony, student loans, taxes, and court-ordered damages (for example, drunk-driving settlements).

>> **Certain assets are protected by bankruptcy.** In every state, you can retain certain property and assets when you file for bankruptcy. Most states allow you to protect a certain amount of home equity; some states allow you to keep all of your home equity regardless of its value. Additionally, you're

allowed to retain some other types and amounts of personal property and assets. For example, most states allow you to retain household furnishings, clothing, pensions, and money in retirement accounts. So don't empty your retirement accounts or sell off personal possessions to pay debts unless you're absolutely sure that you won't be filing bankruptcy.

Filing bankruptcy, needless to say, has it downsides, including the following:

>> **It appears on your credit report for up to ten years.** As a result, you'll have difficulty obtaining credit, especially in the years immediately following your filing. (You may be able to obtain a secured credit card, which requires you to deposit money in a bank account equal to the credit limit on your credit card.) However, if you already have problems on your credit report (because of late payments or a failure to pay previous debts), damage has already been done. And without savings, you're probably not going to be making major purchases (such as a home) in the next several years anyway.

>> **It incurs significant court filing and legal fees.** These can easily exceed $1,000, especially in higher cost-of-living areas.

>> **It can cause emotional stress.** Admitting that your personal income can't keep pace with your debt obligations is a painful thing to do. Although filing bankruptcy clears the decks of debt and gives you a fresh financial start, feeling a profound sense of failure (and sometimes shame) is common.

>> **It becomes part of the public record.** Another part of the emotional side of filing bankruptcy is that you must open your personal financial affairs to court scrutiny and court control during the several months it takes to administer a bankruptcy. A court-appointed bankruptcy trustee oversees your case and tries to recover as much of your property as possible to satisfy the creditors — those to whom you owe money.

Deciphering the bankruptcy laws

If you want to have a leisurely afternoon read, then the bankruptcy laws are definitely not for you. I'm here to help clarify the two forms of personal bankruptcy in case you're considering taking this action:

>> **Chapter 7:** Chapter 7 allows you to discharge or cancel certain debts. This form of bankruptcy makes the most sense when you have significant debts that you're legally allowed to cancel.

>> **Chapter 13:** Chapter 13 comes up with a repayment schedule that requires you to pay your debts over several years. Chapter 13 stays on your credit record (just like Chapter 7), but it doesn't eliminate debt, so its value is

limited — usually to dealing with debts like taxes that can't be discharged through bankruptcy. Chapter 13 can keep creditors at bay until a repayment schedule is worked out in the courts.

The Bankruptcy Abuse and Prevention Act of 2005 contains the elements of personal bankruptcy laws currently in effect, which include the following:

>> **Required counseling:** Before filing for bankruptcy, individuals are mandated to complete credit counseling, the purpose of which is to explore your options for dealing with debt, including (but not limited to) bankruptcy and developing a debt repayment plan.

To actually have debts discharged through bankruptcy, the law requires a second type of counseling called "debtor education." All credit counseling and debtor education must be completed by an approved organization on the U.S. Trustee's website (www.usdoj.gov/ust). Click the link "Credit Counseling & Debtor Education."

>> **Means testing:** Some high-income earners are precluded from filing the form of bankruptcy that actually discharges debts (Chapter 7 bankruptcy) and instead are forced to use the form of bankruptcy that involves a repayment plan (Chapter 13 bankruptcy). The law does allow for differences in income by making adjustments based on your state of residence and family size. The expense side of the equation is considered as well, and allowances are determined by county and metropolitan area. For more information, click the "Means Testing Information" link on the U.S. Trustee's website (www.usdoj.gov/ust) under the link for "Credit Counseling & Debtor Education."

>> **Rules to prevent people from moving to take advantage of a more-lenient state's bankruptcy laws:** Individual states have their own provisions for how much personal property and home equity you can keep. Prior to the passage of the 2005 laws, in some cases, soon before filing bankruptcy, people actually moved to a state that allowed them to keep more. Under the new law, you must live in a state for at least two years before filing bankruptcy in that state and using that state's personal-property exemptions. To use a given state's homestead exemption, which dictates how much home equity you may protect, you must have lived in that state for at least 40 months.

Obtaining sound bankruptcy advice

No one should rush into filing bankruptcy. But you also don't want to make the mistake of not considering the option if your debt has become overwhelming. If you've seriously investigated bankruptcy and want more information than I provide in this chapter, I suggest that you check out the book *The New Bankruptcy: Will It Work for You?* by Cara O'Neill (Nolo Press).

If you're comfortable with your decision to file and you think that you can complete the paperwork, you may be able to do it yourself. The latest edition of the book *How to File for Chapter 7 Bankruptcy* by Albin Renauer and Cara O'Neill (Nolo Press) comes with all the necessary filing forms.

Preventing Consumer Debt Relapses

Regardless of how you deal with paying off your debt, you're at risk of re-accumulating debt if you've run up debt in the past. The following list highlights tactics you can use to limit the influence credit cards and consumer debt hold over your life:

TIP

>> **Replace your credit card with a debit card.** See the section "Discovering debit cards: Convenience without credit temptation" earlier in this chapter for the details.

>> **Think in terms of total cost.** Everything sounds cheaper in terms of monthly payments — that's how salespeople entice you into buying things you can't afford. Pull up the calculator app on your smartphone, if necessary, to tally up the sticker price, interest charges, and upkeep. The total cost will scare you (see my discussion in Chapter 19 regarding total costs for a car). It should.

>> **Stop the junk mail avalanche.** Look at your daily mail (email, snail mail) — I bet half of it is solicitations and mail-order catalogs. And then there are the endless telemarketing calls. You can save some trees and time sifting through junk mail by removing yourself from most mailing lists. To remove your name from mailing lists, including email, and to opt out of telemarketing calls, register through the website www.dmachoice.thedma.org/static/about_dma.php.

TIP

To remove your name from the major credit-reporting-agency lists that are used by credit-card solicitation companies, call 888-567-8688. Also, tell credit-card companies you have cards with, that you want your account marked to indicate that you don't want your personal information shared with telemarketing firms.

>> **Go shopping with a small amount of cash and no plastic.** That way, you can spend only what little cash you have with you!

>> **Identify and treat spending addictions.** Some people become addicted to spending, and it becomes a chronic problem that can interfere with other aspects of their lives. Check out Debtors Anonymous (DA), a nonprofit organization that provides support, primarily through group meetings. To find a DA support group in your area, visit the organization's website at debtorsanonymous.org or contact its headquarters at 800-421-2383.

Chapter **4**

Everything Credit: Scores and Reports

Y ou may not have given much thought to your credit report and may not know what your current credit score is. If you find yourself in that boat, I want you to pay special attention to this chapter. You should care about your credit report and credit score because lenders universally use credit scores to predict the likelihood that you'll repay a loan, and they'll generally only offer you a loan after they've reviewed your credit details. And you will only qualify for the best loan terms (lowest rates) if you have a high credit score.

Building good credit and a high credit score takes some time and effort. And even if you're happy renting an apartment and have no plans to apply for a business loan, you should pay attention to building good credit, which I detail how to do in this chapter. There's no way you can know now what loans or credit lines you may want or need 5, 10, or 20+ years down the road!

If you already have a good grasp of your credit report and credit score, congratulations. You're on the right track, but I hope to show you some additional steps you can take to help your situation.

In this chapter, I explain the difference between your credit report and credit score and how to improve them both. I also detail how lenders and others use your credit information. Finally, I explain how to keep from falling victim to identity theft, which can damage your credit reports and scores and cost you time and money.

A Primer on Credit Reports and Credit Scores

Your credit report and credit score play a vital role in your financial well-being, impacting the rates and terms when you borrow money and affecting other things like your auto insurance premiums, whether or not you're approved to rent housing, and sometimes whether or not you're hired for a job. Therefore, you want to use your credit report and score to your advantage.

The following sections define credit reports and scores, explain how credit bureaus come up with them, point out how lenders use this information, and discuss how you can get the most from your credit during your young-adult years.

Differentiating between credit reports and credit scores

Credit reports and credit scores are different from each other, and you should understand upfront what they are and aren't. The following sections spell out their characteristics in greater detail.

Credit reports

Your personal *credit reports* are a compilation and history (assembled by the three major credit bureaus: Equifax, Experian, and TransUnion) of your various credit accounts.

Your credit report details when each of your debt and loan accounts was opened, the latest balance (amount you still owe), your payment history, and so on. It specifies your track record of making payments in a timely or late fashion and whether you've failed to pay off previous debts.

Lenders and other creditors who have thrown in the towel on money you owe them may report a charge-off on your credit report and your report also details if you've ever declared bankruptcy in order to stop creditors from collecting on debts you owed. Finally, your credit report also shows who has made inquiries on your report when you've applied for credit. Numerous recent credit requests may indicate you're having problems meeting your debt payments and expenses and/or having problems getting approved for a new loan.

Credit scores

Your *credit score* is a three-digit score based on information in your personal credit report. Because each of the big three credit bureaus (Equifax, Experian, and TransUnion) issues its own report, you actually have three different (although typically similar) credit scores.

FICO is the leading credit score in the industry and was developed by the FICO Company (formerly Fair, Isaac and Company). FICO scores range from a low of 300 to a high of 850. Most scores fall in the 600s and 700s, with the median around 720. As with college entrance examinations such as the SAT, higher scores are better. (In recent years, the major credit bureaus have developed their own credit-scoring systems, but most lenders still predominantly use FICO.) You generally qualify for the best lending rates if your credit score is in the mid-700s or higher.

REMEMBER

The higher your credit score, the lower your predicted likelihood of defaulting on a loan (see Figure 4-1). Conversely, consumers with low credit scores have dramatically higher historic rates of falling behind on their loans. Thus, people with low credit scores are considered much riskier borrowers, and fewer lenders are willing to offer them a given loan; those who do so charge relatively high interest rates on those loans.

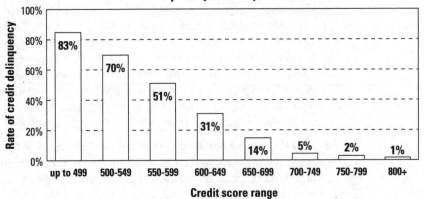

FIGURE 4-1:
Credit scores show the probability of defaulting on a loan.

Understanding how credit scores are determined

You have many credit scores, not just one. The reason you have multiple scores is because each of the three major credit bureau reports has somewhat different information about you and generates a unique score. But most consumers find, not surprisingly, that their three FICO scores from the big-three credit bureaus are fairly similar.

Credit scores change over time as your credit reports change. If you have a low score, the potential for change is good news because you can improve your score, perhaps significantly, in the weeks, months, and years ahead. The bureaus weigh current behavior more heavily than past behavior, though increasing your score is harder to do than decreasing it.

REMEMBER

To have a credit score, you need to use credit. The FICO scoring system requires you to have at least one account open for a minimum of six months on your credit report and one account that has been updated in the most recent six months (it can be the same account).

The factors that determine your credit score include the following:

WARNING

>> **Your payment history:** Your record of paying bills determines about 35 percent of your credit score.

Your score decreases with a recent negative mark (a late payment, for example), with a high frequency of negative marks, and with the severity of the negative mark (for instance, a 60-day late payment is worse than a 30-day late payment).

>> **How much you owe:** This factor, which accounts for 30 percent of your score, examines the total amount you owe, as well as the amount by type of loan. The more you owe relative to your credit limits, the more adverse the effect on your credit score (most Americans use less than 30 percent of their available credit). With revolving debt (credit cards, credit lines), the greater the gap between your balances and your credit limits, the better. Also, paying down installment loans (for example, mortgages, auto loans) relative to the amount you originally borrowed will boost your credit score.

>> **How long you've had credit:** Generally speaking, the longer you've had credit, the better for your credit score. This factor, which comprises 15 percent of your score, considers the average age of your accounts as well as the age of your oldest account.

>> **Your last application for credit:** Applying for and opening new accounts, especially multiple new accounts, can reduce your credit score. This factor accounts for 10 percent of your FICO score.

>> **The types of credit you use:** The FICO score rewards you for having a "healthy mix" of different types of credit (such as a mortgage, credit cards, and so on), although FICO is vague about what the best mix is. This factor accounts for 10 percent of your credit score.

Valuing of a good credit score

Generally, the higher your credit score, the better the loan terms (especially the interest rate) you receive and the more likely your loan applications are approved.

Over the course of your adult life, having a high credit score can save you tens (and perhaps hundreds) of thousands of dollars. Additionally, you can earn more money by being able to borrow money to make investments, such as in real estate or a small business.

REMEMBER

Lenders aren't the only ones that use credit scores. The following individuals and organizations/companies also use credit scores:

>> **Landlords:** A high credit score can lead to the approval of your apartment rental application.

>> **Insurance agents:** A high credit score can help you qualify for lower rates on certain types of insurance such as auto insurance.

>> **Prospective employers:** Significant problems on your credit report can cause some employers to turn you down for a job.

Jump-starting your credit score as a young adult

If you're just starting out financially, you may not have a credit score yet, simply because you don't have enough information on your credit report. Don't despair. To obtain a credit score if you don't yet have credit, the following actions help:

>> **Establish a checking and savings account (and even a debit card).** Doing so demonstrates financial responsibility and stability.

>> **Get added to someone's credit card as a joint or authorized user.** The logical person to ask would be a parent. Make sure this person is very responsible and shares your goal of keeping a terrific credit report and score. And, be sure that you are fully responsible for making your payments in a timely fashion.

>> **Have someone with good credit cosign a loan with you.** I would only advise doing this with a relative, and only if the two of you have a long discussion about what could go wrong and have an agreement in writing to minimize the potential for misunderstandings.

TIP

» **Apply for a credit card after turning 21 years old and when you have a job, because approval is relatively easy.**

Just be sure to get a card with a low annual rate and no or a low annual fee. Consider a rewards card if the benefits you can earn are something you value and will use. And be careful not to rack up balances you can't immediately pay off every month. Most important, don't use credit cards if having them causes you to spend more than you otherwise would.

» **If you can't get a regular credit card, apply for a department store or gas charge card.** Doing so is generally easier, but watch out for high interest rates and other fees if you can't pay your bill in full each month. Alternatively, find out why you don't qualify for a regular card; then work at addressing that shortcoming and reapply when your credit report and credit score have improved.

» **Apply for a secured credit card.** This type of card requires that you keep money on deposit in the bank that issues the card.

WARNING

For what it's worth, I am not a big fan of college students having credit cards. The reason is that most cards allow charging of substantial amounts and may lead to overspending. In the worst cases, some college students end up with large balances at high interest rates upon graduation in addition to all of their student loans. Having one credit card with a low credit limit that you can pay in full each month is worth considering because it can help build your credit rating and score.

Having a debit card is a better choice, in my opinion, for most college students because a debit card is attached to an account with a balance and thus prevents you from spending more than that amount.

Getting Your Hands on Your Credit Reports and Scores

Given the importance of your personal credit report, you may be pleased to know that each year you're entitled to receive a free copy of your credit report from each of the three credit bureaus (Equifax, Experian, and TransUnion).

TIP

If you visit www.annualcreditreport.com, you can view and print copies of your credit-report information from each of the three credit agencies (alternatively, call 877-322-8228 and have your reports mailed to you). After entering some personal data at the website, check the box indicating that you want to obtain all three credit reports, as each report may have slightly different information. You'll then be directed to one of the three bureaus, and after you finish verifying that you

are who you claim to be at that site, you can easily navigate back to www.
annualcreditreport.com so you can continue to the next agency's site.

Your credit reports don't include your credit score because credit bureaus aren't
required to include it by the federal law mandating that the three credit agencies
provide a free credit report annually to each U.S. citizen who requests a copy.
Thus, if you want to obtain your credit score, you generally need to pay for it. (An
exception: You're entitled to the credit score used by a lender who denies your
loan application. For more exceptions, see the following section.)

A recent small perk from some credit-card issuers is that your credit score is listed
on your billing statement. Examples are American Express, Capital One, and
Walmart. While not always a FICO score, they are a close estimate.

Recommended websites for free credit scores

A few websites provide you with a free credit score without forcing you to sign up
for something and/or provide your credit-card information. Here are some reliable sites:

>> After verifying your identity on their website, Discover Financial Services offers
your free Experian credit score with no strings attached or credit-card registration required. Visit their website at www.creditscorecard.com/registration.
(Discover does have its own credit card, and it will pitch you that online.)

>> The credit bureau Experian is behind the website FreeCreditScore.com,
through which you can get your free credit score.

>> Another free option to try is the FICO score simulator at www.myfico.com/
free-credit-score-range-estimator, which provides an estimate of your
FICO score based on your answers to a series of questions about your credit
usage and credit history.

Websites to avoid

Many websites, including the major credit bureaus, purport to offer you your
credit score for free, but more often than not, to obtain this supposedly free score,
you end up having to sign up for an ongoing and decidedly not free credit monitoring service! You may not realize that you're agreeing to some sort of ongoing
credit monitoring service for, say, $50 to $100+ per year. I don't recommend
spending money on those services. Instead, for free, request your credit report
from one of the three agencies every four months to make sure your credit information is accurate (I talk about reviewing your credit report in the upcoming

section) and get your credit score from one of the websites that I recommend earlier in this section.

WARNING

A number of web-based entities such as Credit Karma and WalletHub claim to provide you with your credit score for "free." These sites don't give you the FICO credit score that lenders most often use. Instead, the sites, which do a poor job of disclosure, give you one of the credit scores developed by the credit reporting bureaus, such as the TransUnion VantageScore. As with Discover, you will be pitched a credit-card offer after obtaining your credit score. That's how they keep these sites "free" for consumers seeking their score without paying for it.

In addition to getting a somewhat useless credit score at such sites, remember that you're sharing with them an enormous amount of confidential information about yourself. How some of these sites make money isn't completely obvious, but I can guarantee you that it involves finding ways (legal, hopefully) of tapping into all that information you give them. That would certainly include things like pushing auto loans, credit cards, and home mortgage loans to people in the marketplace for real estate.

Scrutinizing Your Credit Reports to Improve Them

Because your credit score is based on the information in your credit report, the first step to improving your score is to review each of your three reports (head to www.annualcreditreport.com, where you can access your credit report information from each of the three credit agencies). The following sections point out what you need to look for, what you can do to fix inaccurate information, and how you can improve your reports and credit score.

Identifying errors and getting them fixed

Carefully look through your credit reports for any potential inaccuracies. If you find any errors, you want to get them corrected quickly.

INVESTIGATE

Follow these steps to ensure that you properly vet each report:

1. **Review the identifying information to be sure that other folks' information hasn't gotten mixed up with yours.**

Look for the following errors:

- Names that aren't yours
- Incorrect Social Security numbers
- Incorrect date of birth
- Addresses where you haven't lived

2. **Inspect the credit accounts for problems, such as**

- Accounts that don't belong to you
- Negative entries that don't belong to you (such as late payments and *charge-offs,* which are amounts you supposedly borrowed that a lender no longer expects to get back from you)
- Negative entries that are more than seven years old
- Debts that your spouse incurred before marriage
- Incorrect entries due to identity theft or a credit bureau snafu that mixed up someone else's information with yours

3. **Examine the collection actions and public records section of your report for the following errors:**

- Bankruptcies more than ten years old or ones that aren't listed by a specific bankruptcy code chapter (such as a Chapter 7 bankruptcy)
- Lawsuits, judgments, or paid tax liens more than seven years old
- Paid liens or judgments that are listed as unpaid
- Loans that went into collection that are listed under more than one collection agency
- Any negative information that isn't yours

If you identify any errors, you can submit corrections by using one of the online forms for disputing incorrect information that accompany your credit reports. All credit bureaus are mandated to investigate and correct errors within 30 days. Your persistence may be required.

Boosting your credit score

After you get your credit report cleaned up, here are some ways that everyone can improve their credit score:

>> **Pay your bills on time.** The better your credit score, the more a late payment harms your score because such a change in behavior may indicate increasing financial difficulties.

TIP

To avoid making late payments, consider putting your bills on an automatic payment system either through your bank's online bill-pay service or the company's auto-pay option (if they offer one). Major investment firms like Fidelity and Schwab also generally offer cash management accounts that provide similar banking services. If you've never used automatic payments and you're skittish, try the system first with one company you trust the most. Another option is to put the charges on your credit card. Only do this, however, if you *always* pay your credit-card bill in full each month. Be cautious charging large bills on your credit card because using a big portion of your available credit can reduce your credit score. Also be sure that the companies you're paying don't charge an extra fee for using your credit card for payment.

>> **Pay down your debt.** Paying down your debts over time is exactly the kind of responsible credit behavior that lenders want to see in the folks to whom they lend money. The lower the portion your balances are of your credit limits (try to keep them under 30 percent), the better your credit score will be. For this reason, you should avoid both consolidating debts and charging so much on a card in a month that you near the card's credit limit.

>> **Avoid closing credit-card and other revolving accounts.** Closing accounts makes your remaining balances look that much larger in comparison to your total available credit. Also, closing older accounts lowers the average age of your credit accounts, which reduces your credit score.

>> **Apply for credit sparingly.** Applying for credit more frequently lowers your credit score.

Preventing Identity Theft

A study by Javelin Strategy & Research found that young adults are at significantly greater risk for identity theft than people in other age groups. This is largely a function of young people spending so much time online and due to a general lack of experience with being the victim of such problems and learning from the incident. Therefore, you must be proactive in preventing your personal information and accounts (bank, investment, credit, and debit) from being used by crooks to commit identity theft and fraud.

WARNING

Victims of identity theft can suffer trashed credit reports, reduced ability to qualify for loans and even jobs (with employers who check credit reports), out-of-pocket costs, and dozens of hours of time to clean up the mess and clean their credit records and name.

According to the aforementioned study, young adults are at greater risk for identity theft because

- » **Their use of social networking exposes confidential information.** Younger people use social networking websites more heavily than others, and these sites promote the sharing of personal information. Those who use social networking sites are twice as likely to suffer identity-theft problems.

- » **They're common targets of friendly fraud.** Younger people are at far greater risk of *friendly fraud,* in which the perpetrator (family members, domestic workers, employees who have access to personal information, and so on) is known to the victim.

- » **They take much longer than older folks to detect fraud.** Younger people are less likely to closely monitor accounts and credit reports that could reveal that fraud is taking place.

TIP

Here's how to greatly reduce your chances of falling victim to identity theft:

- » **Don't provide personal information over the phone or via text message, unless you initiated the call/exchange, and you know well the company or person on the other end.** And don't fall for incoming calls/texts that your caller ID says are coming from a particular business, because folks have found ways to dupe caller ID systems. Suppose you get a call/text from someone saying he is with Chase Credit Card services and is contacting you about a problem with your credit-card account. If you have an account with Chase, ask the person to provide you with his contact information and name. End the exchange; then get out your credit card, call the phone number listed on the back of your card, and ask the representative you speak with to verify whether the previous contact you received was legitimate or not.

- » **Ignore emails soliciting personal information or action.** Online crooks are clever and can generate a return/sender email address that looks like it comes from a known institution but really does not. This unscrupulous practice is known as *phishing,* and if you take the bait, visit the site, and provide the requested personal information, your reward is likely to be some sort of future identity-theft problem. Never click on links in emails, and only access your online accounts by typing in your bank's URL or by using your own created bookmarks.

- » **Review your monthly financial statements.** Although your bank, mutual fund, and investment company may call, text, or email you if they notice unusual activity on one of your accounts, some people discover problematic account activity by simply reviewing their monthly credit card, checking account, and other statements. Review line items on your statement to be sure that all the transactions are yours.

You can simplify this process by closing unnecessary accounts. The more credit cards and credit lines you have, the more likely you are to have problems with identity theft and to overspend and carry debt balances. Unless you maintain a separate card for your own small business transactions (or carry an extra card or two due to the rewards those cards offer you), you really *need* only one piece of plastic with a Visa or Mastercard logo. Give preference to a debit card if you have a history of accumulating credit-card debt balances.

>> **Periodically review your credit reports.** Some identity-theft victims have found out about credit accounts opened in their name by reviewing their credit reports. Because you're entitled to a free credit report from each of the three major credit agencies every year, you could review one agency report every four months to keep a close eye on your reports and still obtain them without cost. Is it necessary to review your credit reports that frequently, and do I personally do this? The answer to both of those questions is no! But you may want to scrutinize your reports that often if you've had problems or otherwise have reason to be concerned about the security and integrity of your credit. (See the earlier section "Scrutinizing Your Credit Reports to Improve Them" for more information.)

>> **Freeze your credit reports.** Thanks to a change in federal law in 2018, you may freeze your credit reports for free, which is done through a PIN code at each credit bureau. Doing so puts you in total control of who may access your credit report. To "unfreeze" your reports, you will again use your PIN code at each credit bureau. In addition to contacting the three major credit bureaus, the last listing is a credit bureau used by cell-phone companies and utilities:

- **Equifax:** www.equifax.com/personal/credit-report-services/ or call 800-349-9960.

- **Experian:** www.experian.com/freeze/center.html or call 888-397-3742.

- **TransUnion:** www.transunion.com/credit-freeze/place-credit-freeze or call 888-909-8872.

- **National Consumer Telecommunications & Utilities Exchange:** www.exchangeservicecenter.com/Freeze/jsp/SFF_PersonalIDInfo.jsp or call 866-349-5355.

>> **Avoid placing personal information on checks.** Information that's useful to identity thieves and that you shouldn't put on your checks includes your credit-card number, driver's license number, Social Security number, and so on. I also encourage you to leave your home address off your preprinted checks when you order them. Otherwise, everyone whose hands your check passes through gets free access to that information.

When writing a check to a merchant, question the need for adding personal information to the check (in fact, in numerous states, it's against the law to request and place credit-card numbers on checks). Use a debit card instead for such transactions.

>> **Protect your computer.** If you keep personal and financial data on your computer, use up-to-date virus protection software and a firewall, and password-protect access to your programs and files.

MY STORIES OF IDENTITY THEFT (AND RECOVERY)

I can speak from personal experience when it comes to identity theft. It happened to me in my late 20s when a crook withdrew money from my checking account by using personal information that was stolen from my wife's employer payroll department. This is but one of many ways you can fall victim to identity theft. In other cases, the criminal activity may develop with someone opening an account (such as a credit card) using someone's stolen personal information.

In my situation, the bank immediately and without question reimbursed my account for the several withdrawals they had allowed from the fake Eric Tyson. The checking account was closed, and a new one was established. This created some short-term hassle for me, but ultimately, I wasn't out any money from the identity theft.

More recently, someone tried to use my credit-card number to make some purchases at a liquor store hundreds of miles from my home. The person had created a fake card, and the transaction was turned down because the bogus card had an incorrect expiration date. This led to me having to close that account and open one with a new number.

Finally, someone using some of my personal information tried to open a credit-card account with a department store. The attempt failed, and no card was issued.

So, you can see that identity theft attempts and "successes" can happen to anyone! My cases are typical in that nothing major occurred in terms of costs and hassle for me. But, in more unusual cases, more costs and hassles can be involved in cleaning up the mess.

So, if you're ever the victim of identity theft, don't panic and don't despair. Odds are quite good you can recover without financial loss or major hassle. But, if your case is more complicated and challenging, review the good advice offered by the Federal Trade Commission at www.identitytheft.gov/Steps.

>> **Protect your snail mail.** Stealing postal mail from most mailboxes is pretty easy, especially if your mail is delivered to a curbside box. Consider using a locked mailbox or a post-office box to protect your incoming mail from theft. Consider having your investment and other important statements sent to you via email, or simply access them online and eliminate mail delivery of the paper copies. Minimize your outgoing mail and save yourself hassles by signing up for automatic bill payment for as many bills as you can. Drop the rest of your outgoing mail in a secure U.S. postal box, such as those you find at the post office. (If you continue receiving paper statements, consider getting a shredder to shred documents you want to dispose of.)

2
Saving and Earning More

IN THIS PART . . .

Check out strategies and tactics to spend less and get more value.

Find simple and powerful ways to legally and permanently reduce your taxes.

Determine whether to rent or buy a home and, if you decide to buy, how to best finance your purchase.

Manage your money and your relationships.

Get tips to jump-start your career, as well as further your education and training, explore your entrepreneurial options, and handle job changes and loss.

Chapter 5

Proven Ways to Spend Less and Save More

In my work as a financial counselor and teaching courses, I have been surprised at how often people, who were otherwise doing a fine job saving a good portion of their income, have solicited my feedback on their spending. In addition to wanting to know how to save more to accomplish their goals, they also wanted to know how their spending compared to others' and how they could best cut their own spending.

This chapter includes the same advice I gave all of my counseling clients and students about spending money.

In this chapter, I present ideas on how to get the most from spending and how to spend less. (In Chapter 2, I discuss the importance of developing a savings mindset, as well as budgeting and spending strategies.)

How and where you spend your money is a matter of personal choice and priorities, but those choices can affect the amount of money you have left to save. Savings is essential to accomplishing many personal and financial goals. Having more can increase your options and freedom. I must say, though, upfront, that some of the best savers get hooked on the accumulation of money and sometimes have a hard time using their savings and investments in the future for their originally intended purpose. I raise this issue here as food for thought and a reminder that saving more isn't always better. There's something to be said for living for today and striking a balance since we can't know exactly what the future will be. That said, plenty of folks could save more and reduce unproductive and unfulfilling spending.

Containing Housing Costs

Housing and its associated costs such as insurance, utilities, furniture, maintenance, and repairs (for homeowners) are the largest or second-largest expenditure for most people. If you're like many other young adults, you may be renting. Keeping these costs (and taxes) under control, which I explain how to do in this section, goes a long way toward being able to save some money.

Reducing rental costs

When you're a young adult and you don't have dependents, living in a low-cost fashion is typically easier than it is later in life. The living arrangements may have some downsides, but young single people tend to have a broader range of rental options than those available to married people with kids.

The following sections point out what you can do to minimize your rent expense and associated costs.

Share a rental with roommates

Living solo is a pricey luxury most younger people can't afford. Doing so definitely has its benefits — you have more privacy and control over your home environment. Renting may sacrifice some of these advantages to living alone, but having roomies also has its pros. If you share a rental with roommates, the per-person costs should be substantially less than if you live solo.

You must be in a sharing mood, though, to live harmoniously with roommates. They may help themselves to your food or shampoo, stay up late when you need to get up early the next day, or invite over inconsiderate friends. Roommates aren't all bad, though, as they may brighten your social life.

WARNING

Before you choose to share an apartment or other dwelling with someone or multiple other people, make sure (as best you can) that you can live with those people for the length of the rental agreement. If you break the lease, you may owe a hefty amount of money, which defeats the purpose of saving money with a roommate.

When I was in my 20s, I had multiple roommates for a number of years and doing so definitely boosted my ability to save more money. Most of the time, having roommates was a good thing and we all got along pretty well. But there was occasional friction, usually over relatively minor things which could be worked through.

TIP

Be sure to have a rental agreement in place with your landlord and to have all renters listed in the agreement. Don't allow others who aren't listed in the agreement to live in the rental, because you and the other renters could be on the hook for damage they cause and rent (and utilities) they don't pay.

Move to a lower-cost rental

You may realize that you're currently living beyond your means and you need to make some adjustments. You may have allowed your champagne tastes to exceed your beer budget when you went shopping for a home rental. So long as you're completing your current lease, there's no reason you can't move to a lower-cost rental. The less you spend renting, the more you can save toward buying your own place. Just be sure to factor in all the costs of moving to and living in a new rental.

REMEMBER

Of course, a lower-cost rental may be lower quality and not up to your standards. Don't accept living in a high-crime neighborhood, a poorly maintained building, or a location that causes you to burn much of your free time commuting to work.

Negotiate your rental increases

Every year, some landlords increase their tenants' rent no matter how good the tenant has been and regardless of the state of the economy. If your local economy is weak and the rental market is soft or your living quarters are deteriorating, negotiate with your landlord. You have more leverage and power than you probably realize. A smart landlord doesn't want to lose good tenants who pay rent on time. Filling vacancies takes time and money.

TIP

State your case to your landlord through a well-crafted and polite email/note and/ or personal call or visit. Explain how you have been a responsible tenant, always paid your rent on time, and cared for your unit, and convey that your research shows comparable rentals going for less. Briefly explaining any challenging financial circumstances (such as reduced pay from your job) may help your case as well. If you can't stave off the rent increase, perhaps you can negotiate some improvements you value.

Live with relatives

Yes, I realize that living with relatives won't work for some families. However, if your folks or other relatives have the space and temperament to let you live under their roof, it can be a constructive way to keep your rental costs to a minimum. Just be sure to have some lengthy discussions first to set expectations and ground rules, raise concerns, and establish terms, including costs and rental agreements.

If your relative won't accept money from you, how about helping with some chores and other responsibilities around the house? That could start with your own things like doing your own laundry and helping with cleaning, especially and always of the space you live in and regularly use, like the kitchen and bathroom.

During the COVID-19 pandemic, primarily due to government-mandated shutdowns and restrictions, more young people found themselves living back at home instead of with friends in a city. While some lost their jobs, others were able to work remotely. I've spoken with numerous young people who didn't see much value continuing to live in cities, especially costly ones, and other areas enforcing draconian lockdowns.

Get on the path to purchasing your own home

Purchasing a home always seems costly. However, over the long term, owning is usually less costly than renting a similar property. And as a homeowner, you build *equity* (the difference between the home's value and what you owe on it) in your property as you make mortgage payments and as the home's value increases over the long term. If you purchase a property with a 30-year fixed-rate mortgage, the biggest expense of ownership — your monthly mortgage payment — is locked in and remains level. By contrast, as a renter, unless you live in a *rent-controlled unit* (which means that local government dictates and limits the percentage by which the rent may rise annually), your entire monthly housing cost is fully exposed to inflation.

REMEMBER

During periods like 2006–11, the decline in home prices in most parts of the United States coupled with low interest rates made housing the most affordable it had been in decades. At the time, that was great news for renters looking to become future homeowners as well as those who simply wanted to rent a nicer dwelling. While home prices generally rise over the long term, buying during a home price decline can be a great way to get into the housing market when it's having a "sale."

Of course, each local market is unique, and if you happen to live in an area with a strong, diverse economy and little developable land or excess housing, your local housing market may be stronger and more expensive than others. Turn to Chapter 7 for more information on buying real estate.

Slicing homeowner expenses

If you own a home or are about to buy one, you can take many steps to keep your ownership costs down and under control without neglecting your property or living like a pauper. The following sections are my tips.

Buy a home that fits your budget

Purchase a home that you can afford. During the booming real-estate market up until 2005, getting overextended with debt was pretty easy. You didn't need a decent-size down payment or even have to have your income verified to buy a home if you made a larger down payment. Furthermore, interest-only loans allowed borrowers to shrink their mortgage payments by delaying repayment of any of their principal.

I was never a fan of such loans, which is why in our bestselling book *Home Buying For Dummies* (Wiley), my coauthor Ray Brown and I advise that the best way to buy a home is to examine your budget and financial resources before shopping for a home. As the real-estate market declined between 2006–11 in most parts of the United States, some of those people who bought homes that stretched their budgets lost their homes to foreclosure because they got in over their head, fell on hard times, and couldn't afford their monthly mortgage payments.

REMEMBER

Even if you can afford the monthly mortgage payment on a house you're looking to buy, if you have too little money left over for your other needs and wants — such as taking trips, eating out, going out with friends, enjoying hobbies, or saving for retirement — your dream home may become a financial prison. See Chapter 7 for help in figuring how much you can afford to spend monthly on a home and still accomplish your other goals.

Get a roommate (and some rental income)

Owning a home may be more affordable if you have some monthly rental coming in (please see Chapter 7 for tips on buying and affording a home). Consider renting a bedroom (or separate/in-law unit if you're lucky enough to have one) to someone who can pay monthly rent as well as possibly help with utilities. Through services like Airbnb.com, VRBO.com, TripAdvisor.com, Tripping.com, and so on, you can get an idea about what you may be able to charge in rent and find possible renters. You should also inquire with real-estate agents who are active and experienced in your local rental market and consider websites like Trulia.com and Realtor.com for listing your rental.

TIP

If you decide to take on a renter(s), make sure you check the renter(s) thoroughly through references and a credit report, and be sure to discuss ground rules and expectations before renting to someone sharing your space. Vet prospective renters before agreeing to meet them or show them the rental. You don't want to waste your time showing rentals to someone who can't afford it, isn't a good fit for your situation, or has a shady background! Also, ask your insurance company to see whether your homeowner's policy needs adjustments to cover potential liability from renting. For more information, check out *Renting Out Your Property* by Melanie Bien and Robert Griswold (Wiley).

Contain your utility costs

You can take steps to keep your utility costs down whether you own or rent a home. First, don't waste energy, even if you don't pay for it out-of-pocket as a renter. Landlords absolutely factor your energy consumption into future rental-hike decisions. Paying for your own utilities should get you to consider wearing layers in the winter (you shouldn't be walking around then in shorts) and not expecting your home to feel like a meat locker in the heat of summer.

Adjust your thermostat to save energy — allow it to be cooler than normal in winter and warmer than normal in summer — when you're not going to be home for a while (for example, while you're at work or away for a weekend). Smart thermostats can help with this process but aren't required.

Especially if you have to pay for garbage service, recycle as much as possible. Seek the replacement of old, energy-guzzling appliances and, where possible, beef up your property's insulation. Obviously, if you're a renter, you have no control over these things, but you should certainly ask about utility costs and whether any appliances and insulation could be upgraded as necessary.

Cutting Your Taxes

Alongside the costs of owning or renting a home, taxes are the other large personal expenditure for most folks. Everyone gets socked with federal income taxes (and for most people state income taxes) when earning income and when investing and spending money. That's the bad news — the good news is that you can reduce the amount of taxes you pay by using some relatively simple yet powerful strategies. The following two tax trimmers can help:

>> **Use retirement savings plans.** To take advantage of such plans, you must spend less than you earn. Only then can you afford to contribute to these plans. Many of these plans immediately reduce your federal and state income

taxes, and once money is inside such an account, the investment returns are sheltered from taxation. See Chapter 2 for more on retirement (also known as tax reduction) accounts.

>> **Reduce the amount of sales tax you pay.** To do so, you must spend less and save more. When you buy most consumer products, you pay sales tax. Therefore, if you spend less money, you reduce your sales taxes.

For more tax–reduction strategies, please see Chapter 6.

Managing Food and Restaurant Spending

The following culinary strategies can keep you on your feet — perhaps even improve your health — and help you save money.

>> **Discover how to cook.** Take a course and read some good books on cooking. Learn from those around you — parents and friends come to mind — who can teach you a thing or two! Consider that most people eat three meals a day, 365 days a year. That's more than 1,000 meals yearly — a lot of eating! If you don't know how to cook for yourself and how to do so healthfully, you may end up spending a lot more money on food and eating out — and have poor health to boot. Cooking meals for yourself doesn't mean having to make something for each and every meal. You can cook in larger quantities than you need for one meal and put what you don't eat in the refrigerator or freezer to eat at a later meal on another day. Making your own food can save you money, improve your health, allow you to enjoy your food more, and potentially make you more attractive to a mate!

>> **Find out about nutrition and prepared foods.** No, this point isn't contradictory with the first one about learning to cook. Everyone is busy, and buying prepared meals (including some frozen foods) that are easy to heat or ready to eat can make sense for some of your meals. But you want to be sure to buy healthy, nutritious affordable food. Shop at stores like Trader Joe's — to find one near you, visit www.traderjoes.com/stores. I also recommend nutrition websites like Eat This, Not That! (www.eatthis.com), also the name of their popular book series; www.healthline.com; www.LiveStrong.com; and World's Healthiest Foods (www.whfoods.org).

>> **Consider store brands.** Name-brand companies spend a lot of money on advertising and marketing, which you, the consumer, end up paying for through higher prices. You can save a considerable amount of money by buying the store brand (for example, Wal-Mart's Great Value, Target's Good

and Gather, Aldi's, Trader Joe's or Whole Foods 365 Everyday Value), which is usually the same quality (and sometimes the same product) as the name brand but priced lower.

» **Buy in bulk.** You can save substantially by shopping at stores that are able to sell groceries for less because of their operating efficiencies. Topping that list are wholesale superstores such as Costco and Sam's Club. The catch is that you must buy most items in bulk or in larger sizes. An additional advantage to buying in bulk: It requires fewer shopping trips (hence less gasoline) and results in fewer instances of running out of things. You may be able to buy some of the foods you find you like in bulk online. Just be sure to order from a reputable online retailer that stands behind what it sells.

TIP

If you decide to buy in bulk, be careful with items that can spoil. Make sure that you buy what you can reasonably use (or freeze when necessary). If you're single, consider shopping with a friend and splitting the order. If you're looking for a store that sells more organic and natural products at a reasonable price and in smaller sizes, check out Trader Joe's.

» **Kick the bottled water habit.** Although tap water often does leave something to be desired, lab analysis of bottled water shows it has its own problems. You can save hundreds of dollars annually and drink cleaner water by installing a water filtration system at home and improving your tap (or well) water. Also consider pitcher-based water filtration systems like Zero Water and Brita.

» **Pack your lunch sometimes.** Eating out daily can rack up a lot of expense. Brown bag it sometimes.

» **Spend carefully when dining out.** Eating out can be fun and a way to socialize with friends, but keep in mind that you're essentially hiring someone to shop, cook, and clean up for you! You can save some money when eating out by remembering these points:

- **Eat out for breakfast or lunch rather than dinner.** You can generally get the most bang for your buck then. And this may be better for your health; studies show that the meals you eat earlier in the day should be the more substantial ones — not dinner!

- **Go easy on the beverages.** Alcohol is especially expensive when dining out (and at bars), and beverages in general are usually the biggest profit-margin items at restaurants.

Trimming Transportation Expenses

When you're considering the cost of living in different areas, don't forget to factor in commuting costs and wear and tear — not just on your car, but on you! Getting to and fro on a daily basis can get expensive if you don't keep an eye on your expenses. Many people rely on cars for their transportation. Buying and operating a car can be a tremendous financial burden, especially if you borrow to buy or lease the car.

You can control your transportation costs by following my suggestions:

>> **Opt for public transportation.** Choose to live in an area that offers reliable public transportation, such as a subway or bus system. You can often purchase monthly passes at a reasonable rate. If you live close to work, or at least close to a public transit system, you may be able to make do with fewer cars (or no car at all) in your household.

>> **Ride your bike.** During warmer months, consider jumping on your bike to get around. You can save money and get some exercise. Just be sure to be safe! Wear reflective gear and be sure your bike is easily visible. Stay off high-traffic, narrow roads and be on guard for bad and under-the-influence drivers!

>> **If you must have a car, look at cheaper options than financing or leasing one.** Having provided financial advice to many folks over many years, I can tell you from direct observation that spending on cars is one of the leading causes of overspending and under-saving. I understand that in some parts of the United States and Canada going without a car is nearly impossible, and I also understand that driving a car is a wonderful convenience that I have personally enjoyed during most of my adult life.

But if you can avoid having your own car, by all means do so. You can also consider renting a car when needed if you don't find yourself wanting to use one frequently. Or take an occasional taxi or use a Lyft- or Uber-type service.

The main reason people end up spending more than they can afford on a car is that they finance the purchase. When buying a car, you should buy one you can afford with cash, which for many people means buying a good-quality used car. Check out Chapter 19 for more helpful advice.

TIP

When shopping for a car, don't make the mistake of simply comparing sticker prices. Consider the total long-term costs of car ownership, which include gas, insurance, registration fees, maintenance, repairs, and taxes (sales and personal property). And be sure to consider the safety of any car you buy, as driving is surely the most dangerous thing you do. See the National Highway Traffic Safety Administration's website (www.safercar.gov), which has lots of crash-test data as well as information on other car-safety issues. Buy and drive cars that have the highest crash-test safety ratings (five stars).

Finessing Fashion Finances

The good news for you as a consumer is that in the fashion industry, global competition has driven down prices for consumers. Here's what you can do to look like a million bucks (on and off the job) while spending fewer of your bucks:

>> **Don't chase the latest fashions.** Ignore ads that splash celebrities wearing the latest looks. You can enjoy pictures on social media like Instagram, but recognize some of those photos are nothing more than veiled ads to promote particular lines of clothing and brands. (Also keep in mind that the person wearing the clothing and the setting for the photo greatly influence how the clothing appears and appeals to you.) You don't need to buy lots of new clothes every year. If your clothes aren't lasting at least ten years, you're probably tossing them before their time or buying clothing that isn't very durable. Of course, when you enter an office job for the first time, you're probably going to have to buy some new clothing. True fashion, as defined by what people wear, changes quite slowly. In fact, the classics never go out of style. If you want the effect of a new wardrobe every year, store last year's purchases away next year and then bring them out the year after. Or rotate your clothing inventory every third year. Set your own fashion standards.

>> **Shun dry cleaning–required clothing.** Stick with cottons and machine-washable synthetics rather than wools or silks that require costly dry cleaning.

>> **Consider buying gently used fashion at consignment shops, vintage shops, or online.** You can find great bargains at these places that others may have worn only once or twice.

>> **Look for discounts.** Some stores have occasional big sales with major price reductions. Even premium retailers like Bonobos and Lululemon have sales, so be patient and sign up for email lists to be notified. And if you can wait until you're well into a particular season, you can get items on clearance when there's still time left to use them. For example, when stores are ready to put out fall/winter coats in August, they put their swimwear on clearance. Depending on where you live, you may be able to wear that new (discounted!) suit for several weeks and of course in future years.

>> **Minimize accessories.** Shoes, jewelry, handbags, and the like can gobble large amounts of money. Again, how many of these accessory items do you really need? The answer is probably very few, because each one should last many years. Don't purchase accessories and then not use them.

WHY WE BUY THINGS WE DON'T NEED

Whether the products are option-packed cars, high-end home appliances, or the latest designer clothing, marketers motivate consumers to buy on emotion rather than need. Marketers also play on insecurities, fears, and guilt and suggest that you can feel better about yourself and loved ones by buying their products.

This pattern begins at a young age — more than six in ten young teenagers say that buying certain products made them feel better about themselves according to a study conducted for the nonprofit Center for a New American Dream.

You won't be able to overcome this common and constant problem of overspending and accumulating consumer debt until you recognize these pressures and how they influence and corrupt your buying decisions.

An eye-opening book is Pamela Danziger's *Why People Buy Things They Don't Need*. Danziger runs a consulting firm that advises large consumer-product companies on how to design products and convince consumers to buy them. Danziger correctly points out that many of American consumers' purchases are discretionary. "The simple fact is that the contemporary American lives so far above subsistence, we have lost touch with the basic needs of life: food for nutrition, basic clothing, and shelter for warmth and protection," she writes.

The central thesis of Danziger's book is that consumer-products companies can induce consumers to buy costly products they don't really need by appealing to consumers' desires and emotional needs. "In today's consumer-driven society, satisfying consumer needs has less to do with the practical meeting of physical needs and everything to do with gratifying desires based upon emotions. The act of consuming, rather than the item being consumed, satisfies the need," she states.

It really has been in the last couple of generations that we, as a society, have grown quite accustomed to buying consumer items on credit. "Spoiled the younger generations may be, but they are the consumers who express their wants, desires, and dreams in terms of needs and necessities because they have never done without," says Danziger. "Need can wait, but want and desire drive purchases."

Danziger and her consulting firm identify 14 so-called justifiers (I'd call them rationalizations) that consumers employ when making discretionary purchases. Improving the quality of your life; buying on impulse; replacing an existing item (for example, an older sofa), which leads to purchasing numerous related items (armchairs and end tables); and purchasing certain goods for status are examples of common justifiers.

The goal of consumer-product companies and their marketing staff is to persuade and cajole you into buying what they're selling even if you don't really need it. Remember this the next time the thought goes through your mind that you want to buy something that isn't a necessity.

Relaxing on a Budget

Having fun and taking time out for recreation can be money well spent. However, you can easily engage in financial extravagance, which can wreak havoc with an otherwise good budget. Here are my favorite tips for getting the most from your recreation spending:

>> **Don't equate spending (more) money with having (more) fun.** Some entertainment venues offer discount prices on certain days and times. Cultivate some interests and hobbies that are free or low cost. Visiting with friends, hiking, reading, and playing sports can be good for your finances as well as your health.

>> **Hang out with people who share your values and aren't materialistic.** It's especially important that you find a partner who isn't a spendthrift and isn't overly impressed with material things.

>> **Take vacations you can afford.** Don't borrow on credit cards to finance your travels. Try taking shorter vacations that are closer to home. For example, have you been to a state or national park recently? Take a vacation at home, visiting the sites in your local area. For longer-distance travel, go during the off-season and off-peak times and days for the best deals on airfares and hotels. If you've been disciplined about paying your credit-card bill in full each month, check out some of the better reward credit cards that offer benefits like free hotel stays and airline tickets.

THE BENEFITS AND DRAWBACKS OF CREDIT-CARD REWARD PROGRAMS

Credit-card reward point programs, where the cardholder receives points toward gift cards or travel purchases based on the amount the person spends on the card, are a relatively new phenomenon. Let me say upfront, I do have concerns about these cards and their programs for the simple reason that they reward spending! So, if they encourage you to spend more than you otherwise would, you need to factor that into any calculation of the real net benefit such cards are providing you.

Also, to gain the most benefit from rewards programs, you should be the type of credit-card user who pays his bill on time and in full each month. Otherwise, interest charges, late fees, and so on will more than wipe out the value of any rewards the card may offer you. Having your full payment drafted from your bank account insures you stay current and on time.

There are many credit cards that offer points or rewards. In fact, even within a given program, there are often options offering different sign-up bonuses, annual fees, annual bonuses, and so forth. So it takes time and some analysis to select a card that may be right for you. In order to do an informed comparison of these options, you should understand the underlying rewards program and how many points, for example, you need to get a free night's stay in hotels you're likely to choose or how many points or miles you need for a round-trip airline ticket you'd like.

Also, some cards charge an annual fee whereas others do not. It may sometimes be worth paying an annual fee if the extra benefits on that particular card are worth more to you than that annual fee.

Currently, a decent number of rewards cards are out there that offer sizeable sign-up bonuses for all the various major airlines and hotel chains. Some people get those, take advantage of the offer, and then cancel before they get hit with their annual fee after one year. Then, they sign up for a different rewards card. Be careful though, because bank cards that have their own point system will zero out your points in their system if you don't at least retain a no-fee or some other credit card with them.

As you shop for rewards cards, be careful and take with many grains of salt any "advice" you find on blogs or websites that recommend specific cards and provide direct links to sign up for those cards. The reason: These blogs and websites are getting kickbacks known as *affiliate fees,* typically in the neighborhood of about $100 per sign-up for new customers they reel in for the credit-card companies.

Taming Technology Spending

It seems there's no end of ways to stay in touch and be entertained, as well as a never-ending stream of new gadgets. Although I enjoy choices and convenience as much as the next person, the cost for all these services and gadgets adds up, leading to a continued enslavement to your working full-time and earning more money.

Err on the side of keeping your life simple. Doing so costs less, reduces stress, and allows more time for the things that really do matter in life.

Keep the following in mind before you spend money on technology:

>> **Especially when it comes to new technology and gadgets, wait.** You don't have to be the first person to get something new. When something new first hits the market, prices are relatively high and the gadget inevitably has bugs.

Wait at least a couple of years and your patience will be rewarded with much lower prices and more reliable products. If you're considering buying a new cell phone, ask about buying the previous model, which is likely far less than the new model and generally quite similar. Also, do your homework before going shopping. *Consumer Reports* and c|net (www.cnet.com) are useful resources.

>> **Be aware of how much you spend on your cell phone.** Cell phones are a particular device that can encourage the wasting of money. Of course, if your employer pays for your cell phone as a perk or you can afford to buy the latest and greatest gadgets, you can skip what I have to say on this topic. In addition to downloads, text messaging, web surfing, and other services, you can find all sorts of entertaining ways to run up cell-phone bills each month. Apps are especially problematic in this regard. Sure, the company behind most apps claims the app is free, but of course, you'll face numerous tempting ways to make in-app purchases. Ask yourself whether you really need all these costly bells and whistles.

TIP

Be safe with your cell phone, especially when driving, and don't hold a cell phone to your ear when talking because of long-term health concerns about the radiation emitted from these phones. Use the speakerphone or get an ear bud/headset for your phone.

HOW BANKS MAKE MONEY ON CREDIT CARDS

Banks make plenty of money on credit cards, which is why many banks love the business of issuing credit cards. (And why they can "afford" to offer rewards programs.)

Banks make money on credit cards through the so-called interchange fees that they charge merchants for processing transactions made on the credit cards. Such fees average around 2 percent of the transaction amount. So, for example, if you pay most of your monthly bills through your credit card, the monthly interchange fees that the card-issuing bank could be collecting could be $20 per $1,000 charged on your card. If you charge $1,000 per month ($12,000 per year), that's $240 (2 percent of $12,000). If you charge an average of $5,000 monthly ($60,000 per year), that's $1,200 annually in interchange fees!

Keeping Down Insurance Costs

Insurance is a big area — so big, in fact, that Part 4 of this book covers it in detail. The following tips help you minimize your insurance spending while making the most of your insurance, whether health, home, renter's, auto, or life insurance:

» **Use high deductibles.** Each insurance policy has a *deductible,* which is the amount of a loss that must come out of your pocket before coverage kicks in. Higher deductibles can help to greatly lower your premiums. However, if you have a lot of claims, you won't come out ahead by instead choosing a low deductible, because your insurance premiums will escalate.

» **Obtain broad coverage.** Don't buy insurance for anything that won't be a financial catastrophe if you have to pay for it out of your own pocket. For example, buying simple dental or home warranty plans, which cover relatively small potential expenditures, doesn't make financial sense. And if no one's dependent on your income, you don't need life insurance, either.

» **Always shop around.** Rates vary tremendously among insurers. For each of the major insurance policies, I provide you with a short list of the best companies to visit their websites or call for quotes and other cost-saving strategies in Part 4.

» **Take care of your health.** Exercise at least a few times per week and eat healthfully. Lose and keep off that extra weight if you're now overweight. You only get one body and one life, so take care of it.

Getting Affordable and Quality Professional Advice

Although your life may be relatively simple now, sometimes you may have to deal with new challenges, and you may benefit from a seasoned pro at your side. Tax, legal, business, and financial advisors can be worth more than their expense if they know what they're doing and you pay a reasonable fee. Here's how to get the most out of your spending when you hire advisors:

» **Get educated first.** How can you possibly evaluate an expert on a certain topic if you don't know much about the topic yourself? Reading this book, for example, is an excellent thing to do before hiring a financial advisor. Published and software-based resources can be useful, low-cost alternatives and supplements to hiring professionals.

>> **Use professionals only when needed — not constantly.** Most people most of the time should hire a professional only on an as-needed basis. But be wary of professionals who create or perpetuate work and have conflicts of interest with their recommendations.

>> **Scrutinize and interview thoroughly before hiring.** Do background research to evaluate each prospective advisor's strengths and biases. Be sure to check references and conduct an Internet search to see what you can find out about the person. Check regulatory associations in your state for any citations or actions taken against an advisor. The U.S. Securities and Exchange Commission provides an advisory check service at `https://adviserinfo.sec.gov/`.

Chapter 18 provides you more information about different types of professionals you can hire.

Handling Healthcare Expenses

When you're young and in good health, you usually don't give much thought to healthcare expenses and health insurance. But you have health insurance for a reason, and unfortunately, the cost of healthcare continues to rise faster than the overall rate of inflation. Use these tips to protect yourself:

INVESTIGATE

>> **Shop around for health insurance and healthcare.** Many different plan designs are available with a wide variation in costs. Also, like any other profession, medical providers have a profit motive, so they may recommend something that isn't your best option, including extra testing that you may not need or benefit from. Don't take any one physician's advice as gospel. Always get a second opinion for any proposed surgery.

>> **Examine your employer's benefit plans.** Take advantage of being able to put away a portion of your income before taxes to pay for out-of-pocket healthcare expenses, especially in health savings accounts (see Chapter 14).

>> **Investigate alternative medicine and tread carefully.** Alternative medicine's focus on preventive care and treatment of the whole body or person are pluses.

Just keep your antenna up for pie-in-the-sky promises and charlatans out to empty your wallet. Check with your physician before trying any alternatives.

WARNING

>> **Kick your addictions.** Smoking, alcohol, drugs, and gambling can cost you financially and emotionally. Be honest with yourself about the damage that excesses in these areas are causing in your life and take action now to get on a healthier path. Seek support groups and 12-step programs in your area for sustained recovery.

Chapter **6**

Taxes: Reduce Them When You Can!

axes are likely one of your largest expenses along with your housing costs. So you should be highly motivated to reduce your taxes within the boundaries of the law. And you need to understand enough of the tax laws and rules so you don't get whacked with penalties and interest charges. This chapter can help you stay on the right side of the law and understand what strategies you can use to reduce your income taxes legally and permanently.

Understanding Taxable Income

Your *taxable income* is income on which you actually pay income taxes. For example, your employment income and the interest you earn on bank savings accounts and certificates of deposit (CDs) are all federally taxable. By contrast, interest paid on municipal bonds is generally not federally taxable. As I discuss later in this chapter, some income, such as from stock dividends and long-term capital gains, is taxed at lower rates than ordinary income.

STATE INCOME TAXES

While this chapter focuses upon the federal income tax system and strategies to reduce those taxes, most of what is discussed will also help you to reduce your state income taxes, which the vast majority of states levy. Each state income tax system is unique, so it's not possible to cover them all here.

At the time this book was published, 42 states imposed a state income tax. Eight states — Alaska, Florida, Nevada, South Dakota, Tennessee, Texas, Washington, and Wyoming — don't have an income tax. New Hampshire only has a state income tax on dividend and interest investment income.

Does that mean that these eight states with no income tax are where you should move to avoid taxation? Not really, because as you might expect, such states make up for the lack of state income taxes through higher taxes on other things. For example, Florida and Texas have high property and sales tax rates, New Hampshire has high property tax rates, Nevada and Tennessee have a high sales tax rate, and Washington has high gas taxes. Some of these states also have a high cost of living. Finally, keep in mind that employers in those states know that employment income is not taxed by the state so all other things being equal, they can pay employees a little less due to that fact.

Knowing your taxable income is important because it can help you focus on strategies for legally lowering it. When doing your federal income tax return, you calculate your taxable income by subtracting deductions from your income. Certain expenses, such as mortgage interest and property taxes, are deductible in the event that these itemized deductions exceed the standard deduction. (See the later section "Increasing Your Deductions" for more details.) When you contribute to qualified retirement plans, you also get a deduction, just as you do if you put money into a health savings account.

Comparing Marginal Taxes

My purpose in writing this chapter is to help you legally and permanently reduce your taxes. Understanding the tax system is the key to reducing your tax burden.

As an important starting point, you need to understand the concept of marginal tax rates. Get out your most recent year's federal and state income tax returns and look up the total taxes you paid that year. Many people don't know this amount (perhaps in part because it's too often a depressingly large number) but instead can tell me whether they got a refund. Remember — all a refund reflects is the repayment to you of some tax dollars because you overpaid your taxes during the year.

Regarding taxes, not all income is treated equally. This fact is far from self-evident. If you work for an employer and earn a constant salary during the course of a year, a steady and equal amount of federal and state taxes is deducted from each paycheck. Thus, it appears as though all that earned income is being taxed equally.

REMEMBER

In reality, however, you pay less tax on your first dollars of earnings and more tax on your last dollars of earnings. Your *marginal tax rate* is the rate of tax you pay on your last, or highest, dollars of income. For example, if you're single and your taxable income totals $45,000 during 2021, you pay federal tax at the rate of 10 percent on the first $9,950 of taxable income, 12 percent on income between $9,950 and $40,525, and 22 percent on income between $40,525 and $45,000. Your marginal tax rate is 22 percent. Your total marginal rate includes your federal and state tax rates, as well as local income tax rates in the municipalities that have them. You can look up your state income tax rate in your current state income tax preparation booklet or on your state's government website. Table 6-1 shows the federal income tax brackets for single folks and married couples filing jointly for 2021.

TABLE 6-1

2021 Federal Income Tax Rates for Singles and Married Households Filing Jointly

Federal Income Tax Rate	Single Taxable Income	For Married People Filing Jointly
10%	Up to $9,950	Up to $19,900
12%	$9,951 to $40,525	$19,901 to $81,050
22%	$40,526 to $86,375	$81,051 to $172,750
24%	$86,376 to $164,925	$172,751 to $329,850
32%	$164,926 to $209,425	$329,851 to $418,850
35%	$209,426 to $523,600	$418,851 to $628,300
37%	Over $523,600	Over $628,300

REMEMBER

The marginal tax rate is a powerful concept that allows you to determine the additional taxes you have to pay on more income. Conversely, you can calculate the amount of taxes you save by reducing your taxable income, either by decreasing your income or by increasing your deductions.

Changes from the Tax Cut and Jobs Act Bill

Effective 2018, a new set of federal personal and corporate tax rates and rules took effect. Corporate tax reform was long overdue. For too long, the United States had way too high a corporate tax rate, which has caused increasing numbers of companies to choose to do less business in the United States.

Personal income tax rates were reduced across the board with the biggest reductions coming for lower- and moderate-income earners. This resulted in an approximate $2,000 reduction for a moderate-income earning household. In response to these tax cuts, Brian Riedl, a senior fellow at the Manhattan Institute said, "The bottom 80 percent of families currently pay 33 percent of all combined federal taxes, yet would get 37 percent of the tax cuts. By contrast, the top 1 percent currently pays 27 percent of all federal taxes but would get just 18 percent of the tax cuts. The result would be wealthy families paying a larger portion of the federal tax burden."

Here are some of the other major changes in the tax bill:

> » **Increased standard deduction and eliminated personal exemption:** The bill nearly doubled the so-called standard deduction. This amount is deducted from your income before arriving at your taxable income, so a larger standard deduction reduces your taxable income and tax bill. However, Congress also eliminated exemptions that reduced a person's taxable income. The net effect of these changes is some tax simplification in that far fewer taxpayers are filing Schedule A for Itemized Deductions and can instead simply claim the standard deduction.

> » **Increased child tax credit:** The child tax credit, which previously stood at $1,000 per child under the age of 17, was increased to $2,000 per child, and up to $1,400 is refundable for taxpayers not otherwise owing federal income tax. Also, the incomes at which this credit starts phasing out rise from $110,000 for married couples to $400,000, and from $75,000 for non-married filers to $200,000.

> » **State and local tax deductions capped at $10,000:** This includes property taxes on your home, and for homeowners in high cost-of-living areas with high state income taxes (for example, metro areas such as San Francisco, Los Angeles, New York, and Washington D.C.), this cap poses a modest or even significant negative change. Because these taxes are itemized deductions, only being able to take up to $10,000 (previously unlimited) may cause some taxpayers to no longer be able to itemize. Also, by reducing the tax benefits of home ownership (see also the next item), this change effectively raises the cost of home ownership, especially in high-cost and highly taxed areas.

>> **Mortgage-interest deduction for both primary and second homes capped at $750,000 borrowed:** This represents a modest reduction from the previous $1,000,000 limit on mortgage indebtedness deductibility.

Reducing Taxes on Work Income

When you earn money from work, you're supposed to pay income tax on that income. Some people avoid taxes by illegal means, such as by not reporting such income (doing that isn't really possible if you're getting a regular paycheck from an employer), but you can very well end up paying a heap of penalties and extra interest charges on top of the taxes you owe. And you may even get tossed in jail. This section focuses on the legal ways to reduce your income taxes on work-related income.

Contributing to retirement plans

One way you can exclude money from your taxable income is by tucking it away in employer-based retirement plans, such as 401(k) or 403(b) accounts, or self-employed retirement plans, such as an SEP-IRA or Solo 401(k). Besides reducing your federal and state income taxes, retirement plans help you build a nest egg so you don't have to work for the rest of your life.

If your combined federal and state marginal tax rate (see the earlier "Comparing Marginal Taxes" section) is, say, 30 percent and you contribute $1,000 to one of these plans, you reduce your federal and state taxes by $300. Contribute another $1,000, and your taxes drop another $300 (as long as you're still in the same marginal tax rate). And when your money is inside a retirement account, it can compound and grow without taxation. (Some employers offer an additional perk: free matching money simply for your contributing.)

TIP

Single taxpayers with an adjusted gross income (AGI) of less than $33,000 and married couples filing jointly with an AGI of less than $66,000 can earn a tax credit (claimed on Form 8880, "Credit for Qualified Retirement Savings Contributions") for retirement account contributions. (*AGI* is your total wage, interest, dividend, and all other income minus retirement account contributions, self-employed health insurance, alimony paid, and losses from investments.) Unlike a deduction, a tax credit directly reduces your tax bill by the amount of the credit. This credit, which is detailed in Table 6-2, is a percentage of the first $2,000 you contribute to a retirement plan (or $4,000 on a joint return). The credit isn't available to those individuals under the age of 18, full-time students, or people who are claimed as dependents on someone else's tax return.

TABLE 6-2	"Saver's Tax Credit" for Retirement Plan Contributions	
Singles Adjusted Gross Income	Married-Filing-Jointly Adjusted Gross Income	Tax Credit for Retirement Account Contributions
$0–$19,750	$0–$39,500	50%
$19,750–$21,500	$39,500–$43,000	20%
$21,500–$33,000	$43,000–$66,000	10%

WARNING

Many people miss this great opportunity for reducing their taxes because they spend all (or too much of) their current employment income and, therefore, have little or nothing left to put into a retirement account. If you're in this predicament, you need to reduce your spending before you can contribute money to a retirement plan. (See Chapters 2 and 5 for advice on decreasing your spending.)

If your employer doesn't offer the option of saving money through a retirement plan, ask the benefits and human resource(s) person/department whether the company would consider offering such a plan. Alternatively, consider contributing to an individual retirement account (IRA), which may or may not be tax-deductible, depending on your circumstances. You should first maximize contributions to the previously mentioned tax-deductible accounts. (See Chapter 2 for more on retirement accounts.)

However, a retirement account may not be the wisest decision for you at this time. Good reasons not to fund a retirement account include the following:

>> **You have a specific, shorter-term goal.** Such goals include saving to purchase a home or starting a business that necessitates having access to your money.

>> **You're temporarily in a low tax bracket.** This could happen, for example, if you lose your job for an extended period of time or are in school. (In these cases, you're unlikely to have lots of spare money to contribute to a retirement account anyway!) If you have some employment income, consider the Roth IRA. While not offering an upfront tax break on your contributions, a Roth IRA features no taxation on investment earnings over time just as with other retirement accounts. And, unlike those accounts, a Roth IRA allows for tax-free withdrawals after age 59½.

AVOIDING RETIREMENT ACCOUNT WITHDRAWAL PENALTIES

Many young people object to funding retirement accounts because retirement seems so far away and because the money in retirement accounts, once contributed, is only accessible subject to penalties (10 percent federal plus whatever your state charges).

However, if you do put money into a retirement account, you can avoid these early-withdrawal penalties under several different circumstances:

- You can make penalty-free withdrawals from individual retirement accounts for a first-time home purchase (limit of $10,000).

- You can withdraw from your account to help cover higher educational expenses for you, your spouse, your children, or your grandchildren.

- If you have major medical expenses (exceeding 10 percent of your income) or a disability, you may be exempt from the penalties under certain conditions.

- If you get into a financial pinch while you're still employed, be aware that some company retirement plans allow you to borrow against your balance. This tactic is like loaning money to yourself — the interest payments go back into your account. (Important note: If you fail to repay the loan, it's classified as a withdrawal and subject to early withdrawal penalties.)

- If you lose your job and withdraw retirement account money simply because you need it to live on, the penalties do apply. However, if you're not working and you're earning so little income that you need to tap your retirement account, you surely fall into a low tax bracket. The lower income taxes you pay (when compared to the taxes you would have paid on that money had you not sheltered it in a retirement account in the first place) should make up for most or all of the penalty.

- The IRS allows you to withdraw money before age 59½ if you do so in equal, annual installments based on your life expectancy. The IRS has a table for looking up your life expectancy.

Using health savings accounts

You can reduce your taxable income and sock away money for future healthcare expenses by taking advantage of a *health savings account* (HSA). In fact, HSAs can offer superior tax savings versus retirement accounts because in addition to providing upfront tax breaks on contributions and tax-free accumulation of investment earnings, you can also withdraw money from HSAs tax-free so long as the money is used for healthcare costs. No other retirement accounts offer this triple tax-free benefit. For more details on HSAs, see Chapter 14.

Deducting self-employment expenses

When you're self-employed, you can deduct a multitude of expenses from your income before calculating the income tax you owe. Some self-employed folks don't take all the deductions they're eligible for. In some cases, people simply aren't aware of the wonderful world of deductions. Others are worried that large deductions will increase the risk of an audit.

When you're self-employed, going it alone when dealing with your taxes is usually a mistake. You must educate yourself to make the tax laws work for you rather than against you. Spend some time finding out more about tax deductions; you'll be convinced that taking full advantage of your eligible deductions makes sense and saves you money. Hiring tax help is well worth your while, and record keeping is essential. Software such as QuickBooks can assist you with tracking your small business's finances and TurboTax can offer a lower cost alternative for tax return preparation.

More items than you expect are deductible. If you buy a computer or office furniture, you can deduct those expenses. (Sometimes they need to be gradually deducted, or *depreciated*, over time.) Salaries for employees, the cost of office supplies, rent or mortgage interest for your office space, and phone/communications expenses are also generally deductible.

REMEMBER

As a self-employed individual, you're responsible for the accurate and timely filing of all taxes owed on your income and employment taxes on your employees (if you have them) in order to avoid penalties. You need to make estimated tax payments on a quarterly basis. To pay taxes on your income, use Form 1040-ES. You can obtain this form, along with instructions, from the IRS (800-829-3676; www.irs.gov). The form comes with an estimated tax worksheet and four quarterly tax payment coupons. If you want to find the rules for withholding and submitting taxes from employees' paychecks, ask the IRS for Form 941, and for unemployment insurance, look for Form 940. And unless you're lucky enough to live in a state with no income taxes, you need to call your state's department of revenue or a similar entity for your state's estimated income tax package. Another alternative is to hire a payroll firm, such as ADP or Paychex, to do all this work for you.

When you pay with cash, following the paper trail for all the money you spent can be hard to do (for you and for the IRS, in the event you're ever audited). At the end of the year, how are you going to remember how much you spent for parking or client meals if you fail to keep a record? How will you survive an IRS audit without proper documentation? Small business software (for example, QuickBooks) or apps can assist you with expense and cash tracking.

Debit cards are accepted most places and provide convenient documentation. Ditto for credit cards. Be careful about getting a card in your business's name, though, because some banks don't offer protection against fraudulent use of business cards.

TIP

If your children, spouse, or other relatives help with some aspect of your business, consider paying them for the work. Besides showing them that you value their work, this practice may reduce your family's tax liability. For example, children are usually in a lower tax bracket. By shifting some of your income to your child, you cut your tax bill.

Increasing Your Deductions

Deductions are amounts you subtract from your adjusted gross income before calculating the tax you owe. The IRS gives you two methods for determining your total deductions and allows you to select the method that leads to greater deductions and lower taxes.

The two methods are as follows:

>> **Standard deduction:** If you have a relatively simple financial life, taking the standard deduction is generally the better option. Those who are blind or who are age 65 or older get a slightly higher standard deduction. As noted earlier in this chapter in the section, "Changes from the Tax Cut and Jobs Act Bill," the standard deduction now is much higher so more people will be better off claiming it. Before the new tax bill was implemented in 2018, about 70 percent of taxpayers took the standard deduction and 30 percent itemized. Since that time, the portion of those itemizing has dropped by more than half.

>> **Itemized deduction:** Itemizing your deductions on Schedule A of IRS Form 1040 is the other method for determining your allowable deductions. Itemizing tends to make more sense for those who earn a high income, own their own home (mortgage interest and property taxes are itemized deductions), and/or have unusually large expenses from medical bills, charitable contributions, or loss due to theft or catastrophe.

TIP

If you don't currently itemize, you may be surprised to discover that your state income taxes can be itemized. Also, when you pay a fee to the state to register and license your car, you can itemize a portion of the expenditure as a deduction (on Schedule A, "Personal Property Taxes"). The IRS allows you to deduct the part of the fee that relates to the value of your car. The state organization that collects the fee should be able to tell you what portion of the fee is deductible. (Some states detail on the invoice what portion of the fee is tax-deductible.)

Several states have state disability insurance funds. If you pay into these funds (check your W-2), you can deduct your payments as state and local income taxes on Line 5 of Schedule A. You may also claim a deduction on this line for payments you make into your state's unemployment compensation fund.

Lowering Investment Income Taxes

The distributions and profits on investments that you hold outside of tax-sheltered retirement accounts are exposed to taxation. Interest, dividends, and *capital gains* (profits from the sale of an investment at a price that's higher than the purchase price) are all taxed. The good news: You can take action to reduce the taxes in those accounts. This section explains some of the best methods for doing so.

Investing in tax-free money market funds and bonds

When you're in a high tax bracket, you may find that you come out ahead with tax-free investments. Tax-free investments pay investment income, which is exempt from federal tax, state tax, or both. Tax-free investments yield less than comparable investments that produce taxable income. But because of the difference in taxes, the earnings from tax-free investments can end up being greater than what you're left with from taxable investments.

Two tax-free options include the following. (See Chapter 10 for more details on tax-free investments.)

>> **Money market funds:** Tax-free money market funds can be a better alternative to bank savings accounts, the interest on which is subject to taxation.

>> **Bonds:** Likewise, tax-free bonds are intended to be longer-term investments that pay tax-free interest, so they may be a better, more tax-efficient investment option for you than bank certificates of deposit, Treasury bills and bonds, and other investments that produce taxable income.

Selecting other tax-friendly investments

WARNING

Too often, when selecting investments, people mistakenly focus on past rates of return, before-tax. The past, of course, is no guarantee of the future. Selecting an investment with a reportedly high rate of return without considering tax consequences is an even worse mistake because what you get to keep, after taxes, is what matters.

I call investments that appreciate in value and don't distribute much in the way of highly taxed income *tax-friendly.* (Some in the investment business use the term *tax-efficient.*) See Chapter 10 for more information on tax-friendly stocks and stock mutual funds.

Real estate is one of the few areas with preferred status in the tax code. In addition to deductions allowed for mortgage interest and property taxes, you can depreciate rental property to reduce your taxable income. *Depreciation* is a special tax deduction allowed for the gradual wear and tear on rental real estate. When you sell investment real estate, you may be eligible to conduct a tax-free exchange into a replacement rental property.

Making your profits long term

When you buy growth investments such as stocks and real estate, you should do so for the long term. The tax system rewards your patience with lower tax rates on your profits.

TIP

When you're able to hold on to a nonretirement account investment such as a stock, bond, or mutual fund for more than one year, you get a tax break if you sell that investment at a profit. Specifically, your profit is taxed under the lower capital gains tax rate schedule. If you're in the 22 to 35 percent federal income tax brackets, you will generally pay just 15 percent of your long-term capital gains profit in federal taxes. (The same lower tax rate applies to qualified stock dividends.) The long-term capital gains tax jumps up to 20 percent for those income tax filers in the highest income tax brackets of 35 and 37 percent. High-income earners actually face an additional 3.8 percent surtax due to the Affordable Care Act (also known as Obamacare), bringing the highest effective long-term capital gains tax rate to 23.8 percent. If you're in the 10 or 12 percent federal income tax brackets, the long-term capital gains tax rate is 0 percent.

Enlisting Education Tax Breaks

The U.S. tax laws include numerous tax breaks for education-related expenditures. Here are the important tax-reduction opportunities you should know about for yourself and your kids if you have them:

>> **Tax deductions for college expenses:** You may take up to a $2,500 tax deduction on IRS Form 1040 for college costs as long as your modified adjusted gross income (AGI) is less than $70,000 for single taxpayers and less than $140,000 for married couples filing jointly. (**Note:** You may take a partial tax deduction if your AGI is between $70,000 and $85,000 for single taxpayers and between $140,000 and $170,000 for married couples filing jointly.)

>> **Tax-free investment earnings in special accounts:** Money invested in Section 529 plans is sheltered from taxation and is not taxed upon withdrawal as long as the money is used to pay for eligible education expenses. 529 plans

allow you to sock away more than $200,000. However, funding such accounts may harm your kid's qualifications for financial aid.

>> **American Opportunity tax credit:** The American Opportunity credit provides tax relief to low- and moderate-income earners facing education costs. The full credit (up to $2,500 per student) is available to individuals whose modified adjusted gross income is $80,000 or less, or $160,000 or less for married couples filing jointly. The credit is phased out for single taxpayers above $90,000 and married couples filing jointly above $180,000. The credit can be claimed for expenses for the first four years of postsecondary education. You may be able to claim an American Opportunity tax credit in the same year in which you receive a distribution from either an ESA or 529, but you can't use expenses paid with a distribution from either an ESA or 529 as the basis for the American Opportunity credit.

>> **Lifetime Learning tax credit:** The Lifetime Learning credit may be up to 20 percent of the first $10,000 of qualified educational expenses — up to $2,000 per taxpayer. For parents filing tax returns, only this credit or the American Opportunity tax credit may be claimed for each child per tax year. Single taxpayers' phase-out for being able to take this credit is at modified adjusted gross incomes (MAGIs) of $59,000 to $69,000. Other taxpayers' phase-out is from $118,000 to $138,000.

Preparing Your Tax Return and Minimizing Your Taxes

Every year that you earn money, you'll probably complete a federal and state income tax return. Regardless of which approach you use to prepare and file your returns, you should take financial moves during the year to reduce your taxes.

Here are some resources to help:

>> **IRS materials and guidance:** If you have a relatively simple, straightforward situation, filing your tax return on your own by using IRS instructions is okay. However, recognize that their publications don't go out of their way to highlight tax-reduction opportunities. And if you call the IRS with questions, know that the IRS has been known to give wrong information from time to time. For you web surfers, the Internal Revenue Service website (www.irs.gov) is among the better Internet tax sites, believe it or not.

>> **Preparation and advice guides:** Books about tax preparation and tax planning that highlight common problem areas and are written in clear, simple English are invaluable. They supplement the official instructions, not only by helping you complete your return correctly but also by showing you how to save as much money as possible. Please visit my website (www.erictyson.com) for up-to-date recommendations.

>> **Software:** Good tax-preparation software can be helpful. TurboTax is a good program that I've reviewed. If you go the software route, I highly recommend having a good tax advice book by your side.

>> **Professional hired help:** Competent tax preparers and advisors can save you money by identifying tax-reduction strategies you may overlook. They can also help reduce the likelihood of an audit, which can be triggered by blunders. Tax practitioners come with varying backgrounds, training, and credentials. The more training and specialization a tax practitioner has (and the more affluent his clients), the higher his hourly fee usually is. Fees and competence vary greatly.

Enrolled agents (EAs) must pass IRS scrutiny in order to be called an *enrolled agent.* This license allows the agent to represent you before the IRS in the event of an audit. Continuing education is also required; the training is generally longer and more sophisticated than it is for a typical preparer. Returns that require some of the more common schedules (such as Schedule A for deductions) cost about $250+ to prepare. To obtain names and telephone numbers of EAs in your area, contact the National Association of Enrolled Agents (NAEA) at 202-822-6232 or www.naea.org.

If you're self-employed and/or you file lots of other schedules, you may want to consider hiring a certified public accountant (CPA). But you don't need to do so year after year. If your situation grows complex one year and then stabilizes, consider getting help for the perplexing year and then using preparation guides, software, or a lower-cost preparer or enrolled agent in the future. CPAs go through significant training and examination before receiving the CPA credential. In order to maintain this designation, a CPA must also complete a fair number of continuing education classes every year. CPA fees vary tremendously. Most charge $100+ per hour, but CPAs at large companies and in high-cost-of-living areas tend to charge somewhat more.

Chapter **7**

Housing: Comparing Renting and Buying

O ver the decades of your adult life, you need a place to live. Housing is important because you spend a lot of time in it, and its location affects your commute to work, your social life, and the convenience of recreation, shopping, restaurants, and other activities. And you spend plenty of money on housing, whether you rent or own it. Along with taxes, housing expenses are one of the top two expenses for most people.

This chapter explores your housing options and helps you understand the costs of buying and owning a home and compare that option to renting. If you decide to purchase a home, I walk you through the major elements of searching for and negotiating your best deal on a home for purchase.

The Ins and Outs of Renting

Most books on home buying and real estate fail to offer a balanced perspective of renting versus buying. Too many of them only extol the virtues of buying and owning property without discussing the drawbacks. In this section, I discuss the benefits and long-term costs of renting. I also cover the important details of rental applications and contracts.

Seeing the benefits of renting

Although owning a home and investing in real estate generally pay off well over the long term, renting has its advantages. Some of the financially successful renters I've met include people who pay relatively low rent, either because they live in modest housing and/or have roommates, or they live in a rent-controlled building. Some young adults live with a family member who provides them with a great deal on rent, which can have benefits. If you can consistently save 10 percent or more of your earnings, which you may be able to do through a low-cost rental, you're probably on track to achieving your financial goals.

Renting has the following pros:

>> **You can avoid worrying about or being responsible for fixing up the property.** Your landlord is responsible.

>> **You have more financial and psychological flexibility.** You may not be sure that you'll stay with your current employer or chosen career, and you may change direction in the future and not want the financial overhead that comes with a mortgage. And if you want to move, you can generally do so a lot more easily as a renter than you can as a homeowner.

>> **You can have all your money in financial assets that you can tap into more easily.** Some people enter their retirement years with a substantial portion of their wealth tied up in their home, a challenge that you don't face when renting over the long haul. Homeowners who have *equity* (the difference between the market value of the property and the debt owed on it) tied up in a home at retirement can downsize to a less-costly property to free up cash and/or take out a reverse mortgage on their home equity.

Considering the long-term costs of renting

When you crunch the numbers to find out what owning rather than renting a comparable place may cost you on a monthly basis, you may discover that owning isn't as expensive as you thought. Or you may find that owning costs more than renting. This discovery may tempt you to think that, financially speaking, renting is cheaper than owning.

INVESTIGATE

Be careful not to jump to conclusions. Remember that you're looking at the cost of owning versus renting *today*. What about 10, 20, or 30 years from now? As an owner, your biggest monthly expense — the mortgage payment — doesn't increase, assuming that you have a fixed-rate mortgage (for an explanation of fixed-rate and other types of mortgages, see the "Understanding your mortgage options" section later in the chapter). Your property taxes, homeowner's insurance, and maintenance expenses, which are generally far less than your mortgage payment, should only increase with the cost of living. And remember that as a homeowner you build equity in your property; that equity can be significant by your retirement.

When you rent, however, your entire monthly rent is subject to inflation. (Living in a *rent-controlled unit*, where the annual increase allowed in your rent is capped, is the exception to this rule.)

Completing your rental application

When you're in the market for a rental, you'll probably complete an application. You'll be asked to provide such information as your name, current address, date of birth, occupation, employer, banking information, credit history, current landlord and rental terms, and a couple of references.

TIP

Here are some tips to keep in mind as you're completing your rental application:

>> **Put your best foot forward.** Just as a good résumé helps you interest an employer and land a job, your rental application helps you secure a place to live. So, it's important to fill it out accurately and completely. Does that mean you need to list everything on it, including less-than-flattering information? As with your résumé, tell the truth but remember the advertising value of the document.

REMEMBER

With regards to other sources of income, you're under no obligation to detail alimony, child support, or your spouse's annual income unless you want that information considered in your application.

>> **Recognize that you're authorizing the release of personal and confidential information.** Rental applications generally have a section requiring your signature, stating, "I authorize an investigation of my credit, tenant history, banking, and employment for the purposes of renting a house, apartment, or condominium from this owner, manager, brokerage, finder, agent, or leasing company."

>> **Consider the length of the lease commitment.** Most landlords prefer tenants who are stable renters and who remain for long periods of time (years, not months). Especially if you may want to move to buy a place or

relocate for a future job, having a one-year lease that goes month to month after the first year is a good compromise. If you don't expect to stay much more than a year or two, that's probably better left unsaid. Remember, landlords generally want long-term tenants.

>> **Remember lease agreements are negotiable.** Landlords will present you with a standard lease form and hope that you simply accept and sign it, which many people do. Legal agreements don't make for scintillating reading and are often intimidating for non-lawyerly types! Please take the time to read the proposed lease agreement so that you know what you're potentially agreeing to. Ask questions about things you don't understand. And please remember that you can and should negotiate, especially if your local rental market is a bit slow or you're considering a lease that seems a tad expensive for what it is. Ask if there are any promotions (for example, free month's rent).

>> **Rent where you might like to buy.** If you're getting close to wanting to buy your own home, try renting in (or at least near) the area in which you think you'd most like to buy. What better way to test out whether you'll actually enjoy living in an area?

Figuring the Costs of Owning and Making It Happen Financially

Buying a home can be financially rewarding, but owning a property is a big financial commitment that may backfire if you get in over your head or overpay.

In this section, I help you with comparing the costs of buying versus renting, determining what you can afford, figuring out how much to borrow, and accumulating the down payment.

Deciding to buy

Before you determine whether you want to actually buy a home, you want to figure out how long you plan on living in the home.

TIP

Financially speaking, buying a home begins to make more financial sense if you anticipate being there for three to five years or more. Buying and selling a property entails a lot of expenses, including the cost of getting a mortgage (points; application and appraisal fees), inspection expenses, moving costs, real-estate agents' commissions, and title insurance. To cover these transaction costs plus the additional costs of ownership, a property needs to appreciate about 15 percent during the tenure of your ownership.

If you need or want to move in a couple of years, counting on 15 percent appreciation is risky. If you're fortunate and you happen to buy before a sharp upturn in housing prices, you may get it. Otherwise, you'll lose money on the deal.

Comparing the costs of owning versus renting

Some people assume that owning costs more than renting, but owning doesn't have to cost a lot. Owning may even cost less than renting in some geographic areas, especially with the opportunity to buy at lower prices that may occur after a decline in home values (usually around the time of a recession). After the 2008 financial crisis and decline in home values throughout the country, there were attractive values in many areas through and beyond the early 2010s for example.

Buying seems a lot more expensive than renting if you compare your monthly rent (from hundreds of dollars to more than $1,000, depending on where you live) to a property's purchase price, which is usually a much larger number — perhaps $100,000 to $250,000. But you must compare the expenses the same way. When you consider a home purchase, you're forced to think about your housing expenses in one huge chunk rather than in a monthly rent check.

INVESTIGATE

To make a fair comparison between ownership and rental costs, figure what it costs on a monthly basis to buy a place you desire versus what it costs in monthly rent for a comparable place. Remember that mortgage interest and property tax payments for your home are generally tax-deductible subject to certain limitations. The worksheet in Table 7-1 enables you to do a monthly rent versus buy cost comparison.

Now compare Line 9 in Table 7-1 with the monthly rent on a comparable place to see which costs more — owning or renting.

Mortgage

To determine the monthly payment on your proposed mortgage, multiply the relevant number ("multiplier") from Table 7-2 by the size of your mortgage expressed in thousands of dollars (divided by 1,000). For example, if you're taking out a $100,000, 30-year mortgage at 5 percent, you multiply 100 by 5.37 for a $537 monthly payment.

TABLE 7-1   ## Monthly Renting versus Owning Comparison

Figure Out This ($ per Month)	Write It Here
1. Monthly mortgage payment (see "Mortgage")	$
2. Plus monthly property taxes (see "Property taxes")	+ $
3. Equals total monthly mortgage plus property taxes	= $
4. Your income tax rate (refer to Table 6-1 in Chapter 6)	%
5. Minus tax benefits (Line 3 multiplied by Line 4)	– $
6. Equals after-tax cost of mortgage and property taxes (subtract Line 5 from Line 3)	= $
7. Plus insurance ($30 to $150/mo., depending on property value)	+ $
8. Plus maintenance (1% of property cost divided by 12 months)	+ $
9. Equals total cost of owning (add Lines 6, 7, and 8)	= $

TABLE 7-2   ## Your Monthly Mortgage Payment Multiplier

Interest Rate	15-Year Mortgage Multiplier	30-Year Mortgage Multiplier
3.0%	6.91	4.22
3.5%	7.15	4.49
4.0%	7.40	4.77
4.5%	7.65	5.07
5.0%	7.91	5.37
5.5%	8.17	5.68
6.0%	8.44	6.00
6.5%	8.71	6.32
7.0%	8.99	6.65
7.5%	9.27	6.99
8.0%	9.56	7.34
8.5%	9.85	7.69
9.0%	10.14	8.05
9.5%	10.44	8.41
10.0%	10.75	8.78

Property taxes

You can ask a real-estate person, mortgage lender, or your local assessor's office what your annual property tax bill would be for a house of similar value to the one you're considering buying (the average is about 1.5 percent of your property's value). Divide this amount by 12 to arrive at your monthly property tax bill.

Tax savings in home ownership

REMEMBER

Before 2018, mortgage interest and property tax payments for your home were generally tax-deductible on Schedule A of IRS Form 1040 with one limitation — the mortgage interest was for no more than $1 million of debt. Effective 2018, the tax deduction for property taxes combined with your state income tax is now limited to $10,000 annually. And, the mortgage interest deduction now may be claimed on up to $750,000 of mortgage debt.

Because of the Tax Cut and Jobs Act bill that took effect in 2018, determining the tax savings you may realize from home ownership has thus become more complicated. Here's a shortcut that works reasonably well in determining your tax savings in home ownership: Multiply your federal tax rate (see Table 6-1 in Chapter 6) by the portion of your property taxes up to $10,000 when combined with your annual state income tax payments and the portion of your mortgage payment up to $750,000 of mortgage debt.

Technically speaking, even if you're under the $750,000 mortgage debt threshold, not all of your mortgage payment is tax-deductible — only the portion of the mortgage payment that goes toward interest. In the early years of your mortgage, nearly all of your payment goes toward interest. On the other hand, you may earn state tax benefits from your deductible mortgage interest and property taxes, which I'm ignoring here in this simplified analysis.

TIP

If you want to more accurately determine how home ownership may affect your tax situation, get out your tax return and try plugging in some reasonable numbers to estimate how your taxes will change. You can also speak with a tax advisor.

Considering your overall financial health

Before you buy a property and agree to a particular mortgage, take stock of your overall financial health (especially where you stand in terms of retirement planning). Don't trust a lender when he tells you what you can "afford" according to some formulas the bank uses to figure out what kind of a credit risk you are.

To determine how much a potential home buyer can borrow, lenders look primarily at annual income; they pay no attention to some major aspects of a borrower's overall financial situation. Even if you don't have money tucked away in retirement savings, or you have several children to clothe, feed, and help put through college, or you want to financially help your elderly parents, you still qualify for the same size loan as other people with the same income (assuming equal outstanding debts).

Calculating how much you can borrow

One general rule says you can borrow up to about three times your annual income when buying a home. But, the maximum that a mortgage lender will loan you depends on interest rates. If rates fall, the monthly payment on a mortgage also drops. Thus, lower interest rates make real estate more affordable.

To determine how much they're willing to lend you, lenders start by totaling up your monthly housing expenses for a given home. They define your housing costs as

mortgage payment + property taxes + homeowner's insurance

Lenders typically loan you up to about 35 to 40 percent of your monthly gross (before taxes) income for the housing expense. (If you're self-employed, take your net income from the bottom line of your federal tax form Schedule C and divide by 12 to get your monthly gross income.)

Lenders also consider your other debts when deciding how much to lend you. These debts diminish the funds available to pay your housing expenses. Lenders add the amount you need to pay down your other consumer debts (such as auto loans and credit cards) to your monthly housing expense. The total monthly costs of these debt payments plus your housing costs typically can't exceed 40 to 45 percent.

Accumulating your down payment

You generally qualify for the most favorable mortgage terms by making a down payment of at least 20 percent of the property's purchase price. In addition to saving money on interest, you can avoid the added cost of *private mortgage insurance* (PMI) by putting down this much. To protect against their losing money in the event you default on your loan, lenders usually require PMI, which costs several hundred dollars per year on a typical mortgage. (PMI compensates the lender in the event that it has to take over the property and the property ends up being worth less than the outstanding mortgage on it.)

TIP

Many folks, especially folks in their 20s, don't have enough cash on hand to make a 20 percent down payment on a home to avoid paying PMI. Here are a number of solutions for coming up with that 20 percent faster or for buying with less money down:

>> **Minimize your spending.** See Chapter 5 for ideas.

>> **Consider lower-priced properties.** Smaller properties and ones that need some work can help keep down the purchase price and, therefore, the required down payment.

>> **Find financial partners.** Draft a legal contract to specify what happens if a partner wants out, divorces, or passes away.

>> **Seek reduced down-payment financing.** Some property owners or developers may be willing to finance your purchase with 10 percent down, although you can't be as picky about properties because not as many are available under these terms — many need work or haven't been sold yet for other reasons.

>> **Check out the USDA's Single Family Housing Guaranteed Loan Program.** Another way to buy a home with no down payment and a low interest rate in "rural" areas is via the USDA's Single Family Housing Guaranteed Loan Program (https://www.rd.usda.gov/programs-services/single-family-housing-guaranteed-loan-program). These properties are not limited to what one would typically think of as "rural" areas (think more broadly about non-urban areas) and while there are income limits, many young people qualify.

>> **Get family assistance.** If your parents, grandparents, or other relatives have money dozing away in a bank or similar low-interest account, they may be willing to lend (or even give) you the down payment.

For more home-buying strategies, get a copy of the latest edition of *Home Buying Kit For Dummies* (Wiley), which I coauthored with real-estate guru Ray Brown.

Finding the Right Property

In your search for a property to purchase, you have numerous options in today's real-estate market. To find the right property for you, consider your choices:

>> **Single-family home:** Some people's image of a home is a single-family house, perhaps with a lawn and a white picket fence. From an investment perspective, single-family homes generally do best in the long run. Most people, when they can afford it, prefer a stand-alone home.

>> **Higher-density housing:** In some areas, particularly in higher-cost urban areas, you find the following choices:

- **Condominiums:** You own the unit and a share of everything else.

- **Town homes:** These properties are attached or row houses.

- **Cooperatives:** You own a share of the entire building.

The appeal of such higher-density housing is that it's generally less expensive on a per-square-foot-of-living-space basis compared with single family homes in the same area. In some cases, you don't have to worry about some of the general maintenance because the homeowners' association (which you pay for, directly or indirectly) takes care of it.

TIP

If you don't have the time, energy, or desire to keep up a property, shared/higher-density housing may make sense for you. You generally get more living space for your dollar, and it may also provide you with more security than a stand-alone home. However, shared housing is easier to build and hence easier to overbuild.

REMEMBER

With that being said, you should remember that a rising tide generally raises all boats. In a good real-estate market, all types of housing appreciate, although single-family homes tend to do best. Shared-housing values tend to increase the most in densely populated urban areas with little available land for new building.

TIP

From an investment-return perspective, if you can afford a smaller single-family home rather than a larger shared-housing unit, buy the single-family home. Be especially wary of buying shared housing in suburban areas with lots of developable land because values will often be under pressure due to the ease of overbuilding.

INVESTIGATE

Here are some additional tips to keep in mind to help you find the best property for your situation and to buy a home most likely to increase in value:

>> **Cast a broad net and look at different types of properties in a number of communities before you narrow your search.** Be open-minded and figure out which of your many criteria for a home you really care about.

>> **Even (and especially) if you fall in love with a house, go back to the neighborhood at various times of the day and on different days of the week.** Travel to and from your prospective new home during commute hours to see how long your commute will really take. Knock on a few doors and meet your potential neighbors. You may discover, for example, that a flock of chickens lives in the backyard next door or that the street and basement frequently flood.

» **Examine the area schools.** Go visit them. Don't rely on statistics about test scores. Talk to parents and teachers. What's really going on at the school? Even if you don't have kids, the quality of the local school has a direct bearing on the property's value.

» **Determine whether crime is a problem.** Contact the local police department and check out real-estate websites with such data.

» **Talk to the planning department.** What are your property taxes going to be? Will future development be allowed? If so, what type?

» **Identify any other potential risks.** Is the property located in an area susceptible to major risks, such as floods, mudslides, fires, or earthquakes?

Consider these issues even if they're not important to you, because they can affect the property's cost to insure and resale value. Make sure you know what you're getting yourself into before you buy.

GATHERING DATA ON PROSPECTIVE NEIGHBORHOODS

I've long been a fan of Neighborhood Scout as a tool for helping prospective home buyers use data and information to find communities that meet their specific wants and needs. Their website (www.NeighborhoodScout.com) is useful if you are considering a number of places you might live in a given area and are seeking more and unbiased information. The site is especially useful to folks with multiple job possibilities and those who have great flexibility in where they can live (for example, because they are self-employed or can telecommute for their job).

For a fee (detailed later in this sidebar), Neighborhood Scout provides you with access to a treasure trove of just about every type of helpful data you can imagine that may be useful in finding your ideal place to live.

You can find much of this data in other places, but you have to go to different agencies and websites. I haven't found a site as comprehensive as Neighborhood Scout.

Neighborhood Scout uses hundreds of characteristics to build profiles of census tracts, which typically comprise areas where a few thousand people live and are generally much smaller than the areas zip codes comprise. Among the highly useful data available for searching for your best neighborhood are things like school quality; housing costs; crime rates; income levels; the age, size, and style of homes; the density of buildings; rental areas versus owner occupied; the proportion of families with children; the

(continued)

(continued)

ages of people in the neighborhood; ethnic and racial makeup; educational levels; languages spoken; types of careers of those living in the neighborhood; the numbers of farms, coastal properties, and the like; and much more. A feature called "Scout Vision Trends & Forecasts" includes historic home price-appreciation data by neighborhood and estimates for expected appreciation over the next three years.

You can also search for specific types of predetermined "Lifestyle Characteristics" that seek to match you to particular neighborhoods that tend to have certain commonly sought lifestyles or life stages. Among the categories that the site includes are families with children; first-time homebuyers; young, single, and upwardly mobile; and college students.

Using the "Create" feature, you can enter your own criteria for what you're looking for from your desired neighborhood, and Neighborhood Scout will tell you what neighborhoods in a particular area, state, or even nationally are your best fit.

Using the "Match" feature, you can enter an address of a place you like and find other similar neighborhoods that are the closest match.

Neighborhood Scout's pricing structure takes some time to understand. With a "Pro Lite" account, you can get 10 reports per month for $39.99 monthly.

If you anticipate wanting to view many complete neighborhood reports, you may consider a "Pro" level subscription, which costs $79.99 monthly and provides up to 100 reports per month (unused report credits carry forward to future months).

Working with Real-Estate Agents

An experienced and knowledgeable real-estate agent can be a significant help when you purchase or sell a property. But because agents generally work on commission and get paid a percentage of the sale price, they face numerous conflicts of interest. So don't expect an agent to give you objective advice about what you should do given your overall financial situation. Examine your financial situation before you decide to work with an agent.

INVESTIGATE

Interview several agents, examine their activity list for the past 6–12 months, and check references. The activity list is simply a list detailing every transaction where the agent worked with either the buyer and seller along with the property address and sales price. Reviewing the agent's activity list enables you to see how much experience an agent has with properties similar to the type you may buy or sell through them. Ask agents for the names and phone numbers of at least three clients they worked with in the past six months (in the geographical area in which you're looking). For more advice on hiring a good agent, see Chapter 18.

Financing Your Home

A mortgage loan from a bank or other source makes up the difference between the cash you intend to put into the purchase and the agreed-upon selling price of the real estate. This section reviews the different options you have for financing your home, explains which ones are best, and discusses how to get your loan approved.

Understanding your mortgage options

Three major types of mortgages exist — those with a fixed interest rate, those with a variable or adjustable rate, and those that are a combination of the two.

>> **Fixed-rate mortgages:** These are usually issued for a 15- or 30-year period and have interest rates that don't change over the life of the mortgage. Because the interest rate stays the same, your monthly mortgage payment amount doesn't change. With a fixed-rate mortgage, you have no uncertainty or interest-rate worries.

>> **Adjustable-rate mortgages (ARM):** In contrast to a fixed-rate mortgage, an adjustable-rate mortgage (ARM) carries an interest rate that varies over time. Thus, the size of your monthly payment fluctuates. Because a mortgage payment makes an unusually large dent in most homeowners' checkbooks anyway, signing up for an ARM without understanding its risks is dangerous.

So why would anyone want an ARM? Some home buyers are attracted to the potential savings, especially during the first few years of an adjustable loan, when the interest rate is typically lower than it is on a comparable fixed-rate loan.

>> **Hybrid mortgages:** This type of mortgage combines features of both the fixed- and adjustable-rate mortgages. For example, the initial rate may hold constant for three to five years and then adjust once a year or every six months thereafter.

Deciding which mortgage type is best for you

You should weigh the pros and cons of each mortgage type and consider these issues to determine whether a fixed or adjustable mortgage is best for you. Think about the following questions to make that determination:

>> **How much risk can you handle with the size of your monthly mortgage payment?** You can't afford much risk, for example, if your job and income are unstable and you need to borrow a lot or you have little slack in your monthly

budget. If you're in this situation, stick with a fixed-rate loan. If interest rates rise, how will you afford the monthly payments — much less all the other expenses of home ownership? And don't forget to factor in reasonably predictable future expenses that may affect your ability to make payments. For example, are you planning to start a family soon? If so, your income may fall while your expenses rise (as they surely will).

INVESTIGATE

If you can't afford the highest allowed payment on an adjustable-rate mortgage, don't take it. You shouldn't accept the chance that the interest rate may not rise that high — it might, and then you could lose your home! Ask your lender to calculate the highest possible maximum monthly payment on your loan. That's the payment you'd face if the interest rate on your loan were to go to the highest level allowed (the *lifetime cap*).

>> **How long do you plan to keep the mortgage?** The savings on most adjustables is usually guaranteed in the first two or three years, because an adjustable-rate mortgage starts at a lower interest rate than a fixed one. If rates rise, you can end up giving back or losing the savings you achieve in the early years of the mortgage. In most cases, if you aren't going to keep your mortgage more than five to seven years, you're probably paying unnecessary interest costs to carry a fixed-rate mortgage.

You may want to look into a hybrid loan. These loans may make sense for you if you foresee a high probability of keeping your loan seven to ten years or less but want some stability in your monthly payments. The longer the initial rate stays locked in, the higher the rate.

INVESTIGATE

Get a written itemization of charges from all lenders you're seriously considering so you can more readily compare different lenders' mortgages and so you have no surprises when you close on your loan. And to minimize your chances of throwing money away on a loan for which you may not qualify, ask the lender whether you may not be approved for some reason. Be sure to disclose any problems you're aware of that are on your credit report or with the property.

WARNING

Some lenders offer loans without *points* (upfront interest) or other lender charges. Remember: If lenders don't charge points or other fees, they have to make up the difference by charging a higher interest rate on your loan. Consider such loans only if you lack cash for closing or if you're planning to use the loan for just a few years.

Avoiding negative amortization and interest-only loans

As you make mortgage payments over time, the loan balance you still owe is gradually reduced, a process known as *amortizing* the loan. The reverse of this process — increasing your loan balance — is called *negative amortization*. You want to steer clear of negative-amortization mortgages.

Some ARMs allow negative amortization. Your outstanding loan balance can grow even though you're continuing to make mortgage payments when your mortgage payment is less than it really should be.

Taking on negative amortization is like paying only the minimum payment required on a credit-card bill. You keep racking up greater interest charges on the balance as long as you make only the artificially low payment. Doing so defeats the whole purpose of borrowing an amount that fits your overall financial goals. And you may never get your mortgage paid off! Even worse, the increased interest you start to accrue on the unpaid interest added to your mortgage balance may not be tax-deductible because it doesn't qualify as interest incurred as part of the original purchase (what the IRS calls the *acquisition debt*).

WARNING

The only way to know for certain whether a loan includes negative amortization is to ask. Some lenders aren't forthcoming about telling you. You find negative amortization more frequently on loans that lenders consider risky. If you're having trouble finding lenders who are willing to deal with your financial situation, be especially careful.

Some loans cap the increase of your monthly payment but not of the interest rate. The size of your mortgage payment may not reflect all the interest you owe on your loan. So rather than paying off the interest and some of your loan balance (or *principal*) every month, you're paying off some, but not all, of the interest you owe. Thus, the extra unpaid interest you still owe is added to your outstanding debt.

Also tread carefully with *interest-only mortgages,* which are loans in which you pay only interest in the beginning years. Don't consider interest-only loans if you're stretching to be able to afford a home, and consider one only if you understand how they work and can afford the inevitable jump in payments.

Getting your mortgage approved

When you're under contract to buy a property, having your loan denied after waiting several weeks can mean you lose the property as well as the money you spent applying for the loan and having the property inspected. Some property sellers may be willing to give you an extension of time needed to close on the property's purchase, but others won't, especially if the local real estate market is strong. So you want to make sure you get your mortgage approved.

TIP

Here's how to increase your chances of having your mortgage approved:

>> **Get your finances in shape before you shop for real estate.** You won't know what you can afford to spend on a home until you whip your personal finances into shape. Do so before you begin to make offers on properties. This book can help you. If you have consumer debt, pay it down.

>> **Clean up credit-report problems.** If you think you may have errors on your credit report, get a copy before you apply for a mortgage. Chapter 4 details how to obtain a free copy of your credit report and correct mistakes.

>> **Get prequalified or preapproved.** When you get *prequalified,* a lender speaks with you about your financial situation and then calculates the maximum amount it's willing to lend you. *Preapproval* is much more in-depth and includes a lender's review of your financial statements. Just be sure not to waste your time (and money) getting preapproved if you're not really ready to get serious about buying.

>> **Be upfront about problems.** You may be able to stop potential loan rejection by disclosing to your lender anything that may cause a problem before you apply.

>> **Work around low/unstable income.** When you've been changing jobs or you're self-employed, your income may be down or unstable. Making a larger down payment is one way around this problem. You may try getting a cosigner, such as a relative. Be sure to have a written agreement, including who's responsible for payments.

>> **Consider a backup loan.** You certainly should shop among different lenders, and you may want to apply to more than one for a mortgage. Disclose to each lender what you're doing; the second lender that pulls your credit report will see that another lender has already done so.

Putting Your Deal Together

After you do your homework on your personal finances, decide which kind of mortgage to choose, and research neighborhoods and home prices, you'll hope-fully be ready to close in on your goal. Eventually, you'll find a home you want to buy. Before you make that first offer, though, you need to understand the impor-tance of negotiations, inspections, and the other elements of a real-estate deal:

» **Never fall in love with a property.** If you have money to burn and can't imagine life without the home you just discovered, pay what you will. Otherwise, remind yourself that other good properties are out there. Having a backup property in mind can help.

» **Find out about the property and owner before you make your offer.** How long has the property been on the market? What are its flaws? Why is the owner selling? The more you understand about the property and the seller's motivations, the better able you'll be to draft an offer that meets both parties' needs.

» **Get comparable sales data to support your price.** Pointing to recent and comparable home sales to justify your offer price strengthens your case.

» **Remember that price is only one of several negotiable items.** You may be able to get a seller to pay for certain repairs or improvements, to pay some of your closing costs, or to offer you favorable loan terms. Likewise, the real-estate agent's commission is negotiable.

» **Spend the time and money to locate and hire good inspectors and other experts to evaluate the major systems and potential problem areas of the home.** When problems that you weren't aware of are uncovered, the inspection reports give you the information you need to go back and ask the property seller to fix the problems or reduce the property's purchase price to compensate you for correcting the deficiencies yourself.

» **Shop around for title insurance and escrow services.** Mortgage lenders require *title insurance* to protect against someone else claiming legal title to your property. *Escrow charges* pay for neutral third-party services to ensure that the instructions of the purchase contract or refinance are fulfilled and that everyone gets paid. Many people don't seem to understand that title insurance and escrow fees vary from company to company. When you call around for title insurance and escrow fee quotes, make sure you understand all the fees. Many companies tack on all sorts of charges for things such as courier fees and express mail. If you find a company with lower prices and want to use it, ask for an itemization in writing so you don't have any surprises.

Chapter **8**

Relationships and Money

You may plan on getting married someday. Before that day, you'll likely live with other people. Perhaps you'll simply have roommates, or you may choose to live with a significant other.

When you live with others, you may share household expenses and other matters. In this chapter, I discuss how best to handle the financial side of these situations.

Handling Roommates

As I discuss in Chapter 5, sharing the rent with roommates is a time-tested way of containing your housing costs when you're young, single, and need housing. However, having roommates doesn't mean you're free of problems. In fact, how you handle living with roommates can potentially have significant effects on your own personal finances.

If you're going to share a rental with roommates, a wise decision is to draft a roommate agreement and have all your rental mates sign it. A *roommate agreement* basically is a legal agreement of important issues between you and your roommate(s). You can find these templates online on various websites. The following are some characteristics of a standard roommate agreement:

>> The agreement's financial terms are legally enforceable with your roommates, but they aren't legally binding with your landlord.

>> To keep legal fees down, the agreement should include a mediation clause.

>> The agreement should reflect your concerns and priorities. For example, if you need your eight hours of sleep every night, and you therefore require peace and quiet starting at 10 p.m., then the agreement should spell out those sorts of details (within reason of course). Examples of items you may want to cover in the agreement include

- Who pays how much rent, when, and to whom

- How bedrooms are allocated and whether rent depends on which one you have

- Who's responsible for which chores

- How parking is handled if it's limited

- Whether pets and overnight guests are allowed

- How much notice should be given when someone needs to move out

- Whose responsibility it is to find a replacement roommate

If one of your roommates does something in violation of the rental agreement, you all are responsible. Suppose, for example, that one of your roommates fails to pay the rent on time, damages the rental unit in some way, or has loud parties that warrant calls to the police by neighbors. You and your roommates are all responsible for the missing rent, the damages, or the intrusion on your neighbors. The landlord can also add insult to injury and terminate your rental contract. (One exception to this is if you as a renter have subleased to a tenant and that's the person who has violated the rules of the rental agreement. Another related exception is if your rental is subject to local rental control laws and you're designated as a master tenant with authority to approve and evict tenants.)

Some landlords make an effort to identify the bad apple in an otherwise good group of tenants and may not hold the good apples responsible. But don't count on this happening. Choose your roommates wisely and nip problems in the bud before they mushroom into bigger issues. Sit down with everyone and have a candid discussion about problems, and work toward a solution. Communicate respectfully and in a timely fashion with your landlord.

Living-Together Contracts

What if you're involved in a relationship with someone and you're living with that person? That situation may be more complicated than having a roommate and dealing with a contract for a roommate because your finances and personal possessions may be more intertwined. You may want to consider a *living-together contract*, which is used by folks who aren't married to each other.

Practically speaking, your agreement can help you avoid trouble when you mix your money and property, and it can make clear your intentions and expectations regarding property ownership, household expenses, and the like. It can also greatly ease the division or distribution of property after a breakup or death. On a more personal note, the process of negotiating and drafting your agreement may well strengthen your abilities to communicate with and understand each other.

Here's an overview of the legal rules and practical concerns you should think about before drafting a contract of your own. Nearly all states recognize and enforce contracts between unmarried partners. Topics you may want to address in your contract include

>> **Personal property:** You may want to delineate and keep separate any property that you owned before moving in together, as well as property you inherit or receive as a gift. If you want to divide ownership of property purchased during the period of living together some other way than 50-50, specify that.

>> **Living expenses:** Your agreement should specify how your household's expenses are divvied up. You can discuss pooling your money versus keeping separate accounts, as well as sharing expenses equally or through some other method.

>> **Parting ways:** Your agreement should detail how your property, especially jointly owned property, will be divided in the event one of you decides to move out.

>> **Death:** Your agreement (in addition to your will; check out the later sidebar "Preparing wills and other important legal documents" for more information) should also detail what happens to each person's property should one or both of you die.

>> **Dispute resolution:** Providing for mediation and/or arbitration is a time-tested way to effectively resolve disputes.

If you're looking for a helpful book on this topic, check out *Living Together: A Legal Guide for Unmarried Couples* by Frederick Hertz and Lina Guillen (Nolo Press).

Getting Married

To help ensure a happy marriage, couples should discuss all sorts of issues before getting hitched. Money matters are certainly near the top of that list.

Unfortunately, money issues are also on the list of frequently neglected and avoided topics for engaged couples. Not surprisingly, money issues are one of the leading causes of marital discord and divorce. Discussing money with a loved one makes most people uncomfortable, and in many families, money is a taboo topic.

TIP

Merging your financial decisions and resources doesn't have to be unpleasant and a source of stress. Even if you're largely in agreement about your financial goals and strategies, managing as two is far different from managing as one. Here are my tips to prepare for marriage:

>> **Talk money before getting married.** Many couples never talk about their financial and personal goals and expectations before marriage, and failing to do so breaks up way too many marriages. Finances are just one of the many issues you need to discuss. Ensuring that you know what you're getting yourself into is a good way to minimize your chances for heartache. In addition to discussing the topics in the rest of this list, also discuss your feelings and goals pertaining to earning, spending, saving, and investing money. Ministers, priests, and rabbis sometimes offer premarital counseling to help bring issues and differences to the surface.

>> **Discuss merging finances versus maintaining separate accounts.** I generally prefer that couples merge their finances. Marriage is a partnership, and you're supposed to be on the same team. In some marriages, however, spouses may choose to keep some money separate so they don't feel their spouse's scrutiny with regard to different spending preferences. Spouses who've been through divorce may choose to keep the assets they bring into

the new marriage separate in order to protect their money in the event of another divorce. As long as you're jointly accomplishing what you need to financially, some separation of money is okay. But for the health of your marriage, don't hide money from each other, and if you're the higher-income spouse, don't assume power and control over your joint income.

>> **Understand and optimize your employer benefits.** If one or both of you have access to a package of employee benefits through an employer, determine how best to make use of those benefits. Coordinating and using the best that each package has to offer is like getting a pay raise. If you both have access to health insurance, determine which of you has better benefits unless it's advantageous for you to each use your respective plans. Likewise, one of you may have a better retirement savings plan — one that matches your contribution and offers superior investment options. Unless you can afford to save the maximum through both your plans, saving more in the better plan increases your combined assets. (***Note:*** If you're concerned about what will happen if you save more in one of your retirement plans and then get a divorce, in most states, the money is considered part of your joint assets to be divided equally.)

>> **Discuss life and disability insurance needs.** If you and your spouse can make do without each other's income, you may not need any income-protecting insurance. However, if, like many married couples, you both depend on each other's income, or if one of you depends fully or partly on the other's income, one or both of you may need long-term disability and term life insurance policies (see Chapter 15).

>> **Prepare updated wills.** When you marry, you should make or update your wills. Having a will is potentially more valuable when you're married, especially if you want to leave money to others in addition to your spouse, or if you have children for whom you need to name a guardian. Check out the nearby sidebar "Preparing wills and other important legal documents" for more guidance.

>> **Review beneficiaries on investment and life insurance.** With retirement accounts and life insurance policies, you name beneficiaries to whom the money or value in those accounts will go in the event of your passing. When you marry, you should review and reconsider your beneficiaries.

TIP

After you're married, you and your spouse should set aside time once a year or every few years to discuss personal and financial goals for the years ahead. When you talk about where you want to go, you help ensure that you're both rowing your financial boat in unison. Try to pick a time and location for your discussion that will help you both to be relaxed. Selecting times when you're both rested (and full) can help when money topics are challenging!

PREPARING WILLS AND OTHER IMPORTANT LEGAL DOCUMENTS

When you have dependent children, a will is a must-have. The will names the guardian to whom you entrust your children if both you and your spouse die. Should both you and your spouse die without a will (a condition called *intestate*), the state (courts and social-service agencies) decides who will raise your children. Therefore, even if you can't decide at this time who you want to raise your children, you should at least appoint a trusted guardian who can decide for you.

Even if you have no dependents, having a will is wise because it provides your specific instructions on how to handle and distribute your possessions. If you die without a will, your state decides how to distribute your money and other property, according to state law. Therefore, your friends, distant relatives, and favorite charities would probably receive nothing. Without any living relatives, your money may go to the state government!

Without a will, your heirs are legally powerless, and the state may appoint an administrator to supervise the distribution of your assets at a fee of around 5 percent of your estate. A bond typically must also be posted at a cost of several hundred dollars.

A living will and a medical power of attorney are useful additions to a standard will. A *living will* tells your doctor what, if any, life-support measures you prefer. A medical (or healthcare) *power of attorney* grants authority to someone you trust to make decisions regarding your medical care options in the event that you're deemed incapable of making them for yourself.

You don't need an attorney to make a legal will. Most attorneys, in fact, prepare wills and living trusts by using software programs! The simplest and least costly way to prepare a will, a living will, and a medical power of attorney is to use a high-quality, user-friendly software package such as those published by Nolo Press (www.nolo.com). What makes a will valid is that three people witness you signing it. Give copies of these documents to the guardians and executors you name.

Understanding Your Money Beliefs and Practices

Even if you are well educated, including from a personal finance standpoint, you could probably benefit from finding out more about how to make the most of your money and the time and energy that go into making, spending, saving, investing, and protecting it. The basics of good personal financial management — spending less than you earn, investing your savings in proven vehicles for the long term, and securing adequate insurance coverage — are relatively simple in principle, but they can be difficult to put into action.

Many people are unable to follow these rules for the same reasons people can't follow a diet: It's difficult, and it can be emotionally taxing. I've seen many people allow their individual fears, biases, mistaken beliefs, past experiences, and other quirks and demons, along with external pressures from a consumption-oriented society, to color and sabotage their efforts to practice good financial habits.

The following sections and exercises can help you improve your personal money beliefs and tendencies.

Examining your money history

In order to identify, accept, and overcome the money-related obstacles that are currently preventing you from making the most of what you have and reaching a place in life where you're satisfied with your position — financially and personally — start getting a handle on what I call your "money history," particularly the influence of your parents, your childhood, and young-adult environments.

Taking a historical inventory isn't easy, but if you put in the time and want to challenge yourself and your beliefs, the process can be productive.

Set aside time — about an hour should do — for some personal reflection, ideally in a place and at a time that frees you from distractions. Consider going to the library, the beach, or some other place that's away from your home. Reflect upon the following questions:

>> What personal experiences (good and bad) relating to money do you recall from your childhood? Did you work as a kid and teenager? What lessons did you take away from these experiences? If you didn't work, think about why you didn't and what your parents said to you (or implied) about working and making money.

>> What memories of your parents (or other guardians) do you have that relate to finances? Were your parents spenders or savers? What financial crises occurred, and how did your parents handle them? Did money cause tension and problems at home? If you don't have many explicit recollections about money with your caregivers, what implicit messages did you take away from the way they led their lives and the role that money played in it?

>> What efforts did your mom and dad make to teach you about money? How much freedom and latitude did they give you with money? What lessons did you take away from this? If you had to summarize their philosophy and approach to money in a sentence or two, what would it be?

>> How important were financial considerations in what you chose to study and what jobs and career you sought? Did you pursue work based upon what interested you or what you believed you could make more money doing? Were you pushed into your career by someone else for the supposed financial security you could achieve?

>> Thinking back to your childhood and young-adult years, what significant events happened to you and your family that impacted how you felt about money? These events may include, for example, a major illness, a parent being laid off, volunteer work you did, and so on. You need not have a long list of events — the two or three most important and formative occurrences will do.

Exploring your attitudes toward money

Having taken the time to ponder your background and how it colors the way you relate to money (see the preceding section), take the next step and spend some time reflecting on your current feelings and attitudes toward money. There are no right or wrong answers to many of these questions:

>> What stresses you about money?

>> Are you frequently juggling bills and trying to figure out whom to pay next?

>> Do you watch your investments daily, or do you avoid looking at your investment statements out of fear? Why?

>> Are you looking for a hot investment tip that could multiply your money quickly?

>> What financial secrets are you keeping from your spouse (and others)? What would cause you feelings of humiliation and embarrassment?

In working with clients, I've found that simply taking the time to think about and reflect upon one's history with money provides valuable insights that can enable people to cultivate better financial habits. Quite often, people who go through this process say things like, "I never took the time to consider why I do what I do with money or even what I'm doing."

TIP

Don't beat yourself up if you can't handle developing thoughtful responses all in one sitting. Some people find these questions bring up strong memories and emotions, so you may need two or three sessions to complete this task.

Understanding your friends and money

Our peers may have a major influence over how we spend money and even deal with money overall. When I used to teach a personal-finance course at the University of California, I talked about consumer spending and our choice of cars. Over the years, some students confided to me that they had been embarrassed by the shabbiness of their cars. One person told me that his co-workers would get on him about his car "trashing up" the parking lot. Sales professionals who called on clients and took clients out in their car were especially self-conscious about their vehicles.

Here are some examples where money comes into play with others. Consider each and what lessons you can take away about how your friends and peers affect the way you think about, spend, and use your money:

» **Going out to eat or for entertainment:** Do you go out to restaurants, bars, or entertainment venues? Do you go on trips or vacations with others? How do you choose the place? Do the folks you tend to hang out with discuss and care about the cost, or is it not discussed? How are things handled when it comes time to pay the bill?

» **Lending money:** Are you comfortable lending money to friends or family? Have you ever done so with bad results (for example, not being repaid)? If the loan extends over a lengthy time period (years, not months), have you collected a reasonable level of interest?

» **Gift buying/exchanges:** In a typical year, how much do you spend on gifts for others? Do you feel obligated to buy many people gifts? Do you find yourself spending more than you can comfortably afford or giving more than you receive?

INVESTIGATE

Using the listed topics as a guide, spend some time reflecting on your interactions with friends and other acquaintances relating to money. What are you happy about? What would you like to change, and why?

Making sense of your environment and money

Another profound influence on how you deal with and relate to money is your environment. For example, how did you choose where you live? Wanting to live in an area that's safe and convenient is fine, but if you select a location populated by the rich and famous, how will you be able to save money, especially with conspicuous consumption surrounding and tempting you?

In addition to where you live, consider the other circles in which you travel — your work environment, areas where you spend a lot of your free time, and so on.

INVESTIGATE

Write down your thoughts about your environment and how it may impact and reflect your views on money. In what ways is your current environment a positive or negative influence on how you manage your money? What would you like to change about your current environment and why?

Getting a Grip on Procrastination Where Money Is Concerned

In my work as a financial counselor, I often saw signs and symptoms that indicated I was dealing with someone who was a money procrastinator. This isn't a black-and-white issue. Just about everyone I know procrastinates dealing with some aspects of their financial lives and their lives in general.

Diagnosing procrastination

Answer the following questions to identify areas of your financial life where you're procrastinating:

>> **Are you financially disorganized and prone to clutter?** Because avoiders dislike dealing with money and related issues, they don't spend their free time keeping documents organized and easy to find.

>> **Are you late paying your bills and tax payments?** Money avoiders often incur late fees and interest charges on various household bills. Those who are self-employed, and thus responsible for quarterly income tax filings, are at additional risk for falling behind with tax payments, the negative financial consequences of which can be huge.

>> **Do you have unopened financial account statements or emails?** We all get busy with life, but I was amazed at how many money avoiders I worked with who would have piles of unopened account statements (and now emails of the same), even during periods when their types of investments were doing fine, thus eliminating any reason for avoiding opening potentially bad news.

>> **Do you have a sense of unease, and even shame and embarrassment, with having cash sitting around in low-interest accounts?** Money avoiders who are able to save money may have a tendency to allow it to accumulate, for example, in bank accounts that pay little if any interest. While they may know that they could and should do better with investing the money, they can't overcome the inertia.

>> **Do you experience feelings of enormous stress and anxiety over money issues and decisions?** One of the main reasons that avoiders relate to money in the way they do is that for whatever historical reason(s), making financial decisions makes them feel uncomfortable and stressed. (In some cases, for example, growing up in a home where money was an ongoing source of unhappiness, conflicts, and problems can lead to avoidance behavior as an adult.) Other people believe that they lack the skills and knowledge necessary to take control of their finances. Finally, some folks believe, right or wrong, that their current financial picture isn't so bright, so they simply decide to avoid the bad news, even though ignoring the situation will only make things worse in the end.

>> **Do you have a low level of interest regarding money issues and decisions?** While some avoiders shun financial decisions and responsibilities due to anxiety, others are imitating behavior learned from their parents or are rebelling against a parent who was financially or emotionally overbearing.

>> **Do you have an absence of long-term financial planning and thinking?** Many of the money avoiders I dealt with clearly hadn't thought much about what their personal and financial goals were for the years and decades ahead.

>> **Do you have marriage problems relating to money?** Money avoiders typically have conflicts over money with their spouses, and their avoidance may stem from or be exacerbated by that.

Coming to terms with why you may procrastinate with money issues

Understanding some of the common feelings and issues surrounding money-avoidance behavior can help in coming to acknowledge and productively change poor habits. Here are some common reasons folks put off dealing with certain issues:

» **Feelings of incompetence:** Some people have negative memories and associations from prior attempts, with parents or spouses, at dealing with money and making financial decisions. Many money avoiders have similar feelings of incompetence with math and mathematical analysis, which are certainly key abilities to possess for effective personal financial management. Lack of experience making financial decisions certainly plays into feelings of incompetence as well.

» **Disorganization:** Money avoiders have a tendency to be generally disorganized people who avoid dealing with other facets of their lives as well. With only so many hours in the day, people who are poorly organized struggle just to deal with work and family responsibilities. Making financial decisions, especially involving longer-term issues (such as retirement planning and insurance) is easily postponed or never considered.

» **Marital friction:** Money is among the leading causes of marital discord. So, some spouses cope by avoiding the topic altogether in the hopes of keeping more harmony in their marriage. In the short term, this avoidance strategy may reduce some stress and arguments. In the long term, however, it doesn't work, as dissatisfaction gone underground doesn't go away (or get better).

» **Fear of future problems:** People who were abused growing up or lived with a loved one who was a substance abuser often worry about bad things occurring. Ditto for folks suffering from depression or generalized anxiety disorders. Money troubles are often intertwined with these types of issues and lead to plenty of negative associations with money and simply not wanting to deal with the topic.

» **Perfectionism:** While this is a less-common reason for people shunning money matters, some perfectionists continue putting off making decisions and taking action because they can always find flaws in or potential obstacles to their intended course of action. Or, they may feel that they can make a better decision with just a little more thinking and analysis. Of course, no one can predict the future, and everyone is limited in terms of time, money, and analysis.

» **Ability to get away with it:** Some people simply don't want to deal with money issues and decisions and are able to get along sufficiently through good fortune and being surrounded by those who enable the avoiding behavior (perhaps through care giving and taking responsibility). Unfortunately, life changes and unforeseen problems can expose gaps in poor financial management.

>> **Avoidance of difficult issues:** Some people procrastinate doing financial planning for retirement and buying life insurance for the same reason they haven't prepared a will — they'd rather not think about aging, dying, and other difficult and unpleasant topics.

Overcoming money avoidance

If you are a money avoider, my goal isn't to turn you into someone who loves dealing with money. That's probably not going to happen. However, I can show you how to ensure that you can accomplish common financial goals and won't suffer the ill effects that money avoiders so often do by neglecting their finances.

GOING FROM ANXIOUS TO IN CONTROL

"I always felt stupid about math and wholly inadequate. I can't even bring myself to use a calculator out of fear I won't even know how to use that properly," says Heidi, a 40-something-year-old woman. It took Heidi about two years to make some major changes in how she handled her personal finances. She began to make progress when I was able to persuade her that she didn't have to be a math whiz to make positive financial changes. Heidi didn't have major spending problems, but she was sloppy and lazy about saving money and investing it well.

I had her sign up for her employer's retirement savings plan so she could begin to save about 8 percent of her salary. She had the money withdrawn from her salary and directed into a handful of well-diversified mutual funds. "I can't believe how painless it is to do this, and there was virtually no math involved. All I had to do was complete a one-page enrollment form, which required me to say what percentage of my contribution went into each fund that I selected," said Heidi.

With the meager amounts she had been saving that were languishing in a low-interest bank account, Heidi would've needed to work until her mid-70s to achieve the standard of living in retirement that she desired. After working with me, she was on track to be able to stop working by her late 50s.

Seeing these quantifiable changes in her retirement age and gaining a basic understanding of the steps she needs to take to reach her goals was a great motivating source to Heidi and has given her savings a purpose. Equally if not more important, she feels in control of her life financially and has rid herself of that ever-constant anxiety about not being on top of things.

Overcoming money avoidance takes time and patience. That statement isn't meant to provide you with a reason to forgo making changes in your financial life. Instead, I'm relaying a fact and reminding you that change takes time and some steps forward are interrupted by steps back.

The first and most important part of the process is to recognize the tendency to procrastinate when it comes to money management and then understand the reasons behind the procrastination. Many people find it helpful to write down their feelings relating to money avoidance or to speak about their feelings and history with money with someone who is an empathic listener.

In my work as a financial counselor, I found that many avoiders typically felt greatly overwhelmed with a laundry list of financial to-dos. That's why you should prioritize and only work on the top one or two items at a time. I'd tell clients that even though they might have a total of eight or ten things on their longer task lists, they shouldn't expect to complete those next week or even next month. It might take six months to a year to work through the longer list.

The following sections offer simple ways to get control of your money.

Pay your bills automatically

People who are financially disorganized often are late paying bills. Late payments, particularly when it comes to paying taxes, are a problem that can lead to substantial late fees, interest, and penalties. Even if the fees and additional interest from individual late payments of your other bills — $5 here and $30 there — don't seem all that significant on their own, they can add up to a hefty total if you make paying bills late a habit. (Late tax penalties and interest can easily run into the hundreds or thousands of dollars.)

TIP

One of the best things that money avoiders can do with their bills is to set each of them up for automatic payment. Whether the payment in question is your phone, utility, or monthly rent or mortgage bill, you should be able to establish an automatic payment plan that doesn't require you to initiate payment. With just a little upfront work with each creditor or billing company — often not much more effort than paying a monthly bill — you can rid yourself of unnecessary fees and interest and save a little time each month.

Many companies accept (and actually prefer) payment through an electronic transfer from your bank account. Some loan holders (including student-loan holders) may even lessen your interest rate slightly in return for what amounts to a guarantee of an on-time payment every month. If not, you may be able to have some payments charged on your credit card, but be careful with this route if you sometimes don't pay that bill on time! (Another alternative is to use online bill paying through your bank.)

Develop a regular investment program

All money avoiders should make their investing automatic. If you work for an employer, doing so is usually easy. Often, the most daunting part of the process is wading through the pile of retirement plan and investment information and brochures your benefits department may dump on you when you tell them that you want to sign up for their payroll deduction savings program.

REMEMBER

Not only will your money grow faster inside a tax-deferred account, but your employer may also offer free matching money.

The simplest way to navigate through the morass of forms is to look first for the specific document you must complete to sign up for the payroll investment program. Thoroughly read that form first so you know what you need to focus on and get smarter about as you review the other materials. If you get stuck, ask your company's human resource/benefits person for assistance.

If your earnings come from self-employment income, you'll need to establish your own retirement account. Find out about the different retirement account options and choose the one that best meets your needs. SEP-IRAs enable you to sock away large amounts — a self-employed person may contribute up to 20 percent of his business's net income up to a maximum of $58,000 for tax year 2021.

These plans may be established through major mutual-fund companies (I like Vanguard, Fidelity, Schwab, and T. Rowe Price). You can generally set up these accounts so a regular monthly amount is zapped electronically from your local bank account into your mutual fund investment account. (Be careful not to overfund your account, which may happen if you overestimate your business income prior to completing your tax return.)

Close insurance gaps

Nearly every money avoider I've met over the years has problematic gaps in insurance coverage. Solving this problem presents some challenges because understanding various policies and the coverage of each is complicated. Add on top of that the unfortunate fact that to buy most insurance policies, you must deal with a commission-based insurance agent. Talk about a recipe for headaches and conflicts of interest! But these are not acceptable excuses for avoiding this issue because so much is at stake. (For more about insurance, check out Part 4.)

Hire financial help

Money avoiders are clearly a group of people who could benefit from hiring a financial advisor. However, they're also among the people most likely to make a poor choice when hiring. It's difficult to evaluate — or care enough to evaluate — the financial expertise (and potential conflicts of interest) of a financial advisor if you're disinterested in (or suffer anxiety about) and actively avoid money issues.

Your first step, if you're inclined to hire help, is to clearly define what type of assistance you desire. Do you need assistance with analyzing your budget and developing a plan to pay down consumer debt? If so, most financial advisors aren't prepared to help you with that — there's far more money to be made selling investment and insurance products to the affluent.

Advisors are best suited for folks who want to quantify how much they should be saving for specific goals and determining where to invest it. However, there's no getting around it: You do have to do a lot of digging to find a competent and ethical advisor who has reasonable fees. With that information in hand, you can confidently and strategically evaluate potential service providers who can help you overcome your inertia and get you on track managing your money. Turn to Chapter 18 for more information on hiring professionals.

Chapter **9**

Making the Most of Your Career

What's your most valuable asset?

As a young adult, it's probably your future earning potential.

That's why I devote this chapter to helping you make the most of your career and future employment. In addition to tips to jump-start your career, I discuss furthering your education and training, exploring your entrepreneurial options, and handling job changes and loss.

Getting Your Career Going

As you transition from school to the workforce, you can maximize your chances for financial and career success. This section discusses arranging your finances and making decisions to further invest in your education and training.

Putting everything in order

If you just graduated from school, or you're otherwise in the your early years in the workforce, your increased income and reduction in educational expenses are probably a welcome relief to you and your family — but they're no guarantee of future financial success.

Here's how to start on the path to financial success when you first enter the job market:

» **Avoid consumer credit.** The use and abuse of consumer credit can cause long-term financial pain and hardship. Shun making purchases on credit cards that you can't pay for in full when the bill arrives. Here's the simple solution for running up outstanding credit-card balances: Don't carry a credit card unless you are always able to pay it in full when your monthly bill comes due. If you need the convenience of making purchases with a piece of plastic, consider a debit card (see Chapter 3).

» **Cultivate the habits of saving and investing.** I'm often asked, "At what age should a person start saving?" To me, that's similar to asking at what age you should start brushing your teeth. Well, when you have teeth to brush! So I say you should start saving and investing money from your first paycheck. Try saving 5 percent of every paycheck, and then eventually increase your savings rate to 10 percent. Ideally, you should put your savings into retirement accounts (through an automatic deduction) that offer tax benefits, unless you want to accumulate down-payment money for a home or small-business purchase or some other purpose. (You're probably not thinking about buying a new home or retiring, though, if you're just entering the job market.) If you're having trouble saving money, track your spending and make cutbacks as needed (see Chapters 2 and 5 for more assistance).

» **Get insured.** When you're young and healthy, imagining yourself feeling otherwise may be difficult. But because accidents and unexpected illnesses can strike at any age, forgoing health insurance coverage can be financially devastating. When you're in your first full-time job with limited benefits, buying disability coverage, which replaces income lost because of a long-term disability, is also wise. And as you begin to build your assets, make a will so your assets go where you want them to in the event of your untimely passing. (Check out Part 4 for more information about insurance.)

Educating and training your way to career success

The Bureau of Labor Statistics has data that clearly demonstrates that the more education a person has, the more money the person makes and the less likely the person is to be unemployed (see the most recent full year's data and chart in Figure 9-1).

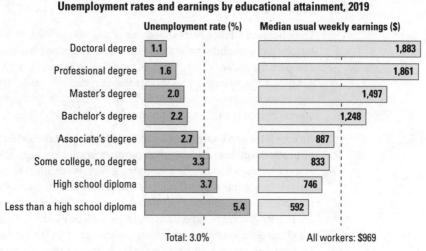

Unemployment rates and earnings by educational attainment, 2019

	Unemployment rate (%)	Median usual weekly earnings ($)
Doctoral degree	1.1	1,883
Professional degree	1.6	1,861
Master's degree	2.0	1,497
Bachelor's degree	2.2	1,248
Associate's degree	2.7	887
Some college, no degree	3.3	833
High school diploma	3.7	746
Less than a high school diploma	5.4	592
	Total: 3.0%	All workers: $969

Note: Data are for persons age 25 and over. Earnings are for full-time wage and salary workers.

Source: U.S. Bureau of Labor Statistics, Current Population Survey

FIGURE 9-1: More education translates into lower unemployment rates and higher earnings.

Now, you must be careful applying group data to your own situation, because assuming that having more education and spending more on education is *always* better would be inaccurate. But the data clearly shows that more education is *generally* better, as it enhances your employability and income-earning potential and reduces your chances of being unemployed.

Seeking value for your education dollars

You and your family probably don't have an unlimited supply of money to spend on furthering your education and training. So, just as with buying anything else — computers, clothing, and so on — you should look for value when spending your education dollars. Value means getting the most (quality) for your money.

Keep the following pointers in mind to ensure you get value for your educational dollars:

>> **Realize that you don't always get what you pay for.** Just because you spend more for education doesn't mean that you'll get better quality than something costing less. For example, the best state colleges and universities offer better value to in-state residents than do some private colleges and universities. Increasing numbers of faster and lower-cost educational alternatives to traditional colleges provide valuable training that leads to in-demand jobs.

>> **Look beyond sticker prices.** Because of the availability of financial aid, including grants and scholarships you don't have to pay back, you can't simply compare the sticker price of various traditional colleges and assume that the price is your actual cost. You should always consider a range of schools and higher-education options, apply for aid when possible, and then compare your expected benefits to the bottom-line cost at each school.

>> **Be careful when examining rankings of colleges (and other higher-education options) and which program's graduates earn the most.** Lots of data and rankings on the best colleges and universities are available. We're starting to see more such data for other higher-education options. One challenge when evaluating this data is that many of the highest-rated schools are private and quite expensive, and they selectively admit the most qualified candidates. So their graduates tend to earn more. Be sure to compare what each school provides and what each costs after factoring in financial aid awards.

>> **Consider employer assistance.** Check out what education assistance your employer may offer. Just be sure that it makes sense for you and your career to stay with that employer for whatever additional time may be required.

>> **If you have specific fields of work in mind, research what education and training best prepares you.** Talk to folks currently in those fields and consider training programs as well as technical training programs where appropriate.

Considering a liberal arts education and alternatives

First it's helpful to define what is generally meant by a "liberal arts education." My alma mater, Yale University, defines a liberal arts education as one that teaches students to think critically and express themselves clearly. Yale asserts that a liberal arts education is a solid foundation for all professions and can help students lead successful and meaningful lives.

That sounds all well and good, and for some people, a liberal arts education may be a good fit. But for others, a liberal arts degree can be a significant waste of time and money.

Also, please keep in mind that many folks like myself, who attended the leading liberal arts colleges and universities, end up going on to graduate school for advanced degrees, for example in business, law, medicine, and so forth.

In our increasingly competitive global economy, I think there are some potentially better alternatives to consider.

>> **Last-mile programs, including "boot camps":** The most popular last-mile programs are "boot camps" that focus mostly on coding — a skill in demand like never before. Coding boot camps are full-time endeavors. Classes are small, and most of the time is spent actually working in teams on projects. In a survey done by job search engine website Indeed, 80 percent of technology hiring managers reported hiring coding boot-camp graduates, and an astounding 99 percent of those said they'd hire more.

>> **College minimal viable products (MVPs):** College minimal viable product (MVP) programs combine the technical skill training and placement of traditional last-mile programs with sufficient cognitive and noncognitive skill development that students get from a good college. Graduates of these programs pay through income-share arrangements (ISAs) in which they repay money owed to the program through paying a portion of their employment income for a short period of time.

>> **Apprenticeships:** Once relegated to industrial trades such as electricians, plumbers, carpenters, and iron and steel workers, apprenticeships are now gaining momentum in industries like advanced manufacturing, healthcare, pharmacy, and IT.

>> **Staffing firms:** Staffing firms like Manpower, Allegis, Adecco, Randstad, and Kelly Services offer last-mile training to workers and staff them out to clients. Revature, an IT staffing company, hires experienced software developers. The founder of Revature noticed around 2011 that his client companies also had an appetite for entry-level software developers. Today, the company has partnerships with numerous colleges such as Arizona State, UNC Charlotte, UVA, Davidson, and more and offers a free 10- to 12-week advanced training program on campus. Meanwhile, Avenica places students from many colleges and offers last-mile training across many industries.

>> **Vocational and trade schools:** Also known as career and technical education (CTE), vocational and trade schools provide gateways to a wide range of jobs. They typically exist in several different entities including community colleges, high schools, and other area CTE centers and are constantly evolving to meet

the changing economic environment and jobs that exist today. Here is a sampling of industries vocational and trade schools provide training for:

- **Automotive industry:** Repair technician, body and paint technician, collision repair and refinishing, diesel mechanic

- **Culinary arts:** Prep cook, sous chef, pastry chef, line cook

- **Emergency services:** Firefighters, paramedics, police officers, CPR and first-aid instructors

- **Healthcare:** Nursing aides, certified nursing assistants, licensed practical nurses, vocational nurses, registered nurses, medical technicians, surgical prep technicians, dental hygienists, dental assistants, phlebotomy, sonography, radiology, pharmacy technician, mammography, laboratory technician, veterinary assisting, veterinary technician

- **Other skilled vocational jobs:** Welding, electrician, plumbing, web designer, carpentry, construction management, pipe-fitting, machining, computer-aided drafting, network administration, civil engineering technician, paralegal, court reporter

» **College cooperative educational experiences:** A number of four-year colleges offer so-called cooperative programs. The idea behind these is that during a portion of the student's college experience, the student works part-time or full-time at an employer. This work for an employer is done during what would normally be the academic part of the year, counts toward school credits, and is paid. These programs vary greatly from school to school, so you really need to do your institution-specific research to find something that is a good fit. Also be aware that at some schools, it may take five years rather than four to complete all the graduation requirements. Some colleges that offer co-op programs include: Cornell University (Ithaca, New York); Drexel University (Philadelphia, Pennsylvania); Georgia Institute of Technology (Atlanta, Georgia); Northeastern University (Boston, Massachusetts); Purdue University (West Lafayette, Indiana); Rensselaer Polytechnic Institute (Troy, New York); Rochester Institute of Technology (Rochester, New York); Stevens Institute of Technology (Hoboken, New Jersey); University of Cincinnati (Cincinnati, Ohio); University of Florida (Gainesville, Florida).

The growing "alternatives" trend is good for you, the higher-education consumer. Competition for your time and dollars is slowly spurring some positive changes at colleges and universities, as it should. Colleges should earn your business, not get it by default.

REMEMBER

Traditional colleges and universities are not the only pathways to success. Keep an open mind about the alternatives available, because they too can lead to career satisfaction and a bright future.

Understanding the world's number-one universal language: Business

I think everyone can benefit from gaining background about business. It's the universal language of the workplace. Even if you want to work for a nonprofit, you should understand concepts such as revenues, customer acquisition and service, marketing, expenses, financial statements, and so on.

If you've already completed your college degree or are attending a college that doesn't offer business courses, don't despair. You can find out about the world and language of business in numerous other ways:

>> During the summers of your latter years of college and immediately after, go to work in business. Find the best organizations that you can, work hard, and be a sponge, soaking up all you can.

>> Read the best business books and publications, especially those on small business and entrepreneurship if that's what you're most interested in. Among books that I recommend are those written by James C. Collins, my *Small Business For Dummies* (coauthored with Jim Schell and published by Wiley), the classic *How to Win Friends & Influence People* by Dale Carnegie (Pocket Books), *The Greatest Salesman in the World* by Og Mandino (Bantam), and *How to Win at the Sport of Business* by Mark Cuban (Diversion Publishing). *Inc. Magazine* is a monthly publication that has lots of worthwhile content, in print and on their website at www.inc.com.

>> Take some free or very-low-cost online business courses from leading colleges and universities. You can do this through Coursera (which offers online courses from top universities like Northwestern, Stanford, the University of Pennsylvania's Wharton School, and Yale), EdX, MIT's OpenCourseWare, and Udacity.

>> Make use of taxpayer funded resources. Check out the short courses/videos offered by the U.S. Small Business Administration. The Small Business Development Centers (www.AmericasSBDC.org) nationwide offer "free" services. Their offices are frequently found on college campuses. They offer feaibility studies for business ideas, use of software to develop your business plan, counseling with social media specialists, cash flow experts, website professionals, and so forth.

>> Watch the best business television shows. Among those worth checking out are *Shark Tank* and *The Profit.*

Investing in your career

In my work with financial counseling clients over the years and from observing friends and colleagues, I've witnessed plenty of people succeed in their careers. What did they have in common? They invested in their careers, and you can and should do the same. Some time-tested, proven ways to do that include

» **Networking:** Some people wait to network until they've been laid off or are really hungry to change jobs. Take an interest in what others do for a living and you'll benefit and grow from the experience, even if you choose to stay with your current employer or in your chosen field. Online services like LinkedIn enable you to network and see what jobs you may qualify for.

» **Making sure you keep growing:** Whether it's reading high-quality books or other publications, learning from experts in a particular field, or listening to good podcasts, find ways to build on your knowledge base.

» **Considering the risk in the status quo:** Many folks are resistant to change and get anxious thinking about what could go wrong when taking a new risk. When I was ready to walk away from a six-figure consulting job with a prestigious firm and open my own financial counseling firm, a number of my relatives and friends thought I was foolish. I'm glad I didn't allow their fears and worries to dissuade me!

Exploring Entrepreneurial Options

Small business has generated more wealth than investing in the stock market or real estate. You can invest in small business by starting a business yourself, buying an existing business, or investing in someone else's small business. The following sections give you an overview in doing so.

Starting a small business

When you have self-discipline and a product or service you can sell, starting your own business can be both profitable and fulfilling. Before you start, consider the following:

» **Determine what skills and expertise you possess that you can use in your business.** You don't need a unique idea or invention to start a small business.

>> **Begin exploring your idea by first developing a written business plan.**
Such a plan should detail your product or service, how you're going to market it, your potential customers and competitors, and the economics of the business, including the start-up costs.

REMEMBER

Of all the small-business investment options, starting your own business involves the most work. Although you can do this work on a part-time basis in the beginning, most people end up running their business full time — it's your new job.

WHAT ABOUT A SIDE HUSTLE OR SECOND JOB?

You will find plenty of people, especially online and in the media, telling you that you can make good money and perhaps even some big bucks with a side hustle. The possibilities are nearly endless. You could be a youth sports referee, tutor, blogger, podcaster, and so on.

In my observation, though, you may confront problems that the side hustle advocates gloss over or more often, fail to mention at all. I would ask you to consider why you have the time, energy, and desire for a side hustle. Do you dislike your full-time job? Are you no longer developing and advancing professionally? I ask these important questions because perhaps you should instead focus on securing a better job to replace the one you currently have or work harder to improve the attributes of your current job. When was the last time you met with your boss/supervisor to discuss your career development?

A side hustle can provide a transition or bridge to something you like better. But it can also cause you to spread yourself thin, or resign yourself to the negatives with your current full-time job rather than getting motivated to fix and address those.

To begin the brainstorming process for a side hustle or completely new line of work, take stock of what skills and expertise you possess and then also consider, of course, what you enjoy doing. Some people are able to find that sweet spot where they can make a decent income doing something they mostly enjoy. Others may have to choose between earning more doing something they don't really enjoy much or earning less doing something that brings them more fulfillment.

In most people's eyes, starting a new business is the riskiest of all small-business investment options. But if you're going into a business that uses your skills and expertise, the risk isn't nearly as great as you may think. Many businesses can be started with little cash by leveraging your existing skills and expertise. You can build a valuable company and job if you have the time to devote to it. To begin your own business, check out the latest edition of *Small Business For Dummies* (Wiley), which I cowrote.

Purchasing a small business

If you don't have a specific product or service you want to sell but you're skilled at managing and improving the operations of a company, buying a small business may be for you. Finding and buying a good small business takes time and patience, so devote at least several months to the search. You may also need to enlist financial and legal advisors to help inspect the company, look over its financial statements, and hammer out a contract.

Good businesses don't come cheap. If the business is a success, the current owner has already removed the start-up risk from the business, so the price of the business should be at a premium to reflect this lack of risk. When you have the money to buy an established business and you have the skills to run it, consider going this route.

Although you don't have to go through the riskier start-up period if you buy a small business, you'll likely need more capital to buy an established enterprise. You'll also need to be able to deal with stickier personnel and management issues. The organization's history and the way it works will predate your ownership of the business. If you don't like making hard decisions, firing people who don't fit with your plans, and getting people to change the way they do things, buying an existing business likely isn't for you.

WARNING

Some people perceive buying an existing business as being safer than starting a new one. Buying someone else's business can actually be riskier. You're likely to shell out far more money upfront, in the form of a down payment. If you don't have the ability to run the business and it does poorly, you have more to lose financially. In addition, the business may be for sale for an undesirable reason — it may not be very profitable, it may be in decline, or it may generally be a pain in the neck to operate.

Investing in a small business

If you don't want the day-to-day headaches of being directly responsible for owning and managing a business but you do like the idea of profiting from a successful one, then investing in someone else's small business may be for you. Although this route may seem easier, few people are actually cut out to be investors in other people's businesses. The reason: Finding and analyzing opportunities isn't easy.

Are you astute at evaluating corporate financial statements and business strategies? Investing in a small, privately held company has much in common with investing in a publicly traded firm (as is the case when you buy stock), but it also has these differences:

>> **Private firms aren't required to produce comprehensive, audited financial statements that adhere to certain accounting principles.** Thus, you have a greater risk of not having sufficient or accurate information when evaluating a small, private firm.

>> **Unearthing private, small-business investing opportunities is harder.** The best private companies that are seeking investors generally don't advertise. Instead, they find prospective investors by networking with people such as business advisors. You can increase your chances of finding private companies to invest in by speaking with tax, legal, and financial advisors who work with small businesses. You can also find interesting opportunities through your own contacts or your experience within a given industry.

REMEMBER

Consider investing in someone else's business only if you can afford to lose all of what you invest. Also, you should have sufficient assets so that whatever money you invest in small, privately held companies represents only a small portion (20 percent or less) of your total financial assets.

Changing Jobs or Careers

During your adult life, you'll almost surely change jobs — perhaps several times a decade. I hope that most of the time you change jobs by your own choice. But in today's increasingly global and rapidly changing economy, job security isn't great. Downsizing has affected even the most talented workers.

REMEMBER

Always be prepared for a job change. No matter how happy you are in your current job, knowing that your world won't fall apart if you're not working tomorrow can give you an added sense of security and encourage openness to possibility. Whether you change your job by choice or necessity, the following financial maneuvers can help ease the transition:

>> **Keep your spending lean.** Spending less than you earn always makes good financial sense, but if you're approaching a possible job change, spending less is even more important, particularly if you're entering a new field or starting

your own company and you expect a short-term income dip. Many people view a lifestyle of thriftiness as restrictive, but ultimately, those thrifty habits can give you more freedom to do what you want to do.

>> **Keep an emergency reserve fund.** You should have a "rainy day" fund to deal with emergencies and the inevitable curveballs that life throws your way. I suggest keeping it in a money market fund or savings account, and it should cover at least three months' worth of living expenses.

>> **Evaluate the total financial picture when relocating.** At some point in your career, you may have the option of relocating. But don't call the moving company until you understand the financial consequences of such a move. You can't simply compare salaries and benefits between the two jobs. You also need to compare the cost of living between the two areas, which includes housing, commuting, state income tax and property taxes, food, utilities, and all the other major expenditure categories. There are various cost-of-living calculators online that enable you to compare different locations.

>> **Track your job-search expenses for tax purposes.** If you're seeking a new job in your current (or recently current) field of work, your job-search expenses may be tax-deductible, even if you don't get a specific job you desire. If you're moving into a new career, your job-search expenses aren't tax-deductible.

The Young and the Unemployed

Your job search may play out like a daytime drama, which is no surprise if you're having a difficult time finding a job. But being unemployed means you need to be especially concerned with your personal finances. The following sections point out why unemployment strikes younger people harder and what you can do during difficult times.

Understanding how joblessness can hit younger adults harder

During the severe recession from 2007–2009, high unemployment rates were all over the news as the unemployment rate surpassed 10 percent in the United States. But that double-digit level of joblessness paled in comparison to the high level of unemployment for young people, especially those who were less well educated.

Despite the multi-year expansion that the U.S. economy enjoyed after 2009, the youngest adults (those under 25) continued to have higher levels of unemployment than the rest of the working adult population. Adults without a high-school diploma have an unemployment rate far greater than the average, followed by high-school graduates who have no college experience. College graduates have by far the lowest unemployment rate. (Figure 9-1 earlier in the chapter helps you understand the rate of unemployment and average weekly earnings based on education level.)

During the government-mandated COVID-19 economic shutdowns that happened to varying degrees in different parts of the United States in 2020 and continuing into early 2021, unemployment quickly spiked higher and then began improving. Thankfully, jobs have been returning far more quickly than during the period after the 2007–2009 Great Recession. But, as with the prior recession, those who were younger and had less formal education generally suffered more with layoffs. Those in industries and careers where work can more easily be done remotely tended to suffer the least.

Although you can't do anything about your age, you can do something about your education and training and career options (see the earlier section "Getting Your Career Going").

Accessing unemployment benefits

If you're laid off and unemployed, you should collect unemployment benefits if you're eligible. You must be actively seeking employment and meet any other eligibility requirements in your state.

TIP

The simplest way to find the state unemployment insurance office nearest you is to visit the website www.CareerOneStop.org and click "Unemployment Benefits Finder" on the home page. CareerOneStop operates this site — a U.S. Department of Labor–sponsored website that provides "career resources and workforce information to job seekers, students, businesses, and workforce professionals to foster talent development in a global economy."

Unemployment benefits are provided at the state level, and each state has its own program. If you're turned down for benefits, be sure to clarify why, and don't be shy about appealing the decision if you feel there's a chance you may get approved if you're able to furnish more information.

Taking action

You can make the most of your finances and be best prepared to handle life's challenges if you stay on top of your financial affairs. That said, losing one's job often comes as a surprise and presents some unusual stresses. Here are some tips to keep in mind if you lose your job:

>> **Batten down the hatches.** Evaluating and slashing your current level of spending may be necessary. Everything should be fair game, from how much you spend on housing to how often you eat out to where you do your grocery shopping. Avoid at all costs the temptation to maintain your level of spending by accumulating consumer debt.

>> **Work at your job search a few hours daily but not on a full-time basis.** Searching for a job is hard work and creates stress for most people. You're probably not going to make the most of your job search by making it your full-time endeavor. Make some calls; arrange some appointments; send some résumés; and do some research on industries, companies, and organizations of interest every day. But I suggest doing so for no more than four to six hours per day. If you can find part-time or temporary work, spend some time doing that to earn some money and to break up the monotony of looking for work.

>> **Try to exercise regularly.** Exercise clears the head and lifts your mood. Daily exercise is best, but if that's not possible, try to get some exercise at least every other day.

>> **Eat healthfully.** As with exercise, eating a balanced and nutritious diet can go a long way toward maximizing your mental (and physical) health and outlook.

3

Investing for Your Future Goals

Understand the range of investments, their risks, and expected returns so you can invest wisely.

Find the right bank to service your needs, whether that be a brick-and-mortar bank, an online bank, or a brokerage account or money market fund.

Match your investments to specific goals and develop and manage a successful portfolio.

Excel at real-estate investing.

Chapter **10**

Successful Investing Principles

One of the most important financial tasks you'll tackle in your 20s and 30s is investing money you've worked hard to earn and save. If you think about it, the investments that you make in your young adult years will have decades to produce great returns for you. So, you really have within your power and grasp the ability to make life-changing investments when you're young.

Investing wisely takes knowledge, discipline, and a sound philosophy. The good news: This chapter can help you get and stay on the right path.

Ignore, for a moment, all the specific investments you've ever heard of. Having a big picture and overarching understanding of the investment world is vital, so I explain and simplify it for you in the following sections. You have two major investment choices: You can be a lender or an owner.

Examining Bonds and Other Lending Investments

When you invest your money in a bank certificate of deposit (CD), a Treasury bill, or a bond issued by a company — such as the telecommunications giant Verizon, for example — you're a *lender.* In each case, you lend your money to an organization — a bank, the federal government, or Verizon. The organization pays you an agreed-upon rate of interest for lending your money and promises to return your original investment (the principal) on a specific date.

Getting paid all the interest in addition to getting back your original investment (as promised) is your hoped-for outcome when you make a lending investment. Given that the investment landscape is littered with carcasses of failed investments, however, this result isn't guaranteed. The following sections outline what happens when you invest in bonds and discuss some lending drawbacks.

Investing in bonds

When you invest in a newly issued bond, you lend your money to an organization. The bond includes a specified *maturity date* — the time at which the principal is repaid — and a particular *interest rate,* or what's known as a *coupon.* This rate is fixed on most bonds. So, for example, if you buy a ten-year, 5 percent bond issued by Boeing, the U.S. aircraft manufacturer, you're lending your money to Boeing for ten years at an interest rate of 5 percent per year. (Bond interest is usually paid in two equal, semiannual installments.)

Some types of bonds have higher yields than others, but the risk-reward relationship remains intact. A bond generally pays you a higher rate of interest when it has a

>> **Lower credit rating:** To compensate for the higher risk of default and the higher likelihood of losing your investment

>> **Longer-term maturity (how many years until bondholders are paid back):** To compensate for the risk that you'll be unhappy with the bond's set interest rate if the market level of interest rates moves up

A bond's value generally moves opposite of the directional change in interest rates. For example, if you're holding a bond issued at 5 percent and rates increase to 6 percent on comparable, newly issued bonds, your bond decreases in value. (The reason: Why would anyone want to buy your bond at the price you paid if it yields just 5 percent when 6 percent can be obtained elsewhere on the same types of bonds?)

Bonds differ from one another in the following major ways:

>> **The type of institution to which you lend your money:** With municipal bonds, you lend your money to a state or local government or agency; with Treasuries, you lend your money to the federal government; with corporate bonds, you lend your money to a corporation.

>> **The credit quality of the borrower to which you lend your money:** Credit quality is a measurement of the likelihood that the borrower will default on the interest and principal you're owed. Knowing this information is important because higher-credit-rating bonds are generally safer but pay lower rates of interest.

>> **The length of the bond's maturity:** Short-term bonds mature within 5 years, intermediate bonds mature within 5 to 10 years, and long-term bonds mature within 30 years. Longer-term bonds generally pay higher yields but fluctuate more with changes in interest rates.

>> **The bond's callability:** Callability means that the bond's issuer can decide to pay you back earlier than the previously agreed-upon date. This event usually occurs when interest rates fall and the bond issuer wants to issue new, lower-interest-rate bonds to replace the higher-rate bonds outstanding. To compensate you for early repayment, the bond's issuer typically gives you a small premium over what the bond is currently valued at.

Considering the downsides to lending

Many folks think that lending investments are safe and without risk, which is wrong. Lending money has the following disadvantages:

>> **You may not get what you're promised.** When a company goes bankrupt, for example, you can lose all or part of your original investment.

>> **Your money's purchasing power may be reduced by inflation.** Many folks have grown complacent with the low inflation the United States has enjoyed for quite some time. But what if inflation increases to 6 percent per year, or even 10 percent per year, as it last did in the early 1980s? After a decade of that much inflation, the purchasing power of your money drops 44 percent at 6 percent annual inflation and a whopping 61 percent at 10 percent yearly inflation. Also, the value of a bond may drop below what you paid for it if interest rates rise or the quality/risk of the issuing company declines.

>> **You don't share in the upside of the organization to which you lend your money.** If a company grows in size and profits, your principal and interest rate don't grow along with it; they stay the same. Of course, such success should ensure that you get your promised interest and principal.

Exploring Stocks, Real Estate, and Small-Business Investments

The three best ways to build long-term wealth are to invest in ownership investments: stocks, real estate, and small business. I've found this to be true from my own personal experiences and from observing many clients and other investors over the decades. The following sections outline these three ways in greater depth.

Socking your money away in stocks

Stocks, which represent shares of ownership in a company, are the most common ownership investment vehicle. You're an *owner* when you invest your money in an asset, such as a company or real estate, that has the ability to generate earnings or profits. Suppose that you own 100 shares of Apple stock. With billions of shares of stock outstanding, Apple is a mighty big company — your 100 shares represent a tiny piece of it.

What do you get for your small slice of Apple? As a stockholder, you share in the company's profits in the form of *dividends* (quarterly cash payments to shareholders from the company) and an increase (you hope) in the stock price if the company grows and becomes more profitable. Of course, you receive these benefits if things are going well. If Apple's business declines, your stock may be worth less (or even worthless!).

As the economy grows and companies grow with it and earn greater profits, stock prices and dividend payouts on those stocks generally increase. Stock prices and dividends don't move in lockstep with earnings, but over the years, the relationship is pretty close.

In fact, the *price-earnings ratio* — which measures the level of stock prices relative to (or divided by) company earnings — of U.S. stocks has averaged approximately 15 the past two centuries (although it tends to be higher during periods of low inflation). A price-earnings ratio of 15 simply means that shares of a company's stock, on average, are selling at about 15 times the company's earnings per share.

When companies go public, they issue shares of stock that people can purchase on the major stock exchanges, such as the New York Stock Exchange. Companies that issue stock are called *publicly held companies.* By contrast, some companies are *privately held,* which means that they've elected to sell their stock only to senior management and a small number of invited, affluent investors. Privately held companies' stocks don't trade on a stock exchange, thus limiting who can be a shareholder.

Not only can you invest in company stocks that trade on the U.S. stock exchanges, but you can also invest in stocks overseas. Many investing opportunities exist overseas. If you look at the total value of all stocks outstanding worldwide, the value of U.S. stocks is in the minority.

A good reason for investing in international stocks is that when you confine your investing to U.S. equities (another word for stocks), you miss a world of opportunities, like taking advantage of business growth in other countries, as well as diversifying your portfolio even further. (For more on diversification, see the later section "Spreading Your Investment Risks.") International securities markets traditionally haven't moved in tandem with U.S. markets.

Investing in the stock market involves setbacks and difficult periods, but the overall journey should be worth the effort. Over the past two centuries, the U.S. stock market has produced an annual average rate of return of about 9 percent (which translates into about 6 percent per year after subtracting inflation). However, as anyone who has invested in stocks over the years has experienced firsthand, stocks can drop sharply — worldwide, stocks were sliced approximately in half during the down market that ended in early 2009. During the government-mandated COVID-19 economic shutdowns in early 2020, stocks plunged about 35 percent in just a few weeks. So if you can withstand down markets here and there over the course of many years, the stock market is a proven place to invest for long-term growth.

You can invest in stocks (and bonds, which I discuss earlier in this chapter) by making your own selection of individual stocks or by letting a mutual (or exchange-traded) fund do the selecting for you.

Investing in individual stocks

Who wouldn't want to own shares in the next hot stock? Few things are more financially satisfying than investing in a stock like Apple or Amazon that multiplies your money many, many times over the years.

But investing in individual stocks entails numerous pitfalls:

>> **You may fool yourself (or let others fool you) into thinking that picking and following individual companies and their stocks is simple and requires little time.**

When you're considering the purchase of an individual security, you should spend a significant amount of time doing research. You need to know a lot about the company in which you're thinking about investing. Relevant questions to ask about the company include: What products and services does it sell? What are its prospects for future growth and profitability? What companies are likely to provide the strongest competition in coming years and how will that affect this particular company you're considering? How much debt does it have? You need to do your homework not only before you make your initial investment but also on an ongoing basis for as long as you hold the investment. Research takes your valuable free time and sometimes costs money.

>> **Your emotions will probably get in your way.** Analyzing financial statements, corporate strategy, and competitive position requires great intellect and insight. However, those skills aren't nearly enough. Will you have the stomach to hold on after what you thought was a sure-win stock plunges 30 or even 50+ percent? Will you have the courage to dump such a stock if your new research suggests that the plummet is the beginning of bigger problems rather than just a bump in the road? When your money's on the line, emotions often undermine your ability to make sound, long-term decisions. Few people have the psychological constitution to handle the financial markets.

>> **You're less likely to diversify.** Unless you have tens of thousands of dollars to invest in dozens of different stocks, you probably can't cost-effectively afford to develop a diversified portfolio. When investing in stocks, for example, you should hold companies in different industries and different companies within an industry. (Diversifying is easier and less costly to do if you invest some of your money in the best mutual funds and exchange-traded funds in addition to individual stocks.) By not diversifying, you unnecessarily add to your risk. (For more on diversification, see the later section "Spreading Your Investment Risks.")

>> **You'll face accounting and bookkeeping hassles.** When you invest in individual securities outside of retirement accounts, every time you sell a security, you must report that transaction on your tax return.

REMEMBER

Investing in individual securities should be done only by those who really enjoy doing it and are aware of and willing to accept the risks in doing so. Researching individual stocks can be more than a full-time job, and if you choose to take this path, remember that you'll be competing against the professionals who do so on a full-time basis. I recommend that you limit your individual stock picking to no more than 20 percent of your overall investments.

Some people are fortunate to work for a growing company that grants them some stock options which may become valuable over time. In the "best" cases that I have observed, stock ownership in your company may end up becoming a significant portion (more than 20 percent) of your overall financial assets. When your employer's stock is rising and your wealth is growing, having such a concentrated position is surely enjoyable. But please recognize the extra risk that comes with having a large portion of your assets tied to the success of one company (your employer). Your future employment depends upon the health of your employer as does much of your investment portfolio in such a situation, so be careful and understand the risks you're accepting with your holdings.

Discovering the advantages of mutual funds and ETFs

Mutual funds (investment pools that hold a collection of securities such as bonds and stocks) span the spectrum of risk and potential returns, from stable-value money market funds (which are similar to savings accounts) to bond funds (which generally pay higher yields than money market funds but fluctuate with changes in interest rates) to stock funds (which offer the greatest potential for appreciation but also the greatest short-term volatility).

Exchange-traded funds (ETFs) are similar to mutual funds except that they trade on a major stock exchange and, unlike mutual funds, can be bought and sold during the trading day. The best ETFs have low fees, and like an index fund (which invests in a fixed mix of securities that track a specific market index), they invest to track the performance of a stock market index.

Investing in stocks through stock mutual funds doesn't mean that you won't end up owning the stocks that produce large returns over time. In fact, the best funds, which I recommend in Chapter 12, have proven track records of owning numerous top-performing stocks and holding them over many years.

REMEMBER

Efficiently managed mutual funds and exchange-traded funds, if properly selected, are a low-cost way for investors of both modest and substantial means to hire professional money managers. See Chapter 12 for sample portfolios of funds. Over the long haul, you're not going to beat full-time professional managers who invest in securities of the same type and risk level.

Generating wealth with real estate

Real estate is another financially rewarding and time-honored ownership investment. Real estate can produce profits when you rent it for more than the expense of owning the property, or you sell it at a price higher than what you paid for it. I know numerous successful real-estate investors (myself included) who've earned excellent long-term profits.

Over the generations, real-estate owners and investors have enjoyed rates of return comparable to those produced by the stock market. However, like stocks, real estate goes through good and bad performance periods. Most people who make money investing in real estate do so because they invest over many years and do their homework when they buy to ensure that they purchase good property at an attractive price.

The value of real estate depends not only on the particulars of the individual property but also on the health and performance of the local economy. When companies in the community are growing and more jobs are being produced at higher wages, real estate does well. When local employers are laying people off and excess housing is vacant because of overbuilding, rent and property values fall.

REMEMBER

Buying your own home is a good place to start investing in real estate. The *equity* in your home (the difference between the home's market value and the loan you owe on it) that builds over the years can become a significant part of your net worth. Over your adult life, owning a home should be less expensive than renting a comparable home. See Chapter 7 for the details on buying and financing your home.

Real estate's attributes

Real estate differs from most other investments in several respects. Here are real estate's unique attributes:

>> **Usability:** Real estate is the only investment you can use (living in or renting out) to produce income. You can't live in a stock, bond, or mutual fund!

>> **Less buildable land:** The demand for land and housing continues to grow with population growth. Scarcer land propels real-estate prices higher over the long term.

>> **Zoning determinations:** Local government regulates the zoning of property, and zoning determines what a property can be used for. In most communities, local zoning boards are against big growth. This position bodes well for future real-estate values. In some cases, a particular property may not have been developed to its full potential. If you can figure out how to develop the property, you can reap large profits.

>> **Leverage with debt usage:** Real estate is also different from other investments because you can borrow a lot of money to buy it — up to 80 percent or more of the property's value. This borrowing is known as exercising *leverage:* With an investment of 20 percent down, you're able to purchase and own a much larger investment. If the value of your real estate goes up, you make money on your investment and on the money you borrowed. (Of course, the reverse happens when real-estate prices go down.)

>> **Diamonds in the rough:** Real-estate markets can be inefficient at times. Information isn't always easy to come by, and you may encounter a highly motivated or uninformed seller. Do your homework and you may be able to reap the rewards of purchasing a property below its fair market value.

>> **Favorable tax treatment:** The tax code preferentially provides additional tax deductions, exclusions, or deferrals of taxes on gains on many types of real estate that aren't available on other types of investments.

Just as with any other investment, real estate has its drawbacks. Buying and selling a property takes time and is costly. When you're renting property, you discover firsthand the occasional headaches of being a landlord. And especially in the early years of rental-property ownership, the property's expenses may exceed the rental income, producing a net cash drain.

Attractive real-estate investments

You can invest in homes, duplexes, or small apartment buildings and then rent them out. In the long run, investment-property buyers usually see their rental income increase faster than their expenses and the value of their property increase. So successful investment-property owners make money monthly and yearly from the cash flow on their properties as well as when they someday sell their investment property for more than they paid for it.

When selecting real estate for investment purposes, remember that local economic growth is the fuel for housing demand. In addition to a vibrant and diverse job base, you want to look for limited supplies of both existing housing and land on which to build. When you identify potential properties in which you may want to invest, run the numbers to understand the cash demands of owning the property and the likely profitability.

If you don't want to be a landlord — one of the biggest drawbacks of investment real estate — consider *real-estate investment trusts* (REITs). REITs are diversified real-estate investment companies that purchase and manage rental real estate for investors. A typical REIT invests in different types of property, such as shopping centers, apartments, and other rental buildings. You can invest in REITs either by purchasing them directly on the major stock exchanges or by investing in a real-estate mutual fund that invests in numerous REITs.

For more information regarding investing in properties, check out my book, *Real Estate Investing For Dummies* (coauthored by Robert S. Griswold and published by Wiley).

Going the small-business investment route

Many folks have also built substantial wealth through small business. You can participate in small business in a variety of ways. You can start your own business, buy and operate an existing business, or simply invest in promising small businesses. See Chapter 9 for more details.

Considering Options, Cryptocurrencies, and Other Hot Vehicles

Seeking out get-rich-quick investments is hardly new. And, unless you're a person who dislikes money for some reason, most people think about where they might invest to make really high returns.

Wouldn't it have been great and feel terrific to have invested in companies like Microsoft, Google, Amazon, Facebook, Tesla, and so forth early on? The best mutual funds actually make such investments, which is why I personally enjoy investing through funds. But some folks still try to gamble on making money fast. The following sections show the more popular routes and what to watch out for.

Opting for options

In recent years, I'm finding that some young people are using options, such as call options, to try and make big money quickly. If you don't understand call options, I'd almost rather not explain them to you because I'd rather you stay away from them! But here's a simple example to explain how they work.

Suppose you're intrigued by the emerging field of artificial intelligence and you hear about the company C3 AI and its stock. You look and see that the stock is trading at $140 per share. Instead of buying the stock, though, you could buy some C3 AI call options. Their $170 call options, which expire in about eight months, are going for just $28 per share. Suppose in the next six months the stock were to zoom higher and hit $300 per share. Your call options would be worth at least $130 per share now, so you would have more than quadrupled your money — a far greater percentage move than you would have enjoyed with the stock. However, if the stock were to instead tread water or go down, your options would end up expiring worthless and you would have lost all the money you invested in them.

So, with options, you are making a short-term bet or gamble on the price of a particular stock rather than making an investment for the years ahead. So, you not only have to be right about the specific stock you are choosing, but you also have to be correct about the specific (short-term) timing of your investment.

Put options work the opposite of call options. If you're expecting a stock's price to go down in the near future, you might profit through buying a put option for that stock.

Calculating cryptocurrencies

In addition to options, I see interest in cryptocurrencies among some young adults today. Bitcoin, the most well-known and highly traded cryptocurrency, has been making headlines as its price climbs to ever dizzying heights. It recently hit breached $61,600 per coin. But there are literally thousands — more than 8,000 at recent count — of other cryptocurrencies.

So, what exactly is Bitcoin (and other cryptocurrencies)? For starters, it's not actually a coin — that's a marketing gimmick to make it sound like a real currency. Bitcoin and other similar cryptocurrencies only exist in the online world. Bitcoin's creators say that they have limited the number of Bitcoins that can be mined and put into online circulation to about 21 million.

As its promoters have talked up its usefulness and rapid rise, many people who have Bitcoins continue to hold onto them like shares of stock in the next Amazon, Apple, or Tesla, hoping for and expecting further steep price increases. People don't hoard real currencies with similar pie-in-the-sky hopes for large investment returns.

WARNING

Online cryptocurrency transactions can be done anonymously, and they can't be contested, disputed, or reversed. So, if you buy something using cryptocurrencies and have a problem with the item you bought, that's too bad — you have no recourse, unlike, for example, a purchase made on your credit card. The clandestine nature of cryptocurrencies makes them attractive to folks trying to hide money or engaging in illegal activities (criminals, drug dealers, and the like). And hackers create another real danger — your cryptocurrency could be stolen as has happened to numerous Bitcoin and other crypto holders.

So, what is a given cryptocurrency like Bitcoin worth? Cryptocurrencies have no inherent value. Contrast that with gold. Not only has gold had a long history of being used as a medium of exchange (currency), but gold also has commercial and industrial uses. Furthermore, gold costs real money to mine out of the ground, which provides a floor of support under the price of gold in the range of $1,000 to $1,200 per ounce for most miners, not far below the price of gold at about $1,700 per ounce at the time of this writing.

While the supply of Bitcoin is currently artificially limited, Bitcoin is hardly unique — it's one of thousands of cryptocurrencies. So, if another cryptocurrency is easier to use online and perceived as attractive (in part because it's far less expensive), Bitcoin will tumble in value.

Even though Bitcoin has been the most popular cryptocurrency in recent years, few merchants actually accept it. And, to add insult to injury, Bitcoin users get whacked with unfavorable conversion rates, which add greatly to the effective price of items bought with Bitcoin.

REMEMBER

I can't tell you what will happen to Bitcoin's or any other cryptocurrency's price next month, next year, or next decade. But I can tell that it has virtually no inherent value as a digital currency, so those paying big bucks for a particular cryptocurrency will likely eventually be extremely disappointed. There are more than 8,800 of these cryptocurrencies, and the field keeps growing as creators hope to get in on the ground floor of the next cryptocurrency that they hope will soar in value.

Noting leveraged and inverse ETFs aren't investments

Since their introduction in 2006, leveraged and inverse exchange-traded funds (ETFs) have taken tens of billions of dollars in assets. Leveraged ETFs purport to magnify the move of a particular index, for example the Standard & Poor's (S&P) 500 stock index, by double or even triple in some cases. So, a double-leveraged S&P 500 ETF is supposed to increase by 2 percent for a 1 percent increase in the S&P 500 index.

Inverse ETFs are supposed to move in the opposite direction of a given index. So, for example, an inverse S&P 500 ETF is supposed to increase by 1 percent for a 1 percent decrease in the S&P 500 index.

The steep 2008 decline in stock market indexes around the globe and increasing volatility theoretically created the perfect environment for leveraged and inverse ETFs. With these new vehicles, you could easily make money from major stock market indexes when they were falling. Or, if you were convinced a particular index or industry group was about to zoom higher, you could buy a leveraged ETF that would magnify market moves two- or even threefold.

Suppose back in early 2008, when the Dow Jones Industrial Average had declined about 10 percent from its then-recent peak above 14,000, you were starting to get nervous and wanted to protect your portfolio from a major market decline. So, you bought some of the ProShares UltraShort Dow 30 ETF (trading symbol DXD), which is an inverse ETF designed to move twice as much in the opposite direction as the Dow. So, if the Dow goes down, DXD goes up twice as much and you make money.

This ETF did indeed rise sharply when the Dow fell sharply in mid to late 2008. By late 2008, with the Dow down about 40 percent, the ETF, rather than being up 80 percent, was only up about 50 percent. In early 2010 — two years after you bought the ETF in early 2008 — the Dow was down about 20 percent. So if you held on that long, your original thinking — that the market was going to fall — proved to be correct. If the ETF did what it was supposed to do and moved twice as much in the other direction, it should have increased 40 percent in value over this period, thus giving you a tidy return. But it didn't — not even close. The ETF actually plummeted nearly 50 percent in value!

My overall investigations of whether the leveraged (and inverse) ETFs actually deliver on their objectives show that they don't. Over the years, ETF issuers have come out with increasingly risky and costly ETFs. Leveraged and inverse ETFs are especially problematic.

Buried in the fine print of the prospectuses of these ETFs, it usually says that these ETFs are only designed to accomplish their stated objectives for one trading day, so they are only really suitable for day traders! Of course, few investors read the dozens of pages of legal boilerplate in a prospectus.

Leveraged and inverse ETFs are not investments. They are gambling instruments for day traders.

For you as an individual investor, if you happen to guess right before a short-term major market move, you may do well over a short period of time (longer than one day but no more than a few months), but the odds are heavily stacked against you.

You can reduce risk through sensible diversification. If you don't want 80 percent of your portfolio exposed to stock market risk, invest a percentage you're comfortable with and don't waste your time and money with leveraged and inverse ETFs.

Getting a Handle on Investment Risks

Many investors have a simplistic understanding of what risk means and how to apply it to their investment decisions. Having a firm handle on investment risk and what it means to you in your young-adult years and as you age is important.

For example, when compared to the gyrations of the stock market, a bank savings account may seem like a less risky place to put your money. Over the long term, however, the stock market usually beats the rate of inflation, while the interest rate on a savings account does not. Thus, if you're saving your money for a long-term goal like retirement/financial independence, a savings account can be a "riskier" place to put your money than a diversified stock portfolio. The following sections take a closer look at determining what you want and identifying potential risks.

Establishing goals and risks

Before you select a specific investment, first determine your investment needs and goals. Ask yourself: Why are you saving money? What are you going to use it for? Establishing objectives is important because the expected use of the money helps you determine which investments to choose.

For example, suppose you've been accumulating money for a down payment on a home you want to buy in a few years. You can't afford much risk with that money. You're going to need that money sooner rather than later. Putting that money in the stock market, then, is foolish because the stock market can drop a lot in a year or over several consecutive years.

By contrast, when saving toward a longer-term goal that's decades away, such as retirement, you're better able to make riskier investments, because your holdings have more time to bounce back from temporary losses or setbacks. You may want to consider investing in growth investments, such as stocks, in a retirement account that you leave alone for many years.

Comparing the risks of stocks and bonds

Given the relatively higher historic returns for ownership investments like stocks, some people think that they should put all their money in stocks and real estate. So what's the catch?

The risk with ownership investments is the short-term drops in their value. During the last century, stocks declined, on average, by more than 10 percent once every five calendar years. Drops in stock prices of more than 20 percent occurred, on average, once every ten calendar years. Real-estate prices suffer similar periodic setbacks.

WARNING

Therefore, in order to earn those generous long-term returns from ownership investments like stocks and real estate, you must be willing to tolerate volatility. You absolutely *should not* put all your money in the stock or real-estate market. You shouldn't invest your emergency money or money you expect to use within the next several years in such volatile investments.

The shorter the time period that you have for holding your money in an investment, the less likely growth-oriented investments like stocks are to beat out lending-type investments like bonds.

TIP

When you invest in stocks and other growth-oriented investments, you must accept the volatility of these investments. That said, you can take several actions, which I discuss in this chapter and in Chapter 12, to greatly reduce your risk when investing in these higher potential–return investments. Invest the money that you have earmarked for the longer term in these vehicles. Minimize the risk of these investments through diversification. Don't buy just one or two stocks; buy a number of stocks. Keep reading for more information about diversification.

Spreading Your Investment Risks

Diversification is a powerful investment concept. It refers to placing your money in different investments with returns that aren't completely correlated. This is a fancy way of saying that when some of your investments are down in value, odds are that others are up in value.

TIP

To decrease the chances of all your investments getting clobbered at the same time, put your money in different types of investments, such as bonds, stocks, real estate, and small business. You can further diversify your investments by investing in domestic as well as international markets.

The following sections point out why diversifying your investments is useful, how you can do it, and why you should avoid the temptation to toss investments that are down during certain times.

Understanding why diversification is key

Within a given class of investments, such as stocks, investing in different types of that class (such as different types of stocks) that perform well under various economic conditions is important. For this reason, mutual funds and exchange-traded funds, which are diversified portfolios of securities such as stocks or bonds, are a highly useful investment vehicle. When you buy into funds, your money is pooled with the money of many others and invested in a diverse array of stocks or bonds.

Diversification reduces the volatility in the value of your whole portfolio. In other words, your portfolio can achieve the same rate of return that a single investment may typically provide with less fluctuation in value.

Keep in mind that no one, no matter whom he works for or what credentials he has, can guarantee returns on an investment. You can do good research and get lucky, but no one is immune from the risk of losing money. Diversification allows you to reduce the risk of unnecessarily large losses from your investments.

Allocating your assets

Asset allocation refers to how you spread your investing dollars among different investment options (stocks, bonds, money market accounts, and so on). Over the long term, the asset allocation decision is the most important determinant of total return and risk for a diversified portfolio. Before you can intelligently decide how to allocate your assets, you need to ponder a number of issues, including your present financial situation, your goals and priorities, and the pros and cons of various investment options.

Although stocks and real estate offer attractive long-term returns, they can sometimes suffer significant declines. Thus, these investments aren't suitable for money that you think you may want or need to use within, say, the next five years.

TIP

Money market funds and shorter-term bond investments are good places to keep money that you expect to use soon. Everyone should have a reserve of money — about three to six months' worth of living expenses in a money market fund — that he or she can access in an emergency. Shorter-term bonds or bond mutual funds can serve as a higher-yielding, secondary emergency cushion.

Investing money for retirement is a classic long-term goal that most people have. Your current age and the number of years until you retire are the biggest factors to consider when allocating money for long-term purposes. The younger you are and the more years you have before retirement, the more comfortable you should be with growth-oriented (and more volatile) investments, such as stocks and investment real estate. Bonds can also be useful for diversification purposes. For example, when investing for retirement, placing a portion of your money in bonds helps buffer stock market declines.

TIP

A useful guideline for dividing or allocating your money between longer-term-oriented growth investments, such as stocks, and more-conservative lending investments, such as bonds, is to subtract your age from 110 (or 120 if you want to be aggressive; 100 to be more conservative) and invest the resulting percentage in stocks. You then invest the remaining amount in bonds.

For example, if you're 25, you invest from 75 (100 − 25) to 95 (120 − 25) percent in stocks. You invest the portion left over — 5 to 25 percent — in bonds. Consider allocating a percentage of your stock-fund money to overseas investments: at least 20 percent to as much as 50 percent for more aggressive investors.

Holding onto your investments and shunning the herd

The allocation of your investment dollars should be driven by your goals and desire to take risk. As you get older, gradually scaling back on the riskiness (and, therefore, growth potential) of your portfolio generally makes sense.

Don't tinker with your portfolio daily, weekly, monthly, or even annually. Every three to five years or so, you may want to rebalance your holdings to get your mix to a desired asset allocation, as I discuss in the preceding section. Don't trade with the hopes of buying into a hot investment and selling your losers. Jumping onto a "winner" and dumping a "loser" may provide some short-term psychological comfort, but in the long term, such an investment strategy often produces subpar returns.

WARNING

When a particular investment is all over the news and everyone is talking about its stunning rise, it's definitely time to take a reality check. The higher the value of an investment rises, the greater the danger that it's overpriced. Its next move may be downward.

During the late 1990s, for example, many technology and Internet stocks had spectacular rises, thus attracting a lot of attention. However, the fact that the U.S. economy is increasingly becoming technology-based doesn't mean that any price you pay for a technology stock is fine. Some investors who neglected to do basic research and bought into the attention-grabbing, high-flying technology stocks lost 80 percent or more of their investments in subsequent years — ouch!

Conversely, when things look bleak (as when stocks in general suffered significant losses in the early 2000s, then again in the late 2000s, and in early 2020), giving up hope is easy — who wants to lose money? However, investors who forget about their overall asset allocation plan and panic and sell after a major decline miss out on a potential rebound in the market and a tremendous buying opportunity. We like buying televisions, computers, and cars on sale. Yet when the stock market is having a sale, many investors panic and sell instead of looking for bargains. Have courage and don't follow the herd.

REMEMBER

Don't let a poor string of events sour you on stock investing. History has repeatedly proven that continuing to buy stocks during down markets increases long-term returns.

Selling your stocks is the worst thing you can do in a slumping market. And don't waste time trying to find a way to beat the system. Buy and hold a diversified portfolio of stocks. The financial markets reward investors for accepting risk and uncertainty.

Selecting an Investment Firm

Thousands of firms sell investments and manage money. Banks, fund companies, securities brokerage firms, insurance companies, and others all want your money. I recommend that you do business with investment companies that

> » **Offer the best value investments in comparison to their competitors.** Value is the combination of performance (including service) and cost. Commissions, management fees, maintenance fees, and other charges can turn a high-performance investment into a mediocre or poor one.

> » **Employ representatives who don't have an inherent self-interest in steering you into a particular type of investment.** Give preference to investing firms that don't tempt their employees to push one investment over another in order to generate more fees. If the investment firm's people are paid on commission, be careful.

Funds are an ideal investment vehicle for most investors. *No-load* fund companies are firms through which you can invest in funds without paying sales commissions, so all your invested dollars go to work in the mutual funds you choose. All funds charge ongoing management fees, and all else being equal, minimizing those fees will help to boost how much of the fund's returns you keep.

Discount brokers generally pay the salaries of their brokers. *Discount brokers* are simply brokers without major conflicts of interest. Of course, like any other for-profit enterprise, they're in business to make money, but they're much less likely to steer you wrong for their own benefit.

TIP

In Chapter 12, I name names and recommend some of the best investments to utilize.

Evaluating Pundits and Experts

Believing that you can increase your investment returns by following the prognostications of certain gurus is a common mistake that some investors make, especially during more trying and uncertain times. Many people want to believe that some experts can predict the future of the investment world and keep them out of harm's way.

During the financial crisis of 2008, all sorts of pundits were coming out of the woodwork, claiming that they had predicted what was unfolding. And when bad things were happening, commentators were all over the place predicting what would happen next.

The sad part about hyped articles and blogs with hyped predictions is that they cause some individual investors to panic and do the wrong thing, like selling good assets such as stocks at depressed prices. The media shouldn't irresponsibly publicize hyped predictions, especially without clearly and accurately disclosing the predictor's track record. Don't fall victim to such hype.

REMEMBER

Ignore the predictions and speculations of self-proclaimed gurus and investment soothsayers. Commentators and experts who publish predictive commentaries and newsletters and who are interviewed in the media can't predict the future. The few people who have a slight leg up on everyone else aren't going to share their investment secrets — they're too busy investing their own money! If you have to believe in something to offset your fears, believe in good information and proven investment managers.

TIP

My website, www.erictyson.com, provides excerpts and updates from the best newsletters to which I subscribe and read. Also check out the "Guru Watch" section of my site in which I evaluate commonly quoted gurus and expose their real records.

Chapter **11**

Making the Best Use of Bank Accounts

While you were in school, you may have had a savings or checking account to help you save money and pay some bills. When you're in the real world and out of school, you have to consider whether you want to make a longer-term commitment with a financial institution, such as a bank.

In this chapter, I walk you through your bank account choices and what investigative work you can do to find the best bank for you. I also address some alternatives to having a bank account in the first place.

Looking at Different Types of Banks

When figuring out where to protect your hard-earned money, you have several choices. You want to select an institution that offers the services and conveniences you need on attractive terms. The following sections outline these choices and provide some helpful information.

Brick-and-mortar banks

The most obvious choice for banking is using a local bank you pass by on a regular basis. Although these types of banks are conveniently located, these banks may not be the most cost efficient. You can find two main types of brick-and-mortar banks:

TIP

>> **Small-town bank:** These banks only have a handful of branches. Some of the tellers may even remember your name and face. Hours are generally limited, and you may encounter extra ATM fees for using ATMs that aren't at one of the bank's branches.

   A sometimes attractive, "small-town" banking option is credit unions. To join, you generally need to work for a particular employer (such as General Electric) or industry/occupation (for example, teachers). Thanks to a federal government exemption on income taxes, credit unions tend to be able to pay higher interest rates on deposits and charge lower rates on loans. Don't assume, however, that a local credit union always has the best deals; be sure to comparison shop. To locate credit unions near you, visit the Credit Union National Association website for consumers at www.asmarterchoice.org and click on the "Find a Credit Union" link or call them at 800-356-9655.

>> **Big banks:** Such banks tend to be regional, national, and sometimes even multinational. You may recognize their name from extensive advertising campaigns. They tend to have extensive ATM networks, which may reduce your ATM fees, but you pay for it in other ways, such as through less-competitive terms (interest rate paid, service fees levied) on checking and savings accounts.

Later in this chapter, in the "Banking Online" section, I identify some universal questions you can ask when searching for a bank, no matter which kind of bank you use.

INVESTIGATE

Be sure to comparison shop among several banks and scrutinize their fees and interest rates on their checking accounts and any other type of account you may be interested in. Also, read the "Understanding Your Bank Account Options" section later in this chapter, and read the rest of the chapter so you're aware of your nonbank and Internet banking options.

Online banks

Although traditional banks with walk-in branch locations are shrinking in number because of closures, consolidations, and some failures, online banking is growing — and for good reason. One of the biggest expenses of operating a traditional retail bank is the cost of the real estate and the related costs of the branch.

Online banks generally don't have any or many retail branches and conduct their business mostly over the Internet and through the mail. By lowering their costs of doing business, the best online banks may offer better account terms, such as paying you higher interest rates on your account balances. Online banks can also offer better terms on loans.

Online banking is convenient, too — you can conduct most transactions more quickly on the Internet, and by banking online, you save the bank money, which enables the bank to offer you better account terms. And because online banking is generally available 24/7, you don't need to rush out at lunchtime to make it to your bank during its limited open hours. (*Note:* Traditional brick-and-mortar banks now generally offer many online services.)

According to a recent customer ratings' summary done by *Consumer Reports,* the highest-rated online banks are (in order, starting with the highest rated): USAA, Schwab Bank, Ally, Discover Bank, EverBank, Synchrony Bank, State Farm Bank, Capital One 360, and E*Trade Bank.

Other choices

You can also place your money in a brokerage account or money market fund. If you want to consider other options that offer more attractive investment accounts and options, check out the later section "Considering Your Alternatives."

Understanding Your Bank Account Options

No matter what type of bank you choose, make sure you have a firm grasp of the different account options. Doing so requires thinking about your banking needs and what's important to you and what's not. The following sections identify how you can protect your moolah with different accounts and access your money when you need it.

Transaction accounts

Whether it's paying monthly bills or having something in your wallet to make purchases with at retail stores, everyone needs the ability to conduct transactions. Two of the most common types of transaction accounts are checking accounts and credit cards.

Checking accounts

The most fundamental of bank accounts, a *checking account* enables you to pay bills (by check or electronic payments) and deposit money from your job (including through direct deposit). Interest paid is generally low or nonexistent, and you need to watch out for various fees.

TIP

During periods of low interest rates, the fees levied on a transaction account, such as a checking account, should be of greater concern to you than the interest paid on account balances. After all, you shouldn't be keeping lots of extra cash in a checking account; you have better options for that. I discuss those options later in this chapter.

Debit cards are excellent transaction cards. They connect to your checking account, thus eliminating the need for you to carry around excess cash. They carry a Visa or Mastercard logo and are widely accepted by merchants for purchases and for obtaining cash from your checking account. Unlike a credit card, debit cards have no credit feature, so you can't spend money that you don't have.

Because of bank regulations, bank customers must give their permission/consent in advance for overdraft protection and the associated fee from a debit-card transaction. (Check and electronic bill payments go through as they always have and can lead to an account being overdrawn.)

WARNING

However, you can rack up overdraft fees if your bank processes debit-card transactions that lead to your account being overdrawn.

Credit cards

These transaction cards, which are offered by banks with either the Visa or Mastercard logo, enable you to make purchases and pay for them over time if you so choose. (Discover and American Express also offer their own credit cards.)

I'm not a fan of some people using credit cards because the credit feature enables you to spend money you don't have and carry a debt balance from month to month. Notwithstanding the lower short-term interest rates some cards charge to lure new customers, the reality is that borrowing on credit cards is expensive — usually to the tune of about 16 percent. The smart way to use such a card is to pay the bill in full each month and avoid these high interest charges.

Options for getting cash

You need a firm understanding of the different features of the transaction accounts your bank offers so you can easily access your cash. You may think choosing a bank that has a large ATM network is your best option, but think again.

REMEMBER

One reason that bank customers have gotten lousy terms on their accounts is that they gravitate toward larger banks and their extensive ATM networks so they can easily get cash when they need it. These ATM networks (and the often-associated bank branches) are costly for banks to maintain. So, you pay higher fees and get lower yields when you're the customer of a bank with a large ATM network — especially a bank that does tons of advertising.

Do you really need to carry a lot of cash and have access to a large ATM network? Probably not. A debit card is likely the better option for some people since these cards are so widely accepted by retailers and other product and service sellers.

Savings accounts

Savings accounts are accounts for holding spare cash in order to earn some interest. Banks and credit unions generally pay higher interest rates on savings account balances than they do on checking account balances. But savings account interest rates have often lagged behind the rates of the best money market funds offered by mutual fund companies and brokerage firms. Online banking is changing that dynamic, however, and now the best banks and credit unions offer competitive rates on savings accounts.

The virtue of most savings accounts is that you can earn some interest yet have penalty-free access to your money. The investment doesn't fluctuate in value the way a bond does, and you don't have early-withdrawal penalties as you do with a certificate of deposit (CD).

Banking Online

No matter whether you choose a brick-and-mortar bank or an online bank, technology has allowed people to do more and more of their banking on the Internet. With this benefit come some important points to remember to protect yourself and your dinero. In this section, I explain the best ways to evaluate an online bank and how to make the most of banking online.

Evaluating a bank: What to look for

When looking for a bank that fits your needs, put on your detective hat and get ready to search for the best deals. You don't want to pick a bank just because that's where your parents or a co-worker banks.

So what do you look for? You first want to look for a bank that participates in the U.S. government–operated Federal Deposit Insurance Corporation (FDIC) program. Otherwise, if the bank fails, your money isn't protected. The FDIC covers your deposits at each bank up to a cool quarter million dollars. If you're doing well, don't ever keep more than the insured amount in a bank account because if your bank fails (and some banks do fail), you could well lose some of the excess money you have on deposit at that bank.

Some online banks are able to offer higher interest rates because they're based overseas and, therefore, don't participate in the FDIC program. (Banks must pay insurance premiums into the FDIC fund, which, of course, adds to a bank's costs.) Another risk for you is noncovered banks that take excessive risks with their business to be able to pay depositors higher interest rates.

When considering doing business with an online bank or a smaller bank you haven't heard of, you should be especially careful to ensure that the bank is covered under the FDIC. And don't simply accept the bank's word for it or the bank's display of the FDIC logo in its offices or on its website.

Check the FDIC's website database of FDIC-insured institutions to see whether the bank you're considering doing business with is covered. Search by going to the FDIC's "BankFind" page (banks.data.fdic.gov/bankfind-suite/). You can search by the bank's name, city, state, or zip code. For insured banks, you can see the date it became insured, its insurance certificate number, the main office location for the bank (and branches), its primary government regulator, and other links to detailed information about the bank. In the event that your bank doesn't appear on the FDIC list yet the bank claims FDIC coverage, contact the FDIC at 877-275-3342.

In addition to ensuring that a bank is covered by the FDIC, also seek answers to these questions:

>> **What's the bank's reputation for its services?** This may not be easy to discern, but at a minimum, you should conduct an Internet search of the bank's name along with the word "complaints" or "problems" and examine the results.

>> **How accessible and knowledgeable are customer-service people at the bank?** You want to be able to talk to a live, helpful person when you need assistance. Look for a phone number on the bank's website and call it to see how difficult reaching a live person is. Ask the customer-service representatives questions to determine how knowledgeable and service-oriented they are.

>> **What are the process and options for withdrawing your money?** This issue is important to discuss with the bank's customer-service people because you want convenient, low-cost access to your money. For example, if a bank lacks ATMs, what does it charge you for using other ATMs?

>> **What are the fees for particular services?** You can probably find this information on the bank's website in a section called "accounts terms" or "disclosures." Also, look for the *Truth in Savings Disclosure,* which answers relevant account questions in a standardized format. Figure 11-1 shows an example of a bank's disclosure for its savings account.

TRUTH IN SAVINGS DISCLOSURE

Initial Deposit Requirement: There is no minimum deposit required to open the account.

Minimum Balance to Obtain Annual Percentage Yield (APY): There is no minimum balance required to obtain the disclosed APY.

Rate Information: The interest rate on your account is **1.09%** with an APY of **1.10%**. Your interest rate and APY may change. At our discretion we may change the interest rate for your account at any time.

Compounding and Crediting: Interest on your account is compounded and credited on a monthly basis.

Balance Computation Method: We use the daily balance method to calculate the interest on your account. This method applies a daily periodic rate to the principal in the account each day.

Accrual of Interest on Noncash Deposits: For all types of noncash deposits, interest begins to accrue not later than the second business day following the banking day on which the funds are deposited.

Fees: If we agree to process a wire transfer for you, the cost per transaction will be up to $40.00.

Transaction Limitations: You may transfer funds out of your savings account only to other accounts you have with us or to your linked account up to six times per monthly statement cycle using a combination of preauthorized, telephone, and automatic transfer services. If you exceed this limit on more than an occasional basis, we will close your account or transfer your funds to a transactional account. You are not limited in the number of transfers that you may make out of your account to repay loans at our bank. Wire transfers, if we agree to process them for you, are limited to $25,000 per day. We may also limit the number of wire transfers you can send each day.

Effect of Closing an Account: If you close your account before interest is credited, you will receive the accrued interest.

FIGURE 11-1:
Sample Truth in Savings Disclosure for a bank's savings account.

Protecting yourself online

The attractions of banking online are pretty obvious. For starters, banking on your computer whenever you want can be enormously convenient. You don't have to squeeze an in-person visit to a local bank branch into your otherwise busy work-day. And thanks to their lower overhead, the best online banks are generally able to offer competitive interest rates and account terms to their customers. Even if you go with a brick-and-mortar bank, you can usually also bank online.

You probably know from experience that conducting any type of transaction online is safe as long as you use some common sense and know who you're doing business with before you go forward. That said, others who've gone before you have gotten ripped off, so you do need to protect yourself.

Folks have been taken online to the tune of more than one billion dollars a year, according to the Internet Crime Complaint Center (ICCC), which is a joint govern-ment effort between the Federal Bureau of Investigation and the National White Collar Crime Center.

WARNING

ICCC and other online security experts recommend that you take the following steps to protect yourself and your identity when conducting business online:

>> Never access your bank accounts from a shared computer or on a shared network, such as the free access networks offered in hotel rooms and in other public or business facilities.

>> Make certain that your computer has antivirus and firewall software that's periodically updated to keep up with the latest threats.

>> Be aware of missed statements that could indicate your account has been taken over.

>> Report unauthorized transactions to your bank or credit-card company as soon as possible; otherwise, your bank may not stand behind the loss of funds.

>> Use a complicated and unique password (including both letters and numbers) for your online bank account.

>> Be careful about the sites you visit. Sites purporting to offer free-access music, games, and movies are often sources of viruses and trojans that fraudsters use to steal your account information.

>> Watch out for *phishers,* people posing to be your bank or bank's representa-tive. If "they" are contacting you, especially through email, it's likely to be fraud. Never follow a bank link directly from an email; always visit the bank website directly by typing in the URL.

>> Log out immediately after completing your transactions on financial websites.

Considering Your Alternatives

Other financial companies have cost advantages similar to — and in some cases even better than — those of banks, which translates into better deals for you. This section addresses two alternatives to bank accounts you may want to consider.

Brokerage accounts with check writing

Brokerage firms enable you to buy and sell stocks, bonds, and other securities. Charles Schwab, E*Trade, TD Ameritrade, and Fidelity are among the larger brokerage firms or investment companies with substantial brokerage operations you may have read or heard about. (See Chapter 12 for my specific recommendations of firms that I like.)

Some of these firms have fairly extensive branch office networks and others don't. But those that have a reasonable number of branch offices have been able to keep a competitive position because of their extensive customer and asset base and because they aren't burdened by banking regulations (because they aren't banks) and the costs associated with operating as a bank.

REMEMBER

A type of account worth checking out at brokerage firms is an *asset management account,* also referred to as a *cash management account.* Although the best deals on such accounts at some firms are only available to higher-balance investors, the best of these accounts typically enable you to

>> Hold and invest in various investments (stocks, bonds, mutual funds, and so on) in a single account.

>> Write checks and use online bill-payment services.

>> Use a Visa or Mastercard debit card for transactions and obtain cash from ATMs.

Money market funds

Basically, a *money market fund* is very similar to a bank savings account except that mutual fund companies offer them, which means they lack FDIC coverage. Historically, this hasn't been a problem, because retail money funds have lost shareholder principal only in one case (the Reserve Primary fund lost less than 1 percent of investors' money).

The attraction of money market funds is that the best ones pay higher yields than bank savings accounts and also come in tax-free versions, which is good for higher-tax-bracket investors. I explain money market funds in greater detail in Chapter 12.

» **Investing inside retirement accounts**

» **Paying for education costs**

Chapter **12**

Portfolios for a Purpose

n Chapter 10, I discuss the principles of intelligent investing. This chapter takes you a step further to help you match the best investments for your specific goals.

Before You Begin Investing

Before you jump into the investing waters, consider the following two often-overlooked ways to put your money to work and earn high returns without much risk:

» **Pay off high-interest debt.** If, for example, you have credit-card debt outstanding at 14 percent interest, paying off that loan is the same as putting your money to work in an investment with a sure 14 percent annual return. Remember that the interest on consumer debt isn't tax-deductible, so you would actually need to earn more than 14 percent investing your money elsewhere in order to net 14 percent after paying taxes.

» **Fund retirement accounts.** If you work for a company that offers a retirement savings plan such as a 401(k), consider contributing as much as you can manage. If you earn self-employment income, consider an SEP-IRA plan. (I discuss the tax benefits of funding retirement plans in Chapter 6.) Keep money for shorter-term goals, like buying a car or a home, in separate, much more liquid accounts.

Investing Nonretirement Account Money

When you invest money outside a retirement account, those investments are exposed to taxation. Therefore, you must understand the tax features of your situation and your investment choices.

TIP

To decide between comparable taxable and tax-free investments, you need to know your *marginal tax bracket* (the tax rate you pay on an extra dollar of taxable income) and each investment's interest rate or yield. (See Chapter 6 to understand your tax bracket.)

In the sections that follow, I give specific advice about investing your money while keeping an eye on taxes.

Emergency money

When you have a few thousand dollars or less, your simplest path is typically to keep this money in a local bank or credit union. Look first to the institution where you keep your checking account. Keeping this stash of money in your checking account, rather than in a separate savings account, makes financial sense if the extra money helps you avoid monthly service charges when your checking account balance would otherwise dip below the minimum. Compare the service charges on your checking account with the potential interest earnings from a savings account. And be sure to comparison shop checking accounts with a close eye on the fees you'll incur given your likely account balance and features of the account you will use.

Another option to consider is putting your money into a *money market fund*, a type of mutual fund, the best of which are usually superior to bank savings accounts because they pay higher yields than bank savings accounts and allow check-writing. And if you're in a high tax bracket, you can select a tax-free money market fund, which pays interest that's free from federal and/or state tax — something you can't get with a bank savings account.

REMEMBER

The yield on a money market fund is an important consideration. The operating expenses deducted before payment of dividends are generally the single biggest determinant of yield. All other things being equal, lower operating expenses translate into higher yields for you. With interest rates as low as they have been in recent years, seeking out money funds with the lowest operating expenses is essential.

Doing most or all of your fund shopping (money market and otherwise) at one good fund company can reduce the clutter in your investing life. Chasing after a slightly higher yield offered by another company is sometimes not worth the extra paperwork and administrative hassle. On the other hand, there's no reason why you can't invest in funds at multiple firms (as long as you don't mind the extra accounts), using each for its relative strengths. (You can buy funds from different fund companies in a single brokerage account — I explain how in the "Discount brokers" section later in this chapter.)

Most fund companies don't have many local branch offices, so you may have to open and maintain your money market mutual fund through the fund's website, toll-free phone line, or the mail.

Distance has its advantages. Because you can conduct business online, by phone, and through the mail, you don't need to go schlepping into a local branch office to make deposits and withdrawals. I'm happy to report that I haven't visited a bank office (or fund branch office) in many years.

Despite the distance between you and your fund company, your money is still accessible via check-writing, and you can also have money transferred electronically to your local bank on any business day. (Fund companies can also mail you a check for a desired amount to your home address on your account.)

Increasing numbers of investment companies are offering you the ability to deposit checks now through a smartphone app. Also, if you need to mail in some checks to deposit, don't fret about a deposit being lost in the mail; it rarely happens, and no one can legally cash a check made payable to you, anyway. Always endorse checks with the notation "for deposit only" under your signature.

Long-term money

If you plan to invest outside retirement accounts, asset allocation for these accounts should depend on how comfortable you are with risk and how much time you have until you plan to use the money. That's not because you won't be able to sell these investments on short notice if necessary. Investing money in a more volatile investment is simply riskier if you need to liquidate it in the short term.

For example, suppose you're saving money for a down payment to buy a house in one to two years. If you had put this money into the U.S. stock market near the beginning of one of the stock market's major downturns (such as what happened in 2000 and then again in 2007), you'd have been mighty unhappy. You would have seen a substantial portion of your money and home-buying dreams vanish in the following year or two. Or consider what happened in 2020 with the COVID-19 government-mandated economic shutdowns. Imagine investing your home down payment in the stock market through early 2020 and preparing to buy a home in 2020 only to see about one-third of your investment wiped out in a few weeks. For those who held on, stocks did come roaring back by year-end, but that timing might not have worked out for you depending upon what your plans had been. I've seen people panic in such situations and sell at what turns out to be the bottom or near bottom.

In the sections that follow, I walk you through common investments for longer-term purposes.

Defining your time horizons

I organize the different investment options in the remainder of this section by time frame and by your tax situation. Following are summaries of the different time frames associated with each type of fund:

>> **Short-term investments:** These investments are suitable for saving money for a home or some other major purchase within a few years. When investing for the short term, look for liquidity and short-term stability — features that rule out real estate and stocks. Recommended investments include shorter-term bond funds, which are higher-yielding alternatives to money market funds. If interest rates increase, these funds will likely drop in value, but relatively less than longer-term bond funds. I also discuss Treasury bonds and certificates of deposit (CDs) later in this section.

>> **Intermediate-term investments:** These investments are appropriate for more than a few years but less than, say, seven years. Investments that meet this requirement are intermediate-term bonds and well-diversified balanced funds (which include some stocks as well as bonds).

>> **Long-term investments:** If you have seven years or more for investing your money, you can consider a portfolio that's balanced between bonds and potentially higher-return (and therefore riskier) investments. Stocks, real estate, and other growth-oriented investments can earn the most money if you're comfortable with the risk involved.

Buying Treasuries direct

Like a few other countries, the U.S. Treasury offers inflation-indexed government bonds. Because a portion of these Treasury bonds' return is pegged to the rate of inflation, the bonds offer investors a safer type of Treasury bond investment option. This portion of your return is reflected as an inflation adjustment to the principal you invested. The other portion of your return is paid out in interest. Thus, an inflation-indexed Treasury bond investor would not see the purchasing power of his investment eroded by unexpected inflation.

Inflation-indexed Treasuries can be a good investment for conservative bond investors who are worried about inflation, as well as taxpayers who want to hold the government accountable for increases in inflation. The downside: Inflation-indexed bonds can yield slightly lower returns because they're less risky compared to regular Treasury bonds.

TIP

If you want a low-cost method of investing in Treasury bonds, you can purchase Treasuries directly from the Federal Reserve Bank. To open an account through the Treasury Direct program, visit their website at `www.treasurydirect.gov`.

You do sacrifice a bit of liquidity, however, when purchasing Treasury bonds directly from the government. In order to sell a bond bought through Treasury Direct, you have to have it transferred to a bank, broker, or dealer, which involves some time and hassle. And, you will surely incur a fee/commission to sell the bond through the bank, broker, or dealer. If you want daily access to your money, buy a recommended Vanguard Treasury fund and pay the company's low management fee.

Purchasing certificates of deposit (CDs)

Bank CDs are popular with generally older, safety-minded investors with some extra cash that they don't need in the near future (typically a year or two). With a CD, you get a higher rate of return than you get on a bank savings account. And unlike with bond and stock funds, your principal doesn't fluctuate in value.

Compared to bonds, however, CDs have a couple of drawbacks:

>> **Inaccessibility:** In a CD, your money isn't accessible unless you pay a penalty — typically six months' interest. With a no-load (commission-free) bond fund, you can access your money without penalty whenever you need it.

>> **Taxability:** Interest from CDs is taxable. Bonds, on the other hand, come in tax-free (federal and/or state) and taxable flavors. So bonds offer higher-tax-bracket investors a tax-friendly option that CDs can't match.

TIP

In the long run, you should earn more and have better access to your money in bond funds than in CDs. Bond funds make particular sense when you're in a higher tax bracket and you'd benefit from tax-free income on your investments (by investing in municipal bond funds). If you're not in a high tax bracket and you have a bad day whenever your bond fund takes a dip in value, consider CDs. Just make sure you shop around to get the best interest rate.

Investing in stocks and stock funds

Stocks have stood the test of time for building wealth. (In Chapter 10, I discuss picking individual stocks versus investing through stock mutual funds.) Remember that when you invest in stocks in taxable (nonretirement) accounts, all the distributions on those stocks, such as dividends and capital gains, are taxable. Stock dividends and long-term capital gains do benefit from lower tax rates (current maximum of 23.8 percent).

Some stock-picking advocates argue that you should shun stock funds because of tax considerations. I disagree. You can avoid stock funds that generate a lot of short-term capital gains, which are taxed at the relatively high ordinary income tax rates. *Index funds*, which invest in a fixed mix of stocks to track a particular market index, are tax-efficient. Additionally, some fund companies offer tax-friendly stock funds, which are appropriate if you don't want current income or you're in a high federal tax bracket and seek to minimize receiving taxable distributions on your funds.

TIP

Vanguard (800-662-7447; www.vanguard.com) offers the best menu of tax-managed stock funds.

Investing Retirement Account Money

If you're in your young-adult years, the good news is that you likely have decades to grow your nest egg before you will want or need to tap that money. The more years you have before you're going to retire, the greater your ability to take risk. As long as the value of your investments has time to recover, what's the big deal if some of your investments drop a bit over a year or two? Of course, you should be concerned with growing your portfolio enough to keep you ahead of the inevitable inflation that occurs over the years.

TIP

Think of your retirement accounts as part of your overall plan to achieve financial independence. Then allocate different types of investments between your tax-advantaged retirement accounts and other taxable investment accounts to get the maximum benefit of tax deferral. This section helps you determine how to distribute your money in retirement plans.

Establishing and prioritizing retirement contributions

When you have access to various retirement accounts, prioritize which account you're going to use first by determining how much each gives you in return. You should generally focus your contributions in this order:

1. **First fund employer-based plans that match your contributions.**

2. **Next, contribute to any other employer or self-employed plans that allow tax-deductible contributions.**

3. **After you contribute as much as possible to these tax-deductible plans (or if you don't have access to such plans), consider an IRA.**

4. **If you max out on contributions to an IRA, consider a Roth 401(k) (employer-offered, after-tax contributions).**

TIP

I would make an exception to these guidelines for folks who believe they are temporarily in a relatively low tax bracket. This can happen, for example, if your employment income is expected to increase significantly once you complete certain training. In such a case, after funding employer plans that match your contributions, you could consider plans like a Roth 401(k) and/or Roth IRA, which don't provide upfront tax breaks but do provide ongoing tax breaks as your investment earnings compound and tax-free withdrawals of your investment returns in the future.

Investments and account types are different issues. People sometimes get confused when discussing the investments they make in retirement accounts — especially people who have a retirement account, such as an IRA, at a bank. They don't realize that you can have your IRA at a variety of financial institutions (for example, a mutual fund company or brokerage firm). At each financial institution, you can choose among the firm's investment options for investing your IRA money.

TIP

No-load, or commission-free, mutual fund and discount brokerage firms are your best bets for establishing a retirement account (see Chapter 10 for more information on these accounts).

Allocating money in employer plans

In some company-sponsored plans, such as 401(k)s, you're limited to a short list of investment choices. I discuss typical investment options for 401(k) plans in order of increasing risk and, hence, likely return:

>> **Money market:** Folks who are skittish about the stock and bond markets are attracted to money market and savings accounts because they haven't dropped in value. In the long run, you won't be doing yourself any favors. Trying to time your investments to attempt to catch the lows and avoid the peaks isn't possible (see Chapter 10).

>> **Bond mutual funds:** Bond funds invest in a mixture of typically high-quality bonds. Bonds pay a higher yield than money funds. Depending on whether your plan's option is a short-term, intermediate-term, or long-term fund (maybe you have more than one type), the bond fund's current yield is probably a percent or two higher than the money market fund's yield. Bond funds carry higher yields than money market funds, but they also carry greater risk because their value can fall if interest rates increase. However, bonds tend to be more stable in value over the shorter term (such as a few years) than stocks. Aggressive, younger investors should keep a minimum amount of money in bond funds (see the asset allocation discussion in Chapter 10).

>> **Guaranteed-investment contracts (GICs), also known as stable value funds:** Guaranteed-investment contracts are backed by an insurance company, and they typically quote you an interest rate a year in advance. The attraction of these investments is that your account value doesn't fluctuate (at least, not that you can see). In GICs, you pay for the peace of mind of a guaranteed return with lower than bond fund long-term returns. And GICs have another minor drawback: Insurance companies, unlike mutual funds, can and do fail, putting GIC investment dollars at risk. Some retirement plans have been burned by insurer failures.

>> **Balanced mutual funds:** Balanced funds invest primarily in a mixture of stocks and bonds. This one-stop-shopping concept offers broad diversification, makes investing easier, and smooths out fluctuations in the value of your investments. Funds investing exclusively in stocks or in bonds make for a rougher ride.

>> **Stock funds:** Stock funds invest in stocks, which often provide greater long-term growth potential but also wider fluctuations in value from year to year. Some companies offer a number of different stock funds, including funds that invest overseas. Unless you plan to borrow against your funds to purchase a home (if your plan allows), you should have plenty of stock funds.

>> **Stock in your employer:** Some companies offer employees the option of investing in the company's stock. I generally suggest avoiding this option because your future income and other employee benefits are already riding on the company's success. If the company hits the skids, you may lose your job and your benefits. You certainly don't want the value of your retirement account to depend on the same factors. If you think strongly that your company has its act together and the stock is a good buy, investing a portion of your retirement account is fine — but no more than 25 percent.

Some employers offer employees an option to buy company stock outside a tax-deferred retirement plan at a discount, sometimes as much as 15 percent, to its current market value. If your company offers a notable discount on its stock, consider taking advantage of it. When you sell the stock, you're usually able to lock in a profit over your purchase price.

Table 12-1 shows a couple of examples of how people in different employer plans may choose to allocate their 401(k) investments among the plan's investment options. See Chapter 10 for more background on asset allocation decisions.

TABLE 12-1   ## Allocating 401(k) Investments

Type of Fund	25-Year-Old Aggressive-Risk Investor	30-Year-Old Moderate-Risk Investor
Bond fund	0%	20%
Balanced fund (50% stock/50% bond)	10%	0%
Larger company stock fund(s)	30–40%	30%
Smaller company stock fund(s)	25%	20%
International stock fund(s)	25–35%	30%

Designating money in plans you design

With self-employed plans (for example, SEP-IRAs), certain 403(b) plans for non-profit employees, and IRAs, you may select the investment options as well as the allocation of money among them. In the sections that follow, I give some specific mixes that you may find useful for investing at some of the premier investment companies.

TIP

To establish your retirement account at one of these firms, call the company's toll-free number and ask the representative to send you an account application for the type of account (for example, SEP-IRA, 403(b), and so on) you want to set up. Most investment firms provide downloadable account applications, and they may allow you to complete the application online.

Vanguard: No-load leader

Vanguard (800-662-7447; www.vanguard.com) is a mutual fund and exchange-traded fund powerhouse and also operates a discount brokerage division. It's the largest no-load fund company and consistently has the lowest overall operating expenses in the business. Historically, Vanguard's funds have excellent performance when compared to those of its peers, especially among conservatively managed bond and stock funds.

For an aggressive portfolio (80 percent stocks, 20 percent bonds), try this:

» Vanguard Star (fund of funds) — 50 percent

» Vanguard Total Stock Market Index — 30 percent

» Vanguard Total International Stock Index — 20 percent

Or you can place 100 percent in Vanguard LifeStrategy Growth, which is a fund of four different Vanguard funds and thus highly diversified.

Fidelity: Investment behemoth

Fidelity Investments (800-544-8888; www.fidelity.com) is the largest provider of mutual funds in terms of total assets, and it operates a discount brokerage division. However, some Fidelity funds assess sales charges (no such funds are recommended in the sections that follow).

For an aggressive portfolio (80 percent stocks, 20 percent bonds), try this:

» Fidelity Puritan (balanced fund) — 35 percent

» Dodge & Cox Stock — 25 percent

» Fidelity Low-Priced Stock — 20 percent

» Vanguard International Growth — 20 percent

Discount brokers

A *discount brokerage account* can allow you centralized, one-stop shopping and the ability to hold mutual funds from a variety of leading fund companies. Some mutual funds and exchange-traded funds are available without transaction fees, although you pay a small transaction fee to buy most of the better funds. The reason: The discounter is a middleman between you and the fund companies.

TIP

You have to weigh the convenience of being able to buy and hold funds from multiple fund companies in a single account versus the sometimes lower cost of buying funds directly from their providers. A small transaction fee can gobble a sizable chunk of what you have to invest, especially if you're investing smaller amounts.

Among brokerage firms or brokerage divisions of mutual fund companies, for breadth of fund offerings and competitive pricing, I like E*Trade (800-387-2331; us.etrade.com), T. Rowe Price (800-225-5132; www.troweprice.com), and Vanguard (800-992-8327; www.vanguard.com).

For an aggressive portfolio (80 percent stocks, 20 percent bonds), try this:

» Dodge & Cox Income and/or Vanguard Total Bond Market Index — 20 percent

» Vanguard Total Stock Market Index and/or Dodge & Cox Stock — 50 percent

» Vanguard International Growth and/or Vanguard Total International Stock — 30 percent

Investing for Education

Whether you're about to begin a regular college investment plan or you've already started saving, your emotions may lead you astray. The hype about educational costs may scare you into taking a financially detrimental path. Quality education for your children (or continued education for yourself) doesn't have to, and probably won't, cost you as much as gargantuan projections suggest. In this section, I explain the inner workings of the financial aid system, help you gauge how much money you'll need, and discuss educational investment options.

Understanding the importance of applying for financial aid

Just as your child shouldn't choose a college based solely on whether he thinks he can get in, he shouldn't choose a college on the basis of whether you think you can afford its full sticker price. Except for the affluent, who can pay for the full cost of college, everyone else should apply for financial aid. Some parents who don't think they qualify for financial aid are pleasantly surprised to find that their children have access to loans as well as grants (which don't have to be repaid).

REMEMBER

Completing the Free Application for Federal Student Aid (FAFSA) is the first step in the financial aid process. (See the form online at www.fafsa.ed.gov.) Some private colleges also require completing the Financial Aid Form (FAF), which asks for more information than the FAFSA. Some schools also supplement the FAFSA with PROFILE forms; these forms are mainly used by costly private schools to differentiate need among financial aid applicants. States have their own financial aid programs, so apply to these programs as well if your child plans to attend an in-state college.

FINANCIAL AID REALLY ISN'T AID AT ALL BUT A PRICING SYSTEM

Now, I must point out that "financial aid" isn't really aid at all. What typically happens at most colleges and universities is that some of the families are expected to pay the full charges, many are expected to pay a good portion of the full price, and some don't pay anything at all. So, even though a given private school may charge, say, $70,000 per year, their average "customer" may actually pay something closer to $35,000 per year.

Which, logically, raises the question as to why the college doesn't simply charge everyone $35,000 per year and do away with the cumbersome, invasive, and often unfair financial aid process. Under the current system, the customers of college are first asked to provide personal financial information so the schools can assess how much they can afford to pay. That way the schools can collect more from those who have more, and that money effectively helps pay the way for those who are deemed able to pay less than average.

Is this a fair system? Some people don't think so. Is there a better way to do this? Perhaps. For now, this is the system that traditional colleges and universities generally use.

The data you supply through student aid forms is run through a financial needs analysis, a standard methodology approved by the U.S. Congress. The analysis calculates how much money you, as the parent(s), and your child, as the student, are expected to contribute toward educational expenses. Even if the needs analysis determines that you don't qualify for needs-based financial aid, you may still have access to loans that are not based on need. So be sure you apply for financial aid.

Using your retirement accounts

Under the current financial needs analysis, the value of your retirement plans isn't considered an asset. By contrast, money that you save outside retirement accounts, especially money in the child's name, is counted as an asset and reduces your eligibility for financial aid.

TIP

Fund your retirement accounts, such as 401(k)s and SEP-IRAs, before saving for your child's education. In addition to getting an immediate tax deduction on your contributions, your earnings grow without taxation while you're maximizing your child's chances of qualifying for aid. Forgoing contributions to your retirement savings plans to save in a taxable account for your kid's college fund is foolish because you'll be expected to contribute more to your child's educational costs.

Putting money in kids' names

Save money in your name rather than in your children's names if you plan to apply for financial aid. Colleges expect a much greater percentage of the money in your children's names to be used for college costs than the money in your name.

However, if you're affluent enough to foot your child's college bill without outside help, investing in your kid's name can save you money in taxes. Prior to your child's reaching age 18, the first $1,100 (for 2021) of interest and dividend income is tax-free; the next $1,100 is taxed at the child's tax rate. Any income above $2,200 is taxed at the parents' marginal tax rate.

Upon reaching age 19 (or age 24 if your offspring are still full-time students), income generated by investments in your child's name is taxed at your child's presumably lower tax rate. Parents control a custodial account until the child reaches either the age of 18 or 21, depending on the state in which you reside.

Using 529 college savings plans

Section 529 plans are named after Internal Revenue Code Section 529 and are also known as qualified state tuition plans. A parent or grandparent can generally put more than $200,000 per beneficiary into one of these plans.

The attraction of the Section 529 plans is that money inside the plans compounds without tax, and if it's used to pay for college tuition, room and board, and other related higher-education expenses, including graduate school expenses, the investment earnings and appreciation can be withdrawn tax-free. Parents can also use up to $10,000 per year per child toward K–12 educational expenses. Some states provide additional tax benefits on contributions to their state-sanctioned plan.

You can generally invest in any state plan to pay college expenses in any state, regardless of where you live.

WARNING

A big potential drawback of the Section 529 plans — especially for families hoping for some financial aid — is that college financial aid offices treat assets in these plans as parental nonretirement assets. Even worse, the assets can be considered as belonging to an older child when an independent young adult no longer reports parental financial information for financial aid purposes.

Please also be aware that a future Congress could change the tax laws affecting these plans, diminishing the tax breaks or increasing the penalties for nonquali-fied withdrawals.

INVESTIGATE

Section 529 plans make sense for affluent parents (or grandparents) to establish for children who don't expect to qualify for financial aid. Do your research and homework before investing in any plan. Check out the investment track record and fees in each plan, as well as restrictions on transferring to other plans or changing beneficiaries.

Weighing home equity

Your family's assets may also include equity in real estate and businesses that you own. Although the federal financial aid analysis no longer counts equity in your primary residence as an asset, many private (independent) schools continue to ask parents for this information when making their own financial aid determinations. Therefore, paying down your home mortgage more quickly instead of funding retirement accounts can harm you financially: You may end up with less financial aid and a higher tax bill.

Paying for educational costs

Although you may not have children yet or your children may be young, you've probably started thinking about how you're going to pay for their college expenses. College can cost a lot. The total costs, including tuition, fees, books, supplies, room, board, and transportation, vary substantially from school to school. The total average annual cost is running around $55,000 per year at private colleges and around $27,000 (in-state rate) at public colleges. Figuring out how you're going to pay these expenses can be overwhelming.

TIP

You should generally put as much money as possible in your retirement accounts. If you have money left over after taking advantage of retirement accounts, try to save for your children's college costs. Save in your name unless you know you aren't going to apply for financial aid, including those loans that are available regardless of your economic situation.

Be realistic about what you can afford for college expenses given your other financial goals. Being able to personally pay 100 percent of the cost of a college education, especially at a four-year private college, is a luxury of the affluent. If you're not a high-income earner, consider trying to save enough to pay a third or, at most, half of the cost. You can make up the balance through a wide variety of means, such as the following:

>> **Loans:** A host of financial aid programs, including a number of loan programs, allow you to borrow at reasonable interest rates. Federal government educational loans have variable interest rates, which means that the interest rate you're charged floats, or varies, with the overall level of interest rates. The rates

are also capped so the rate can never exceed several percent more than the initial rate on the loan.

TIP

A number of loan programs, such as unsubsidized Stafford Loans and Parent Loans for Undergraduate Students (PLUS), are available even when your family is not deemed financially needy. Only subsidized Stafford Loans, on which the federal government pays the interest that accumulates while the student is still in school, are limited to students deemed financially needy. For more information about these loan programs, call the Federal Student Aid Information Center at 800-433-3243 or visit its website at www.studentaid.ed.gov.

>> **Grants:** In addition to loans, a number of grant programs are available through schools, the government, and independent sources. You can apply for federal government grants via the FAFSA. Grants available through state government programs may require a separate application. Specific colleges and other private organizations (for example, employers, banks, credit unions, and community groups) also offer grants and scholarships.

>> **Your home's equity:** If you're a homeowner, you may be able to borrow against the equity (market value less the outstanding mortgage loan) in your property. This option is useful because you can borrow against your home at a reasonable interest rate, and the interest is generally tax-deductible. Some company retirement plans, such as 401(k)s, allow borrowing as well.

>> **IRAs:** Parents may make penalty-free withdrawals from individual retirement accounts if the funds are used for college expenses. Although you won't be charged an early-withdrawal penalty, the IRS (and most states) will treat the amount withdrawn as taxable income. On top of that, the financial aid office will look at your beefed-up income and assume that you don't need as much financial aid. (You can make qualified withdrawals from Roth IRAs and not be taxed.)

>> **Your child's employment:** Your child can work during the summer and save that money for educational expenses. On campus work-study jobs are another possibility. Besides giving your child a stake in his own future, this training encourages sound personal financial management.

Chapter **13**

Real-Estate Investing

I f you've already bought your own home (and even if you haven't), using real estate as an investment may interest you. Over the decades and generations, real-estate investing, like the stock market and small-business investments, has generated notable wealth for participants. (See Chapter 10 for more on the rate of return from various investments.)

REMEMBER

Real estate is like other types of ownership investments, such as stocks, where you have an ownership stake in an asset. Although you have the potential for significant profits, don't forget that you also accept greater risk. Real estate isn't a gravy train or a simple way to get wealthy. Like stocks, real estate goes through good and bad performance periods. Most people who make money investing in real estate do so because they invest and hold property over many years. The vast majority of people who don't make money in real estate don't because they make easily avoidable mistakes. In this chapter, I discuss how to make successful real-estate investments and minimize your chances for poorly performing investments.

Understanding Real-Estate Investment Pros and Cons

Many people build their wealth by investing in real estate. Real estate, like all investments, has its pros and cons.

Some people focus exclusively on property investments, but many others build their wealth through the companies they started or through other avenues and then diversify into real-estate investments. What do these wealthy folks know, and why do they choose to invest in real estate? Here are real estate's main attractions:

>> **Limited land:** The supply of buildable, desirable land is generally limited. And because the population in desired areas grows over the years, demand for land and housing continues to grow. Land and what you can do with it are what make real estate valuable.

>> **Leverage:** Real estate is different from most other investments because you can borrow 75 to 80 percent (or more) of the value of the property to buy it. Thus, you can use your down payment of 20 to 25 percent of the purchase price to buy, own, and control a much larger investment; this concept is called *leverage.* For example, suppose you purchase a rental property for $200,000 and make a $40,000 down payment (and borrow the other $160,000). Over the next five years, the property appreciates to $260,000. Thus, your $40,000 investment has appreciated $60,000. Thus, you've made a 150 percent return on your investment.

>> **Ongoing income:** In addition to appreciation potential, you also hope and expect to make money from renting the investment property to make a profit based on the property's rental income in excess of its expenses (mortgage, property taxes, insurance, maintenance, and so on). Unless you make a large down payment, your monthly operating profit is usually small (or nonexistent) in the early years of rental property ownership. Over time, your operating profit, which is subject to ordinary income tax, should rise as you increase your rental prices faster than your expenses. During soft periods in the local economy, however, rents may rise more slowly than your expenses (or rents may even fall over a short period of time).

>> **Tax-deferred growth:** With investment property, the appreciation of your properties compounds without tax during your years of ownership. You don't pay tax on this profit until you sell your property, and even then you can roll over your gain into another investment property to avoid paying tax. (If you choose to simply take your profits and not roll them over, the federal tax rate on gains from property held more than one year — known as *long-term capital gains* — is no more than 23.8 percent.) When you sell a stock or fund investment that you hold outside a retirement account, you must pay tax on your profits. By contrast, if you roll over your real-estate gain into another like-kind investment real-estate property, you can avoid paying tax on your rental property profit when you sell. The rules for properly making one of these (IRS code section) *1031 exchanges* (also known as *Starker exchanges*) are complex. Make sure you find an attorney or tax advisor who's an expert at these transactions to ensure that everything goes smoothly (and legally).

>> **Ability to add value:** You, as a small investor, can't add value to stocks by "fixing them up," but you may have some good ideas about how to improve a property and make it more valuable. Perhaps you can fix up a property or develop it further and raise the rental income and resale value accordingly. Through hard work, ingenuity, persistence, and good negotiating skills, you may also be able to make money by purchasing a property below its fair market value. Relative to investing in the stock market, tenacious and savvy real-estate investors can more easily buy property below its fair market value. You can do the same in the stock market, but the legions of professional, full-time money managers who analyze stocks make finding bargains more difficult.

>> **Longer-term focus:** One problem with investing in the securities markets, such as the stock market, is that prices are constantly changing. Cable TV channels, websites, smartphones, and other communication devices constantly report the latest prices. From my observations and work with individual investors, I've seen that the constant reports cause some investors to lose sight of the long term and the big picture. Because all you need to do is tap your smartphone app, click your computer mouse, or dial a toll-free phone number to place your sell or buy order, some stock market investors fall prey to snap judgments. While the real-estate market is constantly changing, short-term, day-to-day, and week-to-week changes are invisible. Publications don't report the value of your real-estate holdings daily, weekly, or even monthly, which is good for encouraging a longer-term focus. (Exception: Some real-estate price-tracking websites purport to have monthly and even weekly price updates on your property.) If prices do decline over months and years, you're much less likely to sell in a panic with real estate. Preparing a property for sale and eventually getting it sold take a good deal of time, and this barrier to quickly selling helps keep your vision in focus.

WARNING

Real-estate investing isn't for everyone. Most people do better financially when they invest their ownership holdings in a diversified portfolio of stocks, such as through stock funds. Definitely shy away from real-estate investments that involve managing property if you fall into either of the following categories:

>> **You're time-starved and anxious.** Buying and owning investment property and being a landlord take a lot of time. If you fail to do your homework before purchasing real estate, you can end up overpaying or buying a heap of trouble. You can hire a property manager to help with screening and finding good tenants and troubleshooting problems with the building you purchase, but this step costs money and still requires some time involvement. Also, remember that most tenants don't care for a property the same way property owners do. If every little scratch or carpet stain sends your blood pressure skyward, avoid distressing yourself as a landlord.

>> **You're not interested in real estate.** Some people simply don't feel comfortable and informed when it comes to investing in real estate. If you've had experience and success with other investments, such as stocks, it's fine to stick with them. Over long periods of time, both stocks and real estate provide comparable returns.

Investing in real estate is time-intensive, and it carries risks. Invest in real estate because you enjoy the challenge and because you want to diversify your portfolio. Real estate's value doesn't move in lockstep with other investments, such as stocks or small-business investments that you hold, so it's a useful diversification tool.

Evaluating Simpler Real-Estate Investments

Investing in rental real estate that you're responsible for can be a lot of work. Think about it this way: With rental properties, you have all the headaches of maintaining a property, including finding and dealing with tenants, without the benefits of living in and enjoying the property.

Unless you're extraordinarily interested in and motivated to own investment real estate, begin with these simpler yet still profitable methods:

>> **Investing at home.** For the long term, because you need a place to live, why not own real estate instead of renting it? Real estate is the only investment that you can live in or rent to produce income — you can't live in a stock, bond, or mutual fund! Unless you expect to move within the next few years or live in an area where owning costs much more than renting, buying a place probably makes good long-term financial sense. In the long term, owning usually costs less than renting, and it allows you to build equity in an asset. See Chapter 7 to find out more about profiting from homeownership.

>> **Convert your home into a rental when you move.** If you plan to move and want to keep your current home as a long-term investment property, you can. Be aware of the potential tax downsides of doing so. You owe tax on the profit if your property is a rental when you sell it and you don't buy another rental property. You can purchase another rental property through a 1031 exchange to defer paying taxes on your profit.

>> **Evaluate real-estate investment trusts.** *Real-estate investment trusts* (REITs) are entities that generally invest in different types of property, such as shopping centers, apartments, and other rental buildings. For a fee, REIT

managers identify and negotiate the purchase of properties that they believe are good investments, and then they manage these properties, including all tenant relations. Thus, REITs are a good way to invest in real estate if you don't want the hassles and headaches that come with directly owning and managing rental property.

You can research and purchase shares in individual REITs, which trade as securities on the major stock exchanges. An even better approach is to buy a mutual fund or exchange-traded fund that invests in a diversified mixture of REITs (Vanguard has a good, low-cost one). In addition to providing you with a diversified, low-hassle real-estate investment, REITs offer an additional advantage that traditional rental real estate doesn't: You can easily invest in REITs through a retirement account (for example, an IRA).

Assessing Residential Housing Investments

TIP

A solid bet for real-estate investing is to purchase residential property. People always need places to live. Residential housing is easier to understand, purchase, and manage than most other types of property, such as office and retail property. If you're a homeowner, you already have experience locating, purchasing, and maintaining residential property.

The most common residential housing options are single-family homes, condominiums, and townhouses. You can also purchase multi-unit buildings. In addition to the considerations that I address in Chapter 7, from an investment and rental perspective, consider the following issues when you decide what type of property to buy:

>> **Tenants:** Single-family homes with just one tenant (which could be a family, a couple, or a single person) are simpler to deal with than a multi-unit apartment building that requires the management of multiple renters and maintenance of multiple units.

>> **Maintenance:** From the property owner's perspective, condominiums are generally the lowest-maintenance properties because most condo associations deal with issues such as roofing, gardening, and so on for the entire building. Note that as the owner, you're still responsible for maintenance that's needed inside your unit, such as servicing appliances, interior painting, and so on. Beware, though, that some condo complexes don't allow rentals. With a single-family home or apartment building, you're responsible for all the

maintenance. Of course, you can hire someone to do the work, but you still have to find the contractors and coordinate, oversee, and pay for the work they do.

>> **Appreciation potential:** Look for property where simple cosmetic and other fixes may allow you to increase rents and increase the market value of the property. Although condos may be easier on the unit owner to maintain, they tend to appreciate less than homes or apartment buildings, unless the condos are located in a desirable urban area.

>> **Cash flow:** The difference between the rental income you collect and the expenses you pay out is known as your *cash flow*. With all properties, as time goes on, generating a positive cash flow generally gets easier as you pay down your mortgage debt and (hopefully) increase your rents. Unless you can afford a large down payment of 25 percent or more (to help pay down your debt), the early years of rental-property ownership may financially challenge you. Making a profit in the early years from the monthly cash flow of a single-family home may be hard because some properties sell at a premium price relative to the rent that they can command. Remember, you pay extra for the land, which you generally can't rent. Also, the downside to having just one tenant is that when you have a vacancy, you have no rental income. Apartment buildings, particularly those with more units, can generally produce a small positive cash flow, even in the early years of rental ownership.

REMEMBER

Unless you really want to minimize maintenance responsibilities, avoid condominium investments. Similarly, apartment-building investments are best left to sophisticated investors who like a challenge and can manage more-complex properties. Single-family home investments (and smaller multi-unit properties) are generally more straightforward for most people. Run the numbers on your rental income and expenses to see whether you can afford the negative cash flow that often occurs in the early years of ownership (I show you how in the "Estimating cash flow" section later in this chapter). And do thorough inspections before you buy any property that will be used as a rental.

Investing in Commercial Real Estate

Ever thought about owning and renting out a small office building or strip mall? If you're really motivated and willing to roll up your sleeves, you may want to consider commercial real-estate investments. However, you're generally better off not investing in such real estate because it's much more complicated than investing in residential real estate. It's also riskier from an investment and tenant-turnover perspective. When tenants move out, new tenants sometimes require extensive and costly improvements.

If you're a knowledgeable real-estate investor and you like a challenge, here are two good times to invest in commercial real estate:

>> When your analysis of the local market suggests that it's a good time to buy (I explain how in a moment in this section and the section, "Researching Where and What to Buy," later in this chapter)

>> When you can use some of the space to run your own small business

Just as owning your home is generally more cost-effective than renting over the years, so it is with commercial real estate if — and this is a big *if* — you buy at a reasonably good time and hold the property for many years.

INVESTIGATE

So how do you evaluate the state of your local commercial real-estate market? Examine the supply-and-demand statistics over recent years. Determine how much space is available for rent and how that number has changed over time. Also investigate the vacancy rate and find out how it has changed in recent years. Finally, research the rental rates, usually quoted as a price per square foot. See the section "Researching Where and What to Buy" later in this chapter to find out how to gather this kind of information.

TIP

Here's one sign that purchasing a commercial property in a particular area is not wise: The supply of available space in the market has increased faster than demand, leading to falling rental rates and higher vacancies. A slowing local economy and an increasing unemployment rate also spell trouble for commercial real-estate prices. Each market is different, so make sure you check out the details of your area.

Shunning Sure-to-Lose Real-Estate Investments

While I discuss time-tested real-estate investments, I would be remiss if I also didn't highlight real-estate investments you should avoid due to their terrible track records. Here are the details of real-estate investments that you should generally avoid:

>> **Time shares:** Time shares are near-certain money losers. With a *time share*, you buy a week or two of ownership or usage of a particular unit, usually a condominium, in a resort location. If you pay, for example, $10,000 for a week of "ownership," you would pay the equivalent of about $520,000 a year for the whole unit. However, a comparable unit nearby may sell for only $175,000.

The extra markup pays the salespeople's commissions, administrative expenses, and profits for the time-share development company. (This little analysis also ignores the not-so-inconsequential ongoing time-share maintenance fees.) Vacationers are easy prey for salespeople who, often using high-pressure sales tactics and the lure of a free stay in a unit for a night or two, want to sell them a souvenir of the trip. Why commit yourself to taking a vacation to the same places at the same time each year? Many time shares let you trade your weeks; however, doing so is a hassle, and you're limited by what time slots you can trade for, which are typically dates that other people don't want.

>> **Second (vacation) homes:** Some folks dream of having a weekend cottage or condo — a place they can retreat to when crowded urban or boring suburban living conditions get on their nerves. Most second-home owners I know rent out their property very little — 10 percent or less of the time. As a result, second homes are usually money drains. I've seen more than a few cases in which the second home is such a cash drain that it prevents its owners from contributing to and taking advantage of tax-deductible retirement savings plans. If you don't rent out a second home most of the time, ask yourself whether you can afford such a luxury. Can you accomplish your other financial goals (for example, saving for retirement, paying for the home in which you live) with this added expense? Keeping a second home is more of a consumption than an investment decision.

>> **Limited partnerships:** High sales commissions and ongoing management fees burden limited partnerships (LPs) sold through stockbrokers and financial planners who work on commission. Quality real-estate investment trusts (REITs), which I discuss earlier in this chapter, are far better investments. REITs, unlike LPs, are also highly liquid.

>> **High-priced real-estate seminars:** Beware the pitches and promises of hucksters selling grossly overpriced seminars and the like that purport to teach you the simple secrets to getting rich. I've seen the pitches too many times (often with real estate and stock investing) and warned about them often over the decades. Cable television infomercials and websites bring investors a never-ending stream of real-estate hucksters. The faces and names change over the years, but the pitch is the same. If you're a cable television viewer, you've likely seen some of the chirpy and lengthy real-estate infomercials on cable television channels. Quite often, you will find pitched books, audio tapes, and DVDs that are filled with excessive motivational nonsense wherein the guru preaches about the importance of having the right mindset and attitude to succeed as a real-estate investor. He provides little in the way of details and how-to information. It turns out that there's a good reason for this lack of information. After customers buy a book or DVD set directly from his company, his salespeople use high-pressure tactics to sell personal real-estate coaching services for thousands of dollars.

If a real-estate investment "opportunity" sounds too good to be true, it is. If you want to invest in real estate, avoid the hucksters and scams and instead invest directly in properties that you can control or invest through reputable REITs (or REIT mutual funds), which I discuss earlier in this chapter.

Researching Where and What to Buy

If you're going to invest in real estate, spend some time and energy to do some research regarding where and what to buy. I'm not suggesting that you need to conduct a nationwide search for the best areas. In fact, investing in real estate closer to home is typically best because you're probably more familiar with the area, allowing you to have an easier time researching and managing the properties. This section discusses the important research to do.

Considering economic issues

People need places to live, but an area doesn't generally attract homebuyers if jobs don't exist there. Ideally, look to invest in real estate in communities that maintain diverse job bases. If the local economy relies heavily on jobs in a small number of industries, that dependence increases the potential risk of your real-estate investments. If one of those industries falls on hard times, people may move away, leaving a glut of housing behind. That doesn't bode well for a rental property in that area. The U.S. Bureau of Labor Statistics compiles this type of data for metropolitan areas and counties. Visit www.bls.gov for more information.

Also, consider an area's likelihood of appreciation or depreciation. Determine which industries are more heavily represented in the local economy. If most of the jobs come from slow-growing or shrinking employment sectors, real-estate prices are unlikely to rise quickly in the years ahead. On the other hand, areas with a greater preponderance of high-growth industries stand a greater chance of faster price appreciation.

Finally, check out the unemployment situation and examine how the jobless rate has changed in recent years. Good signs to look for are declining unemployment and increasing job growth. The Bureau of Labor Statistics also tracks this data.

Taking a look at the real-estate market

The price of real estate, like the price of anything else, is driven by supply and demand. The smaller the supply and the greater the demand, the higher prices usually climb. An abundance of land and available credit, however, inevitably lead to overbuilding. When the supply of anything expands at a much faster rate than demand, prices generally fall.

Upward pressure on real-estate prices tends to be greatest in areas with little buildable land. In the long term, the lack of buildable land in an area can be a problem. Real-estate prices that are too high (as has happened in recent years, for example, in the San Francisco Bay Area) may cause employers and employees to relocate to less-expensive areas. If you want to invest in real estate in an area with little buildable land and sky-high prices, run the numbers to see whether the deal makes economic sense. (I explain how to do this later in this chapter.)

INVESTIGATE

In addition to buildable land, consider these other important real-estate market indicators to get a sense of the health, or lack thereof, of a particular market:

>> **Building permits:** The trend in the number of building permits tells you how the supply of real-estate properties may soon change. A long and sustained rise in permits over several years can indicate that the supply of new property may dampen future price appreciation.

>> **Vacancy rates:** If few rentals are vacant, you can assume that the area has more competition and demand for existing units, which bodes well for future real-estate price appreciation. Conversely, high vacancy rates indicate an excess supply of real estate, which may put downward pressure on rents as landlords compete to attract tenants.

>> **Listings of property for sale and number of sales:** Just as the construction of many new buildings is bad for future real-estate price appreciation, increasing numbers of property listings may indicate potential future trouble. As property prices reach high levels, some investors decide that they can make more money cashing in and investing elsewhere. When the market is flooded with listings, prospective buyers can be choosier, exerting downward pressure on prices. At high prices (relative to the cost of renting), more prospective buyers elect to rent, and the number of sales relative to listings drops. A sign of a healthy real-estate market is a decreasing and relatively low level of property listings, indicating that the demand from buyers meets or exceeds the supply of property for sale from sellers. When the cost of buying is relatively low compared with the cost of renting, more renters can afford and choose to purchase, thus increasing the number of sales.

>> **Rents:** The trend in rental rates that renters are willing and able to pay over the years gives a good indication of the demand for housing. When the demand for housing keeps up with the supply of housing and the local economy continues to grow, rents generally increase. This increase is a positive sign for continued real-estate price appreciation. Beware of buying rental property subject to rent control; the property's expenses may rise faster than you can raise the rents.

Examining property valuation and financial projections

How do you know what a property is really worth? Some say it's worth what a ready, willing, and financially able buyer is willing to pay. But some buyers pay more than what a property is truly worth. And sometimes buyers who are patient, do their homework, and negotiate well are able to buy property for less than its fair market value.

TIP

Crunching some numbers to figure what revenue and expenses a rental property may have is one of the most important exercises that you can go through when determining a property's worth and making an offer. In the sections that follow, I walk you through these important calculations.

Estimating cash flow

Cash flow is the money that a property brings in minus what goes out for its expenses. If you pay so much for a property that its expenses (including the mortgage payment and property taxes) consistently exceed its income, you have a money drain on your hands. Maybe you have the financial reserves to withstand the temporary drain for the first few years, but you need to know upfront what you're getting yourself into.

WARNING

Here are two big mistakes that novice rental–property investors make:

>> **They fail to realize all the costs associated with investment property.** In the worst cases, some investors end up in personal bankruptcy from the drain of *negative cash flow* (expenses exceeding income). In other cases, negative cash flow hampers investors' ability to accomplish important financial goals.

>> **They believe the financial statements that sellers and their real-estate agents prepare.** Just as an employer views a résumé with some skepticism, you should always view such financial statements as advertisements rather than sources of objective information. In some cases, sellers and agents fib or spin things in the most favorable way. In most cases, these statements contain lots of projections and best-case scenarios.

TIP

For property that you're considering purchasing, ask for a copy of Schedule E (Supplemental Income and Losses) from the property seller's federal income tax return. When most people complete their tax returns, in order to minimize their income taxes, they try to minimize their revenue and maximize their expenses — the opposite of what they and their agents normally do on the statements they produce to help make the property sale. Confidentiality and privacy aren't an issue when you ask for Schedule E because you're asking only for this one schedule and not the person's entire income tax return.

You should prepare financial statements based on facts and a realistic assessment of a property. Take your time and make the decision with your eyes and ears open and with a healthy degree of skepticism.

Valuing property

Estimating a property's cash flow is an important first step to figuring a property's value. But on its own, a building's cash flow doesn't provide enough information to intelligently decide whether to buy a particular real-estate investment. Just because a property has a positive cash flow doesn't mean you should buy it. In areas where investors expect to earn lower rates of appreciation, real estate generally sells for less and may have better cash flow.

Just as you should evaluate a stock versus other comparable stocks, so, too, should you compare the asking price of a property with the prices of comparable real estate. But what if all real estate is overvalued? Such a comparison doesn't reveal the state of inflated prices. So, in addition to comparing a real-estate investment property to comparable properties, you need to perform some local area evaluations of whether prices from a historic perspective appear too high, too low, or just about right.

Here are the pros and cons of the different approaches you can use to value property:

>> **Appraisers:** The biggest advantage of hiring an appraiser is that she values property for a living. An appraisal also gives you some hard numbers to use for negotiating with a seller. Hire a full-time appraiser who has experience valuing the type of property you're considering. Ask her for examples of a dozen similar properties in the area that she has appraised in the past three months.

The drawback of appraisers is that they cost money. A small home may cost several hundred dollars to appraise, and a larger multi-unit building may cost $1,000 or more. The risk or downside is that you can spend money on an appraisal for a building that you don't end up buying.

>> **Real-estate agents:** If you work with a good real-estate agent, ask him to draw up a list of comparable properties and help you estimate the value of the property you're considering buying. The advantage of having your agent help with this analysis is that you don't pay extra for this service.

WARNING

The drawback of asking an agent what to pay for a property is that his commission depends on your buying a property and on the amount you pay for that property. The more you're willing to pay for a property, the more likely the deal is completed, and the more the agent makes on commission.

» **Do-it-yourself:** If you're comfortable with numbers and analysis, you can try to estimate the value of a property yourself. The hard part is identifying comparable properties. Finding identical properties is usually impossible, so you need to find similar properties and then make adjustments to their selling prices so you can do an apples-to-apples comparison.

Among the factors that should influence your analysis of comparable properties are the date each property sold; the quality of the location; the lot size; the building age and condition; the number of units; the number of rooms, bedrooms, and bathrooms; the number of garages and fireplaces; and the size of the yard. A real-estate agent can provide this information, or you can track it down for properties you've seen or you know have recently sold.

Through a series of price adjustments, you can then compare the value of your target property to others that have recently sold. For example, if a similar property sold six months ago for $250,000 but prices overall have decreased 3 percent in the last six months, subtract 3 percent from the sales price. Ultimately, you have to attach a value or price to each difference between comparable properties and the one you're considering buying.

Digging for a Good Deal

Everyone likes to get a deal or feel like they bought something at a relatively low price. How else can you explain the American retail practice of sales? Merchandise is first overpriced, and what doesn't sell quickly enough is then marked down to create the illusion that you're getting a bargain! Some real-estate sellers and agents do the same thing. They list property for sale at an inflated price and then mark it down after they realize no one will pay their asking price. "A $30,000 price reduction!" the new listing screams. Of course, such reductions are rarely a deal.

REMEMBER

It's possible to get a good buy on a problem property that provides a discount larger than the cost of fixing the property. However, these opportunities are hard to find, and sellers of such properties are often unwilling to sell at a discount that's big enough to leave you much room for profit. If you don't know how to evaluate the property's problems thoroughly and correctly, you can end up overpaying.

Some real estate hucksters claim to have the real-estate investment strategy that can beat the system. Often these promoters claim you can become a multimillionaire through investing in distressed properties. A common suggested strategy is to purchase property that a seller has defaulted on or is about to default on. Or how about buying a property in someone's estate through probate court? Maybe you'd like to try your hand at investing in a property that has been condemned or has toxic-waste contamination!

In some cases, the strategies that these real-estate gurus advocate involve taking advantage of people's lack of knowledge. For example, some people don't know that they can protect the equity in their home by filing for personal bankruptcy. If you can find a seller in such dire financial straits and desperate for cash, you may get a bargain buy on the home. (You may struggle with the moral issues of buying property cheaply this way, however.)

Other methods of finding discounted property take lots of time and digging. Some involve cold-calling property owners to see whether they're interested in selling. This method is a little bit like trying to fill a job opening by interviewing people you run into on a street corner. Although you may eventually find a good candidate this way, if you factor in the value of your time, the deal seems like less of a bargain.

Without making things complicated or too risky, you can use some of the following time-tested and proven ways to buy real estate at a discount to its fair market value:

>> **Find a motivated seller.** Be patient and look at lots of properties, and sooner or later you'll come across one that someone needs to sell (and these aren't necessarily the ones advertised as having motivated sellers). Perhaps the seller has bought another property and needs the money to close on the recent purchase. Having access to sufficient financing can help secure such deals.

>> **Buy unwanted properties with fixable flaws.** The easiest problems to correct are cosmetic. Some sellers and their agents are lazy and don't even bother to clean a property. One single-family home that I bought had probably three years' worth of cobwebs and dust accumulated. It seemed like a dungeon at night because half the light bulbs were burned out.

Painting; tearing up old, ugly carpeting; refinishing hardwood floors; and putting new plantings in a yard are relatively easy jobs. They make the property worth more and make renters willing to pay higher rent. Of course, these tasks take money and time, and many buyers aren't interested in dealing with problems. If you have an eye for improving property and are willing to invest the time that coordinating the fix-up work requires, go for it! Just make sure you hire someone to conduct a thorough property inspection before you buy.

Be sure to factor in the loss of rental income if you can't fully rent the property during the fix-up period. Some investors have gone belly up from the double cash drain of fix-up expenses and lost rents.

>> **Buy when the real-estate market is depressed.** When the economy takes a few knocks and investors rush for the exits (as in the downturn before, during, and after the 2008 financial crisis), it's time to go shopping! Buy real estate when prices and investor interest are down. Interest rates are usually lower then too. During times of depressed markets, obtaining properties that produce a positive cash flow (even in the early years) is easier.

>> **Check for zoning opportunities.** Sometimes you can make more productive use of a property. For example, you can legally convert some multi-unit apartment buildings into condominiums. Some single-family residences may include a rental unit if local zoning allows for it. A good real-estate agent, contractor, and the local planning office in the town or city where you're looking at property can help you identify properties that you can convert. However, if you're not a proponent of development, you probably won't like this strategy.

If you buy good real estate and hold it for the long term, you can earn a healthy return from your investment. Over the long haul, having bought a property at a discount becomes an insignificant issue. You make money from your real-estate investments as the market appreciates and as a result of your ability to manage your property well. So, don't obsess over buying property at a discount and don't wait for the perfect deal, because it won't often come along.

4

Insurance: Protect Yourself, Your Loved Ones, and Your Assets

Chapter **14**

Taking Care with Health Insurance

When you're young and living under your parents' roof, you're unlikely to be concerned with health insurance. School-aged kids generally get their health insurance through a parent's coverage, a practice that's usually continued through college.

Welcome to the young-adult world of health insurance! Health insurance was in the news soon after the election of President Barack Obama in 2008 because he promised during the campaign, and then pushed for, a national health insurance program (Obamacare passed in 2010) mandated by the federal government.

Health insurance was front and center once again during the 2016 presidential election. Candidate Donald Trump promised over and over again that he would "repeal and replace" Obamacare with "something so much better." Once elected, President Trump soon discovered that the U.S. healthcare and health insurance industries are much more complicated than he realized, as is getting members of Congress to agree on a specific repeal-and-replace plan. "Now, I have to tell you, it's an unbelievably complex subject . . . Nobody knew healthcare could be so complicated," President Trump said in his second month in office.

I could have told Mr. Trump that the healthcare industry and reforming it is complicated — but he didn't ask me! In fact, I've had involvement with and interest in the healthcare and insurance industry since my first professional job after college as a management consultant. Most young adults are fortunate to not be big consumers of healthcare. But, because you never know what the future holds and people of all ages should get checkups and preventative care, this chapter discusses the best and most affordable ways to secure health insurance in your 20s and 30s. I also cover the ramifications of the healthcare bill (known as Obamacare) that was signed into law in 2010 and what possible changes may be coming in the future.

Making Sure You're Covered

Having health insurance is essential for nearly everyone, no matter your age. Many people get health insurance through their employers. Numerous people don't have coverage because it is or seems costly.

Historically, some people who can afford health insurance choose not to buy it because they believe they're healthy and they're not going to need it. Others who opt not to buy health insurance figure that if they ever really need healthcare, they'll get it even if they can't fully afford it.

WARNING

Although you may think you're healthy and don't need health insurance, think again. People without health insurance are more prone to put off getting routine and preventative care, which can lead to small problems turning into big ones. Besides this being an unwise approach to optimizing your health, it often costs more because of advanced illness, emergency room visits, and so on.

This section discusses transitioning from your parents' coverage to your own and how the healthcare laws help you get coverage.

Transitioning your coverage

Each state once had its own laws as far as health insurance coverage went, so there was no one-size-fits-all approach. In the past in most states, an adult child generally lost health insurance coverage under a parent's policy upon college graduation or when turning a particular age (for example, 25 or 26). Each state had a unique set of laws. Consider, for example, three state rules I pulled at random:

>> Connecticut required that group comprehensive and health insurance policies extend coverage to unwed children until the age of 26, provided they remained residents of Connecticut or were full-time students.

>> Florida allowed for dependent children up to age 25 who lived with a parent or were students, and those up to 30 who were also unmarried and had no dependent children of their own, to remain on their parents' insurance.

>> Wyoming allowed a child who was unmarried and a full-time student to remain on a parent's insurance up to age 23 if the parent was covered by a small group policy.

Then the Affordable Care Act, also known as Obamacare, was passed in 2010 so states had to amend their approach to conform with Obamacare's requirements — detailed in the next section, "Seeing how Obamacare changed your coverage."

So, what are the best ways to negotiate keeping health insurance coverage in your 20s without spending a small fortune for coverage? Here's my advice:

>> **Consider staying on your parents' policy until you secure full-time employment.** As soon as you're eligible for your employer's health plan, sign up for it. (You can and should offer to help pay for your share of the coverage if you're financially able to do so.)

>> **If you don't have access to your own coverage through your employer, look to COBRA.** The Consolidated Omnibus Budget Reconciliation Act (COBRA) enables you to stay on your parents' policy for up to 18 months from the time you lose coverage on that policy. Just be aware that you have to pay the full premiums.

>> **If you're self-employed, or your employer doesn't offer health coverage or the coverage isn't very good, get your own policy with a high deductible.** A deductible is the amount of medical claims you must first pay out of your pocket before insurance coverage kicks in. Check out the later section "Finding Your Best Health Plan" for advice. You can then sock money away in a health savings account (HSA) if you desire. See the section on HSAs later in this chapter.

Seeing how Obamacare changed your coverage

In 2010, Congress passed, and President Obama signed, two comprehensive healthcare reform bills that affect how you can get health insurance coverage. Summarizing thousands of pages of legislation in a concise space is challenging, but the reality is that the highlights that apply to young adults aren't that extensive.

Obamacare implemented the following changes to group health plans offered through employers:

>> Employers must offer coverage to their employees for their adult children up to age 26 who aren't eligible for coverage under another employer's health plan. So if your mother or father is covered under a group health plan, you may get coverage through that plan through age 26, even if you aren't a dependent for income tax purposes. The coverage isn't taxable to the employee or dependent.

>> Insurers may not impose lifetime limits on claims paid (annual limits became prohibited as of 2014).

>> Employers must offer minimum coverage to full-time employees or make payments to the government.

>> Group health plans must limit cost sharing and deductibles to those in a health savings account–eligible, high-deductible health plan.

>> Group health plans must remove all preexisting-condition exclusions on all participants.

Higher-income earners are subjected to some higher taxes to help pay for the health bill:

>> Single taxpayers with earned income above $200,000 and married couples filing jointly with earned income above $250,000 pay an extra 0.9 percent Medicare tax on wages and self-employment income in excess of these thresholds.

>> Taxpayers with modified adjusted gross income (MAGI) from any source (including investments) above these thresholds are subject to a 3.8 percent additional tax on the lesser of their net investment income (for example, interest, dividends, and capital gains) and the amount by which their modified adjusted gross income exceeds the thresholds.

Recent developments and likely future changes

Major changes to Obamacare can only occur when both the House and the Senate can get a majority to agree to those changes and the president is willing to go along as well. Efforts to "repeal and replace" Obamacare failed in 2017 in the Senate.

There have been a number of incremental changes to Obamacare in recent years including:

>> **Elimination of mandate (penalties):** Previously, if you didn't secure an Obamacare approved/mandated policy, you were forced to pay a sizeable financial penalty on your annual federal income tax return. That has since been eliminated.

>> **Short-term scaled-down plans allowed:** Health insurance plans that offer coverage for up to one year and renewability for a total of three years are allowed as short-term alternatives to Obamacare compliant plans.

>> **Open enrollment time frame modified:** The period each year when you can enroll in a new or different Obamacare health insurance plan has been changed to the 45-day period from November 1 through December 15.

>> **Expansion of subsidies:** The income levels at which Obamacare policies can be at least partially subsidized was expanded. See the subsidy calculator on the Kaiser Family Foundation website at `https://www.kff.org/interactive/subsidy-calculator/`.

>> **States allowed to have work requirements for Medicaid coverage:** Each individual state can choose to have work requirements, for those who are able, as a condition for being under the state's Medicaid program (health insurance program for lower-income people).

President Biden's election and the fact that he was vice president at the time of Obamacare's passage and Congress is also under his party's control (the mid-term elections in 2022 are likely to change that) may lead to changes to counter-act some of the modifications that occurred under the prior administration's tenure.

Finding Your Best Health Plan

Most working-age folks obtain health insurance through their employer. Employer-provided coverage eliminates the hassle of having to shop for coverage from scratch. Also, thanks to the purchasing power of a group, employer-provided coverage may provide a higher level of benefits, given the cost, than individually purchased coverage.

If you're self-employed, out of work, or working for an employer that doesn't offer health coverage, you need to shop for and secure health insurance. And even if your employer does offer health policies, you may well have choices to make.

In the following sections, I discuss the important issues to consider when selecting among available health insurance plans.

Selection of doctors and hospitals

Open-choice plans that allow you to use any doctor or hospital you want are less common and generally more expensive than *restricted-choice plans*, such as *health maintenance organizations* (HMOs) and *preferred provider organizations* (PPOs). These plans keep costs down because they negotiate low rates with selected providers.

HMOs and PPOs are more similar than they are different. The main difference is that PPOs still pay the majority of your expenses if you use a provider outside their approved list. If you use a provider outside the approved list with an HMO, you typically aren't covered at all.

TIP

If you want to use particular doctors or hospitals, find out which health insurance plans they accept as payment. Weigh whether the extra cost of an open-choice plan is worth being able to use the services of particular medical providers if they're not part of a restricted-choice plan. Also be aware that some plans allow you to go outside their network of providers as long as you pay a bigger portion of the incurred medical costs. If you're interested in using alternative types of providers, such as acupuncturists, find out whether the plans you're considering cover these services.

Plan benefits and features

Healthcare plans typically offer some important features. The following list identifies the key features to search for to ensure a quality plan at the most reasonable cost:

>> **Major medical coverage:** This includes hospital care, physician visits, and ancillary charges, such as X-rays and laboratory work. If you're a woman and you think you may want to have children, make sure your plan has maternity benefits.

>> **Deductibles and copayments:** To reduce your health insurance premiums, choose a plan with the highest deductible and *copayment* (the amount you pay when service is rendered, such as $10 to $30) you can afford. As with other insurance policies, the more you're willing to share in the cost of your claims, the less you'll have to pay in premiums. Most policies have annual deductible options (usually $250, $500, $1,000, or higher) as well as copayment options, which are typically 20 percent or so of the claim amount. With the passage of

Obamacare and plans compatible with health savings accounts, many plans have a deductible of several thousand dollars. Insurance plans generally set a maximum out-of-pocket limit such as $1,000 or $2,000 on your annual copayments. The insurer covers 100 percent of any medical expenses that go over that cap. Many HMO plans don't have deductible and copayment options.

TIP

If you have existing health problems and you have a choice of group plans through your employer, consider plans with low out-of-pocket expenses. Because you're part of a group, the insurer won't increase your individual rates just because you file more claims.

>> **Lifetime maximum benefits:** Health insurance plans specify the maximum total benefits they'll pay over the course of time you're insured by their plan. The national health insurance bill signed into law in 2010 prevents insurers from setting lifetime maximums. If you're ever examining a short-term or other plan that is outside of the government-mandated plan network, keep in mind that with the high cost of healthcare, you should choose a plan that has no maximum or that has a maximum of at least $5 million. See the section "Seeing how Obamacare changed your coverage" earlier in this chapter.

Shopping for Health Insurance

Yes, health insurance is among the more complicated things to shop for, but it's like other products and services — there's a marketplace of providers competing for your business. This section explains how to unearth your best options and what to do in case you're ever denied coverage in the future.

Uncovering the best policies

When shopping for health insurance, you basically have two options: You can buy a health plan through an agent or you can buy directly from an insurer. When particular health insurance plans are sold both ways, buying through an agent usually doesn't cost more.

Obamacare, which includes a federal marketplace, provided a new way in some states to buy health insurance — through state-based exchanges.

If you're self-employed or you work for a smaller employer that doesn't offer health insurance as a benefit, get proposals from the larger and older health insurers in your area. Larger plans can negotiate better rates from providers, and older plans are more likely to be here tomorrow. Nationally, Blue Cross Blue

Shield, Kaiser Permanente, Aetna, UnitedHealth, CIGNA, Assurant, and Anthem are among the older and bigger health insurers.

Many insurers operate in a bunch of different insurance businesses. You want an insurer that's one of the biggest in the health insurance arena and is committed to, understands, and has more experience in that business. If your coverage is canceled, you may have to search for new coverage.

Also check with professional or other associations that you belong to, as such plans sometimes offer decent benefits at a competitive price because of the purchasing clout they possess. A competent independent insurance agent who specializes in health insurance can help you find insurers who are willing to offer you coverage.

WARNING

Health insurance agents have a conflict of interest that's common to all financial salespeople who work on commission: The higher the premium plan they sell you, the bigger the commission they earn. So, an agent may try to steer you into higher-cost plans and avoid suggesting some of the cost-reducing strategies that I discuss in this chapter, such as opting for a higher deductible.

Dealing with Obamacare's high health insurance prices

When millions of health insurance policyholders had their plans canceled during the years when Obamacare (also known as the Affordable Care Act) was implemented, many of them faced big rate hikes when shopping for a replacement policy. That's because of the essential health benefits that, by law, must be included in health insurance policies. These benefits include maternity and newborn care, mental health and substance use disorder services, prescription drugs, and pediatric services (including dental and vision care), to give a partial list. In the past, you were able to pick and choose from plans that excluded some of these services and thus were less expensive.

Plus, Obamacare includes consumer protection provisions that have elevated prices. For example, it prohibits health insurance companies from limiting or excluding coverage related to preexisting health conditions. In order to absorb this cost and costs related to other provisions, insurance companies have raised rates substantially.

While many people faced much higher priced policies due to Obamacare, some folks qualify for government subsidies that help reduce the effective price of said policies. (Of course, this money doesn't come out of thin air; it comes from the federal government and therefore, taxpayers.)

Qualifying for a subsidy depends on your family income and how many children you have. Subsidies are available to qualified individuals and families whose incomes fall in the range of 138 percent to 400 percent of the poverty line (assuming they buy a policy on a government exchange). At the top of the spectrum for 2021, an individual making under $51,040 would be eligible for a subsidy, as would a family of four earning less than $104,800.

In recent decades, health insurance prices have consistently increased faster than the overall rate of inflation. That has continued under Obamacare. Here are a few tips for health insurance shoppers to make the most of their spending:

>> If your plan is/was canceled, don't just go with the plan mentioned in the cancelation letter. Shop around. Contact an agent who focuses on health insurance plans and ask to see a side-by-side comparison of various plans. Check out other companies. If you're eligible for a subsidy, check out the exchanges. Chances are you'll find something more reasonable if you're willing to make tradeoffs in the area of deductibles and out-of-pocket expenses.

>> Be patient and do your homework. Talk to insurers and agents. Spend some time on the computer; the Affordable Care Act marketplace website is www.healthcare.gov. Ask friends and colleagues what they're doing. Although you do need to be mindful of enrollment deadlines, you don't want to rush into what is an important financial decision.

>> If you go with a bronze plan, consider one that is compatible with a health savings account (HSA). A bronze plan may be best for people who are generally healthy. These have the lowest premiums. Of course, they also have the highest deductibles, which means that in the event you do get sick, you'll have to cover more of your costs out of pocket. And that is why it's important to select a bronze plan that's compatible with an HSA (not all of them are). I have always recommended HSAs as a great tax-saving strategy, and now that deductibles are so high, they make more sense than ever. After all, if you have to have a high deductible anyway, at least getting the tax break on the out-of-pocket expenses you have to pay makes sense. See the section, "Health Savings Accounts: Tax Reduction for Healthcare Costs," later in this chapter.

>> Do what you can to get and stay healthy. Chances are you'll now be paying more out of pocket for non-preventative care, so good health should be your top priority. Of course, health insurance is needed because some conditions are unpreventable, but you can affect plenty of others with lifestyle improvements. Obviously, if you smoke, stop now; smoking is the only "preexisting condition" health insurance companies are allowed to charge you more for. But it's also important to eat healthfully, exercise, and lose weight if you need to. The healthier you are, the less you'll need to seek medical care — and the less you'll have to pay out of pocket for your care.

Handling insurance rejection

Before the passage and implementation of Obamacare, those with so-called preexisting conditions sometimes got turned down when applying for health insurance or had to pay substantially higher premiums. A similar phenomenon happens with other types of insurance when you're deemed too great a risk. For example, you may have problems with getting life or disability insurance or have to pay a much greater price if you're not in the best of health.

When you try to enroll in a particular life or disability insurance plan (discussed in Chapter 15), you may be turned down because of current or previous health problems. That may happen (but isn't likely to) in the future with health insurance, depending on what happens with Congress and President Biden. If your current health causes you to be charged a high premium for life or disability insurance or be denied such coverage outright, try these strategies to find out why and get approved:

TIP

>> **Ask the insurer why you were denied.** If you're denied coverage because of a medical condition, find out what information the company has and determine whether it's accurate. Perhaps the company made a mistake or misinterpreted some information that you provided in your application.

>> **Request a copy of your medical information file.** Just as you have a credit report file that details your use (and misuse) of credit (see Chapter 4), you also have a medical information report. Once per year, you can request a free copy of your medical information file (which typically highlights only the more significant problems over the past seven years, not your entire medical history) by calling 866-692-6901 or visiting www.mib.com (click on "Request Your MIB Consumer File"). If you find a mistake on your report, you have the right to request that it be fixed. However, the burden is on you to prove that the information in your file is incorrect. Proving that your file contains errors can be a major hassle — you may even need to contact physicians you saw in the past because their medical records may be the source of the incorrect information.

INVESTIGATE

>> **Shop around.** Just because one company denies you coverage doesn't mean that all insurance companies will deny you. Some insurers better understand certain medical conditions and are more comfortable accepting applicants with those conditions. Although most insurers charge higher rates to people with blemished medical histories than people with perfect health records, some companies penalize them less than others. An agent who sells policies from multiple insurers, called an independent agent, can be helpful because she can shop among a number of different companies.

» **Find a job with an employer whose insurer doesn't require a medical exam.** Of course, this shouldn't be your only reason for seeking new employment, but it can be an important factor. If you're married, you may also be able to get into an employer group plan through your spouse's plan.

Health Savings Accounts: Tax Reduction for Healthcare Costs

Health savings accounts (HSAs) are terrific for reducing your taxes while saving money for healthcare expenses. They especially make sense if you're self-employed or an employee of a smaller company with no health plan or a high-deductible health plan.

An HSA is fairly simple: You put money earmarked for medical expenses into an investment account that offers tax-deductible contributions and tax-deferred compounding, just like a retirement account (withdrawals aren't taxed so long as the money is used for qualified healthcare expenses). For tax year 2021, you can sock away up to $3,600 for an individual account and $7,200 for a family account. To qualify for an HSA, you must have a high-deductible health insurance policy — at least $1,400 for individuals and $2,800 for families.

You don't have to deplete the HSA by the end of the year: Money can compound tax-deferred inside the HSA for years. If you qualify, you can begin to investigate an HSA through insurers offering health plans you're interested in or with the company you currently have coverage through (also see my website, www.erictyson.com, for the latest information on the best HSAs).

You may also be able to save on taxes if you have a substantial amount of healthcare expenditures in a year relative to your income. You can deduct medical and dental expenses as an itemized deduction on Schedule A to the extent that they exceed 10 percent of your adjusted gross income.

TIP

If you expect to have out-of-pocket medical expenses and can't qualify for an HSA because of your employer's plans, find out whether your employer offers a *flexible spending* or *healthcare reimbursement account.* These accounts enable you to pay for uncovered medical expenses with pretax dollars. If, for example, you're in a combined 35 percent federal and state income tax bracket, these accounts allow you to pay for necessary healthcare at a 35 percent discount. These accounts can also be used to pay for vision and dental care.

WARNING

Be forewarned of the major stumbling blocks you face when saving through medical reimbursement accounts:

>> **You need to elect to save money from your paycheck prior to the beginning of each plan year.** The only exception is at the time of a "life change," such as marriage, a spouse's job change, divorce, the birth of a child, or a family member's death.

>> **You also need to use the money within the year you save it.** These accounts contain a "use it or lose it" policy.

» Figuring out the fine points of life insurance

» Taking time to get your finances in order for loved ones

Chapter **15**

Safeguarding Your Income

I f you're like most younger adults and in good health, you probably don't think much about possible health problems. And why should you?! You can and should enjoy your youth and hopefully being and staying healthy.

But, through no fault of your own, or because of bad luck, you might experience some health challenges. It's also possible that like plenty of other folks some aspect of your lifestyle may contribute to a health issue for you. So, you should take sensible steps to make sure you protect your primary source of employment income in case of an unexpected health problem.

If you are dependent upon the income you get from working, you probably need some insurance to protect that stream of income, not only for yourself but also possibly for loved ones if they're dependent on you financially.

In this chapter, I discuss the two forms of insurance — disability and life insurance — that can help you address these needs. I also discuss other simple yet powerful steps beyond insurance that you can take to get things in order for your loved ones.

Protecting Your Income for You and Yours: Disability Insurance

Disability insurance protects your employment income for yourself and perhaps also for your dependents. But even if no one depends on you financially, you need long-term disability insurance if you depend on your own income. After all, if you suffer a disability, you probably won't be able to earn employment income, but your living expenses will continue. And therein lies the need for disability insurance.

REMEMBER

When you're young and healthy, dismissing the need for disability insurance is easy to do because the odds of suffering a long-term disability seem — and are — relatively low. But the occurrence of a long-term disability is unpredictable, and numerous long-term disabilities affect younger people. Some disabilities happen because of accidents, and those can happen to you regardless of age. Others are caused by medical problems, and more than one-third of all such disabilities are suffered by people under the age of 45. The vast majority of these medical problems can't be predicted in advance.

In the following sections, I assist you with understanding what coverage you may already have and determining whether it's the right amount, how much to get, what features to seek in a policy, and where to actually buy a policy.

Understanding disability coverage you may already have

Through payment of employment-related taxes, you may have some disability coverage through state and federal government insurance programs. However, this coverage is more short term than long term in nature:

>> **State disability programs:** A handful of states have disability insurance programs, but the coverage is typically Spartan. Benefits are paid over a short period of time (usually one year at most). State programs are also generally not a good value because of the cost for the small amount of coverage they provide.

>> **Social Security disability:** Social Security pays long-term benefits only if you're unable to perform any substantial, gainful activity for more than a year or if your disability is expected to result in death. Furthermore, Social Security

disability payments are quite low because they're intended to provide only for basic, subsistence-level living expenses. Also, if you've only been working for a short amount of time, you haven't paid much into Social Security and thus won't have a high level of earned benefits.

What about coverage you have through your employer? If you're self-employed or work for a small company, you probably don't have long-term disability coverage. By contrast, most large employers offer disability insurance to their employees. Ask your employer's benefits department or person for details on your current policy and then compare those with the features that I recommend you get on a policy that you buy for yourself.

REMEMBER

Workers' compensation, if you have such coverage through your employer, pays out if you're injured on the job, but it doesn't pay any benefits if you get disabled away from your job. You need coverage that pays no matter where and how you're disabled.

Determining how much disability insurance you need

You should carry sufficient long-term disability insurance coverage to provide you with adequate income to live on should you become disabled. If you don't have many financial assets and you want to maintain your current lifestyle if you suffer a disability, get enough coverage to replace your entire monthly take-home (after-tax) pay.

TIP

The benefits you purchase on a disability policy are quoted as the dollars per month you receive if disabled. So if your job provides you with a $3,000-per-month income after taxes, get a policy that provides a $3,000-per-month benefit.

If you pay for your disability insurance, the benefits are tax-free (but hopefully you won't ever have to collect them). If your employer picks up the tab, your disability benefits will be taxable, so you need a greater amount of benefits.

REMEMBER

In addition to the monthly coverage amount, you also need to select the duration for which you want a policy to pay you benefits. You should select a policy that pays benefits until you reach an age at which you become financially self-sufficient. For most people, that's around the age when their Social Security benefits kick in. (Folks born after 1959 get full Social Security benefits at age 67 and reduced benefits before that age.)

Identifying useful disability policy features

If you go shopping for a long-term disability (LTD) insurance policy, you need to master some jargon. LTD policies have numerous options, some of which you need and some of which you don't. Here's what you need to know:

>> **Definition of disability:** An *own-occupation* disability policy provides benefit payments if you can't perform the work you normally do. The extra cost of such policies is worthwhile if you're in a high-income or specialized occupation and you'd have to take a significant pay cut to do something else (and the reduced income and required lifestyle changes wouldn't be acceptable to you). Other policies pay you only if you're unable to perform a job for which you're reasonably trained.

>> **Noncancelable and guaranteed renewable:** These desirable features ensure that your policy can't be canceled because of your developing health problems.

>> **Waiting period:** The lag time between the onset of your disability and the time you begin collecting benefits is a disability policy's *deductible.*

TIP

As with other types of insurance, you should take the highest deductible (longest waiting period) that your financial circumstances allow. A longer waiting period significantly reduces the policy's cost. The minimum waiting period on most policies is 30 days. The maximum waiting period can be up to one to two years. Try a waiting period of three to six months if you have sufficient emergency reserves.

>> **Residual benefits:** This useful option pays you a partial benefit if you have a disability that prevents you from working full time.

>> **Cost-of-living adjustments (COLAs):** This feature automatically increases your benefit payment by a set percentage annually or in accordance with changes in inflation. The advantage of a COLA is that it retains the purchasing power of your benefits. A modest COLA, such as 3 percent, is worth having.

>> **Future insurability:** This allows you, regardless of health, to buy additional coverage in the future. You may benefit from the future insurability option if your income is artificially low now and your career trajectory suggests that your income will rise significantly in the future.

>> **Insurer's financial stability:** Choose insurers that will be here tomorrow to pay your claim. But don't obsess over the company's stability; benefits are paid even if an insurer fails, because the state or another insurer almost always bails out the unstable insurer.

Shopping for coverage

When you start to shop for LTD, focus your attention first on group plans, which generally offer the best value. You may have access to buy group disability insurance through your employer or a professional association. Just be sure that the group plan policy includes the features I discuss and recommend in the preceding section.

If you don't have access to a group policy, you'll likely end up buying an individual policy through an agent. Some agents are called *independent agents* because they sell policies from numerous insurance companies. Other agents are dedicated to selling policies from a single company. Both types are fine to use so long as you shop the marketplace and get a cost-effective policy with the features that I suggest in the preceding section.

WARNING

Tread carefully when purchasing disability insurance through an agent. Some agents try to load your policy with all sorts of extra bells and whistles to pump up the premium — along with their commission.

Protecting Your Income for Dependents: Life Insurance

You generally need life insurance when others, such as a spouse or a child, depend on your income, especially if you have major financial commitments such as a mortgage or years of child rearing ahead. You may also want to consider life insurance if an extended family member currently depends on your income or is likely to do so in the future.

You generally don't need life insurance if you're

>> Single with no children

>> Part of a working couple that can maintain an acceptable lifestyle on one of your incomes

>> Independently wealthy (financially independent) and don't need to work

These sections explain how to figure out how much life insurance coverage you may already have, how much you need, and how to purchase it.

Assessing your current life insurance coverage

In a moment, I discuss how much coverage you may need if you've decided you need life insurance protection. First, though, take stock of your current coverage. Start with your current employer and determine whether the company offers you any life insurance coverage at its own expense.

Next, consider possible coverage you may have through Social Security that provides survivor's benefits to your spouse and children. Be aware, however, that if your surviving spouse works and earns even a modest amount of money, he or she will get little, if any, survivor's benefits. Prior to reaching Social Security's full retirement age (67 for those born after 1959), your survivor's benefits get reduced by $1 for every $2 you earn above $18,960 (in 2021).

TIP

If either you or your spouse anticipates earning a low enough income to qualify for survivor's benefits, you should factor those benefits into how much life insurance to buy. For example, if your annual after-tax income is $40,000 and Social Security provides a survivor's benefit of $12,000 annually, you'd need enough life insurance to replace $28,000 annually ($40,000 − $12,000).

The Social Security Administration (SSA) used to mail an annual statement to working adults that showed their earnings history and estimated future Social Security benefits. In an effort to save on printing and mailing costs, they no longer do this and only mail a statement to those age 60 and older who are not yet collecting benefits and who haven't set up an online account through the SSA website. If you haven't reviewed your earnings history and estimated Social Security benefits in recent years, be sure to set up an account through www.ssa.gov.

Determining how much life insurance to buy

To figure the amount of life insurance to buy, ask yourself how many years of income you want to replace. Table 15-1 provides a simple way to calculate how much life insurance you need to consider purchasing. To replace a certain number of years' worth of income, multiply the appropriate number in the table by your annual after-tax income. Because life insurance policy payouts aren't taxed, you need to replace only after-tax income and not pre-tax income.

TABLE 15-1

Figuring Life Insurance Needs

To Replace This Many Years of Income	Multiply Your Annual After-Tax Income By
5	4.5
10	8.5
20	15
30	20

TIP

You can figure your annual after-tax income in one of two ways. You can calculate it by getting out last year's tax return (and Form W-2) and subtracting the federal, state, and Social Security taxes you paid from your gross employment income. Alternatively, you can estimate your annual after-tax income by multiplying your gross income by 80 percent if you're a low-income earner, 70 percent if you're a moderate-income earner, or 60 percent if you're a high-income earner.

Deciding what type of life insurance to buy

Before you purchase any life insurance, you need to know your options. Life insurance comes in two major types:

>> **Term insurance:** You pay an annual premium (as you do for your auto insurance), for which you receive a particular amount of life insurance protection. If you die during the term, your beneficiaries collect; otherwise, the premium is gone but you're grateful to be alive!

>> **Cash value insurance:** All other life insurance policies (whole, universal, variable, and so on) combine life insurance with a supposed savings feature. A portion of your premiums is credited to an investment account that grows in value over time.

TIP

Purchase low-cost term insurance and do your investing separately. Life insurance is rarely a permanent need; over time, you can reduce the amount of term insurance you carry as your financial obligations lessen and you accumulate more assets. Cash value life insurance can make sense for some people, such as small-business owners who own a business worth millions of dollars and who don't want their heirs to possibly be forced to sell the business to pay estate taxes in the event of their death.

WARNING

Insurance salespeople aggressively push cash value policies because of the high commissions that insurance companies pay them. That's why these policies explicitly penalize you for withdrawing your cash balance within the first seven to ten years. You're paying for these high commissions when you buy one of these policies. Also, you're more likely to buy less life insurance coverage than you need because of the high cost of cash value policies relative to the cost of term. The vast majority of life insurance buyers need more protection than they can afford to buy with cash value coverage.

MAKING SENSE OF LIFE INSURANCE POLICY ILLUSTRATIONS

One of the ways that agents make cash value life insurance appear more attractive is through the policy illustrations that they send you during the sales process. To convince you to buy cash value life insurance, agents will prepare illustrations (projections) showing you how large the cash value of various policies will grow over the years, and they may compare it to after-tax investments. It's easy for insurers' illustrations to make the cash value life insurance look best by simply skewing the assumptions used in the projections.

For example, insurance companies pay a somewhat better interest rate on your cash balance in the first year or first few years of the policy. They do this to lure you into a policy. However, after that initial period expires, the insurer can set the interest rate (your return) at whatever level they desire as long as it's above whatever minimum is delineated in the policy. You can't get out of the policy in the early years without paying a substantial penalty (because the insurer needs to recoup the hefty commissions they paid the agent), so don't think you can simply take your money and run once the interest rate is lowered.

Not to get too technical, but you must keep in mind that the illustrations are based upon "actuarial assumptions" made by each insurer. Insurers may assume, for example, that their policyholders' "cost of insurance" (mortality charges for likelihood of dying) may be less in the future when in fact there is no basis for that assumption.

Another way that agents can make cash value life insurance seem more attractive is to neglect to mention that the policy illustrations don't show any future taxation. Future taxation of the cash value in excess of the premiums that have been paid should be considered. You will owe ordinary income tax rates on this money unless you keep the policy in force until your passing.

So, don't pay much attention to policy projections. If you're going to consider a cash value policy, you should instead examine the historic (past) rates of return of given insurers and how that compares with their peers. But, be sure to strongly consider the pros and cons of term insurance versus cash value policies.

Shopping for life insurance

You can purchase term life insurance so that your premium increases annually or it increases after 10, 15, 20, 25, or 30 years. The advantage of a premium that locks in for, say, 20 years is that you have the security of knowing how much you'll be paying each year for the next two decades. You also don't need to go through medical evaluations as frequently to qualify for the lowest rate possible.

The disadvantage of a policy with a long-term rate lock is that you pay more in the early years than you do on a policy that adjusts more frequently. In addition, you may want to change the amount of insurance you carry as your circumstances change. Thus, you may throw money away when you dump a policy with a long-term premium guarantee before its rate is set to change. Policies that adjust the premium every five to ten years offer a balance between price and predictability.

TIP

Be sure to get a policy that's *guaranteed renewable*, which assures that the policy can't be canceled because of your health worsening. Don't buy a life insurance policy without this feature unless you expect that your life insurance needs will disappear when the policy is up for renewal.

Here are some sources for high-quality, low-cost term insurance (the first three are independent agencies):

>> **AccuQuote:** www.accuquote.com; 800-442-9899

>> **ReliaQuote:** www.reliaquote.com; 800-940-3002

>> **Term4Sale:** www.term4sale.com; 888-798-3488 (this company provides quotes and refers you to agents who sell life insurance in your area)

>> **USAA:** www.usaa.com; 800-531-8722 (this company sells low-cost term life insurance directly to the public; some of its other insurance products are only available to members of the military and their families)

Caring for Your Loved Ones: "Peace of Mind" Insurance

Buying an insurance policy isn't the only thing you should do to provide for your loved ones. Consider taking the following steps, most of which involve only your time and forethought and no expense:

>> **Centralize your important financial records.** Keep your most recent investment account records (either electronic or paper), insurance policies,

employee benefits documents, small-business accounting records, and other important documents in one place (such as a file drawer) that your loved ones know about. If you only access your accounts and statements electronically, be sure your loved ones know about your various accounts and policies and how to access them.

>> **Prepare an up-to-date will.** You can do this yourself with a good software package such as those made by Nolo Press (www.nolo.com).

>> **Provide a list of key contacts.** This list includes experts you recommend calling (or material you recommend reading) in the event of legal, financial, or tax quandaries.

>> **Prepare sentimental remembrances.** You may want to give some thought to sentimental leave-behinds for your loved ones, especially for kids. These can be something like a short note telling them how much they meant to you and what you'd like them to remember about you.

Chapter **16**

Home, Auto, Renter's, and Other Insurance Policies

N o one likes to pay his hard-earned money to an insurance company. But if you were to wreck your car or someone were to break into your home and steal some valuable personal property, you'd be mighty unhappy if you lacked the right coverage and had to fully pay at your own expense to replace those items.

So I understand that reading this chapter isn't on your short list of fun things to do today. But I do promise to clearly explain how to get the insurance protection you need on your property and personal possessions and to do so for the best price that you can. I also discuss smaller-type insurance policies that are likely to be a waste of your money and thus are best avoided.

Protecting Your Home and Possessions: Homeowner's and Renter's Insurance

When you buy a home (typically with a mortgage), the mortgage lender mandates that you get homeowner's insurance. The lender wants to protect its investment in the property for the same reason that you should want to protect your stake in the property. This kind of policy insures your personal property and also provides some liability protection should a lawsuit arise out of something that happens at the property (an accident, for example).

If you're renting, you may consider renter's insurance coverage for these same reasons — personal property coverage and liability protection. This section will help you consider, though, the pros and cons of considering renter's insurance when you have the choice as to whether to carry it. (Some landlords require you carry basic coverage.)

Although homeowner's insurance and renter's insurance are completely separate and different policies, they share many important features, which I discuss in the following sections.

Dwelling coverage

When you buy a home, you'll get a policy with *dwelling protection*, the amount of which is determined by the cost of rebuilding in your area. The insurer details the size and features of your home so, for example, in the event of a fire that destroys the property, the policy will pay out enough money for you to rebuild the property and replicate what you started with. (If you're a condominium owner, check out whether the insurance the condo association bought for the entire building is sufficient.)

TIP

When buying a homeowner's policy, seek out coverage that includes *guaranteed replacement cost.* This ensures that the insurance company will rebuild the home even if the cost of construction is more than the policy coverage. If the insurance company underestimates your dwelling coverage, it has to make up the difference. Each insurer defines guaranteed replacement cost differently, so be sure to ask insurers how they define it. Some companies pay for the home's full replacement cost, no matter how much it ends up being, while other insurers set caps or limits. For example, some insurers may pay up to 25 percent more than the dwelling coverage on your policy.

When you're renting, you don't need to have dwelling protection because you don't have an ownership stake in the building. Should something happen to the building, it could, of course, affect your ability to live there or affect your possessions, but those are different matters not covered by dwelling coverage, which is strictly for the benefit of the building's owner.

Personal property protection

Personal property coverage basically covers the contents of your home — furniture, clothing, and other possessions. On a homeowner's policy, the amount of personal property coverage is usually dictated by the amount of dwelling coverage. For example, you may get personal property coverage that's equal to 50 to 75 percent of the dwelling coverage, which should be more than enough for most people. Unless you own a ton of expensive furnishings, ask your insurer if you can choose a lower percentage for this coverage than they use as an automatic default. Otherwise, you will be throwing away money on coverage you'll never use.

When you're renting or you're the owner of a condominium, you need to select the level of personal property coverage you desire. You can estimate this figure by totaling up the cost of replacing all your personal items.

TIP

You need to have a good grasp of what you own. Take an inventory of all your personal property, even if you don't need to total its value. The best way to do so is to take pictures or make a video. Be sure to take an inventory again every year or two or after you make some larger purchases. Also consider keeping receipts for the bigger-ticket items you buy for documentation purposes. No matter how you document your belongings, don't forget to keep the documentation somewhere besides your home — otherwise, it could be destroyed along with the rest of your house in a fire or other disaster.

I generally don't recommend paying for a *rider* for extra coverage (a rider is add-on coverage that specifically covers particular items not covered in your standard policy) unless you have items of significant value (such as artwork, jewelry, and so on).

Liability insurance

We live in a litigious society, so even though you may rightfully say the odds of someone suing you over an incident at your home are low, there's still a risk. *Liability insurance* protects you against legal claims due to an injury that occurs on your property. Get enough liability insurance to cover one to two times your financial assets.

As a renter, it's potentially useful to have liability protection if you like the idea of having some liability protection in the highly unlikely event that you are sued by someone harmed at your apartment. For example, suppose you have a wild room-mate or two who like throwing parties where people may not behave themselves. In addition to placing your security deposit at risk, there's a small chance of being sued in some unusual cases when there's trouble. So, in addition to insuring your personal property, another useful feature with renter's insurance is liability coverage.

Renter's insurance

If you don't have a lot of personal possessions or losing them wouldn't be a financial hardship given your overall financial situation, you can probably skip renter's insurance. In my own case, when I was renting for a few years after college, I chose not to carry renter's insurance. Consider renter's insurance if having to replace your possessions at your own expense would be a big deal financially or perhaps not even possible without taking on consumer debt.

And, as I just discussed, you might also consider renter's insurance for the liability protection. For sure, lawsuits are unusual in rental situations, but they do occasionally happen.

Plenty of apartment complexes and landlords now require their renters to carry and provide proof of renter's insurance coverage. They mandate this because they would rather not have disagreements over who is at fault for a problem that leads to damage of personal property, for example. Suppose the apartment directly above yours has a significant water leakage one day while you're at work, and by the time you return home, some of your furniture and other property is damaged. If you and the other tenant have renter's insurance, that should cover the personal property loss, and the two of you won't have to battle it out possibly with each other or the building owner as to who is at fault and financially liable.

If the landlord for an apartment you'd like to rent mandates renter's insurance, they may be able to suggest insurers that specialize in such coverage for you to contact. You can also use my short list of home insurers in the "Shopping for homeowner's insurance" section later in the chapter. Comparison shop the minimal coverage you are required to carry and get price quotes for different deductibles.

Natural disaster protection

A deficiency of homeowner's insurance is that it generally doesn't cover damage to your home and personal property caused by earthquakes and floods. To cover such situations, you need to buy separate natural disaster protection coverage.

The Federal Emergency Management Agency (FEMA) provides coverage of up to $250,000 for your dwelling and $100,000 for your personal property. Some private insurers also sell flood insurance policies that you should comparison shop with the FEMA policy. Private insurers can accommodate higher-value properties and also include loss-of-use coverage so you have money to rent a replacement property while your dwelling is repaired or rebuilt.

TIP

The National Flood Services' website (nationalfloodservices.com/new-mfq-floodtools/) can show you the relative flood risk for a given address and where floods have occurred historically nearby. You can also see how many flood insurance claims have been filed in your area over the past decade and the average dollar amount of those claims.

In terms of costs, for example, if your insurer estimates it would cost $200,000 to rebuild your home, you can buy a flood insurance policy through FEMA that provides $200,000 of building coverage and $80,000 of contents coverage for about $467 annually if you live in a low-risk area. If you're a renter, simply get the $80,000 contents-only coverage for $280 per year.

Inquire with your current insurer or the insurers you shop among (such as those I recommend later in this chapter). If the cost of flood or earthquake insurance seems expensive, compare that expense to the costs you'd likely incur should your home and personal property be a total loss.

Shopping for homeowner's insurance

To get the best homeowner's insurance for the least cost, you can be proactive. Try these money-saving strategies:

>> **Take a high deductible.** Because the objective of homeowner's insurance is to protect against large losses, not small ones, take the highest deductible with which you're comfortable. Take into consideration how large an emergency reserve you have and the stability of your employment income.

>> **Ask about special discounts.** If your property has a security system or you have other policies with the same insurer, you may qualify for a lower rate.

>> **Improve your credit score.** Many insurers use your credit score (see Chapter 4) as a factor in setting some of your insurance rates. They do this because their studies have shown that folks who have higher credit scores tend to have fewer insurance claims.

>> **Shop around.** Each insurance company prices its homeowner's and renter's policies based on its own criteria. So the lowest-cost company for your friend's property may not be the lowest-cost company for you. You have to shop around at several companies to find the best rates. Here's a list of companies

that usually have lower-cost policies and do a decent job with customer satisfaction and claims paying:

- **Amica:** This company isn't the cheapest, but it boasts consistently high customer-service ratings. Call Amica at 800-242-6422 or visit its website at www.amica.com.

- **Erie Insurance:** This firm operates mainly in the Midwest and Mid-Atlantic region. Check your local phone listings for agents. Call 800-458-0811 for a referral to a local agent or visit the company's website at www.erieinsurance.com.

- **GEICO:** You can contact this company by calling (800) 841-2964 or by visiting its website at www.geico.com.

- **Liberty Mutual:** Check your local phone listings for agents, call 800-837-5254, or visit the company's website at www.libertymutual.com.

- **Nationwide Mutual:** Check your local phone listings for agents, call 877-669-6877, or visit the company's website at www.nationwide.com.

- **State Farm:** Check your local phone listings for agents, call 844-803-1573, or visit the company's website at www.statefarm.com.

- **USAA:** This company offers insurance to members of the military and their families. Call the company at 800-531-8722 or visit its website at www.usaa.com to see whether you qualify.

TIP

If you're interested in more information specific to your state, you may benefit from the information that your state insurance department collects regarding insurers' prices and complaints (not all states do this, however). Look up your state's department of insurance phone number online or visit the National Association of Insurance Commissioners website at www.naic.org/state_web_map.htm to find links to each state's department of insurance site.

Insuring Your Car

Although cars can be money pits, most people need them to get around. Cars are popular for good reason. You can transport yourself when and where you want in a car.

TIP

Especially if you live in an urban area where you may have to pay for parking, if you don't anticipate using a car frequently, consider not having one. In addition to public transit, you can use cabs and ride-share services like Lyft and Uber and/or rent a car from time to time. Some young adults borrow their friends' cars — be sure to work out a fair payment arrangement and understand your insurance coverage.

DRIVING SAFELY

Without a doubt, the most dangerous thing you probably do is get behind the wheel of a car or travel as a passenger in someone else's vehicle. Yet, many people give insufficient thought to taking sensible measures to reduce their risk in cars.

For starters, we minimize and trivialize the risk. We say things to ourselves such as, "I drive short distances," or "My large SUV will protect me."

Car buyers often do little if any research on the safety records of cars they ultimately buy. Only 12 percent (about one in eight) of prospective new-car buyers said in a survey that safety features were the most important consideration in their planned purchases. That's amazing given the danger.

Compounding the fact that many people don't research and buy the safest cars, we overestimate how good our driving skills are. Consider how drivers responded to the following multiple-choice options in a survey conducted by the Insurance Institute for Highway Safety:

- My driving skills are much better or better than average: 74 percent

- My driving skills are average: 25 percent

- My driving skills are below average: 1 percent

Seventy-four times as many people said their driving skills were above average than those who said they were below average! And, 99 percent of all respondents rated their skills as average or above! Clearly, that can't possibly be the case in the real world.

More than 30,000 people die annually in accidents on America's roads. Although this number has declined over the decades, it's still sad and tragically high, especially when you consider that many of these deaths are preventable. Here's what you can do to be on the good side of those statistics:

- **Drive a safe car.** Don't make the mistake of assuming that driving a safe vehicle requires buying a $50,000 high-end car. You don't need to spend buckets of money to get a car with desirable safety features. Visit www.safercar.gov/Vehicle-Shoppers for up-to-date information on the safety ratings on new and used cars.

- **Drive safely.** Wear your seat belt! A U.S. Department of Transportation study found that 60 percent of auto passengers who were killed were *not* wearing their seat belts. Stay within the speed limit and don't drive while you're intoxicated or tired. And don't try to talk or text on your cell phone while driving. Use hands-free devices and minimize conversations while on the road.

(continued)

(continued)

- **Avoid/minimizing driving during the most dangerous times.** Extensive driving in the very late night/early morning hours and on major holidays (New Year's Eve, Independence Day, and so on) is asking for trouble given the preponderance of drunk drivers on the road. Also, be thoughtful about going on the road when the weather creates hazardous driving conditions.

- **Be selective about whom you allow to drive you.** When you take a ride in someone else's car, you are literally putting your life in their hands. So, if a taxi or rideshare driver shows up in an unsafe car or is driving recklessly, don't be shy about opting out or speaking up. Make up an excuse — just do what you feel is necessary to protect yourself.

For more auto safety tips, please visit my website at `www.erictyson.com`.

INVESTIGATE

To evaluate buying your own car, tally the annual total expected cost. Use Edmunds "True Cost to Own" calculator at `www.edmunds.com/tco.html` to see what it will cost you year by year over the first five years of owning a given make and model of a car. (*Note:* If you're smart and save to pay for your car in cash, be sure to subtract the financing costs that Edmunds assumes in its calculations. You may also want to tinker with some of its other assumptions if, for example, you anticipate driving much less or more than assumed in the calculations.)

If you choose to own a car, you can take important steps to minimize the car's costs. You need insurance, but you don't need to waste money on it. This section explains exactly what you need and what you should shun and how to get the best pricing.

Liability protection

Because of the inevitable accidents that happen with cars, auto insurance provides *liability protection* for injury caused to people and property. In fact, most states require this coverage by law. Liability protection comes in a couple of different forms:

- » **Bodily injury liability:** This type covers injury to people. You should have sufficient bodily injury liability insurance to ideally cover at least twice the value of your assets.

WARNING

  If you have little in the way of assets, know that your future earnings may be garnished in a lawsuit.

>> **Property damage liability:** This type covers the property, which includes other people's cars. The level of property-damage liability coverage in an auto policy is generally set based on the amount of bodily injury liability protection. Coverage of $50,000 is a good minimum to start with.

>> **Uninsured or underinsured liability:** Auto policies also allow you to buy liability coverage for other motorists you may have an accident with who lack coverage or whose liability protection is minimal. This uninsured or underinsured motorist liability coverage allows you to collect for lost wages, medical expenses, and pain and suffering incurred in the accident.

REMEMBER

If you already have comprehensive health and long-term disability insurance, uninsured or underinsured motorist liability coverage isn't really necessary. Just be aware that if you skip this coverage, you can't sue for general pain and suffering or insure passengers in your car who may lack adequate medical and disability coverage.

Collision and comprehensive

Collision coverage applies to claims arising from collisions of your car (and usually covers cars you rent as well). *Comprehensive coverage* is for claims for damage not caused by collision. For example, comprehensive coverage would cover damage done by someone breaking into your car.

Both collision and comprehensive coverage have their own deductible. For reduced auto insurance premiums, take the highest deductibles you can comfortably afford (I suggest at least $500 and ideally $1,000).

REMEMBER

As your car ages and declines in value, you can eventually eliminate your comprehensive and collision coverage. Remember that insurers won't pay you more than your car's book value, regardless of what it costs to repair or replace it. You can easily research your car's approximate current value on websites such as Kelley Blue Book (www.kbb.com).

Riders you should bypass

You can add various optional coverages, known as *riders*, which appear to be inexpensive but really aren't when you compare the cost against the small amount of protection they provide. Here are common ones that auto insurers and agents pitch and that I would generally bypass:

>> **Roadside assistance and towing:** These provisions provide coverage if your car breaks down. You may already have this protection if you belong to an

auto club like AAA. If you (or your parents on your behalf) want the peace of mind of knowing a particular service will come to your aid if your car breaks down, bypass this coverage and sign up for AAA or a similar service.

>> **Rental car reimbursement:** This rider provides for a limited coverage amount for a rental car should your car be stolen or damaged and not drivable.

>> **Riders that waive the deductible under certain circumstances:** The point of the deductible is to reduce your policy cost and eliminate the hassle of filing small claims.

>> **Medical payments coverage:** This coverage typically pays a few thousand dollars for medical expenses. If you and your passengers carry major medical insurance coverage, this rider isn't really necessary. Besides, a few thousand dollars of medical coverage doesn't protect you against catastrophic expenses.

Getting a good buy

In the previous sections, I explain what you do and don't need on your auto insurance policy. Here are some additional ways to get the most for your money:

>> **Consider insurance costs before buying your (next) car.** The cost of insuring a car should factor into your decision of which car you buy, because the insurance costs represent a major operating expense. Call insurers and ask for insurance price quotes for the different models you're considering before you buy.

>> **Ask for special discounts.** A security alarm, antilock brakes, or having another policy with the same insurer may qualify your car for lower rates. And make sure you're given appropriate "good driver" discounts if you've been accident- and ticket-free in recent years. Some insurers may not penalize you for one recent ticket — ask what their policy is.

>> **Shop among the best companies.** Use the insurers list I provide in the "Shopping for homeowner's insurance" section earlier in this chapter to obtain quotes for auto insurance. In addition, also try Progressive (800-776-4737; www.progressive.com).

UMBRELLAS AREN'T JUST FOR BAD WEATHER

A good problem is having enough assets that you need additional liability protection beyond what's economical and available to buy on a home and auto policy. Enter *excess liability insurance* (also known as *umbrella insurance*), which is additional liability insurance that's added on top of the liability protection on your home and car(s).

Expect to pay $200+ annually for $1 million of coverage. Each year, thousands of people suffer lawsuits of more than $1 million related to their cars and homes.

So how do you decide how much you need if you have a lot of assets? You should have at least enough liability insurance to protect your assets, and preferably enough to cover twice the value of those assets.

Avoiding Policies That Cover Small Possible Losses

A good insurance policy can seem expensive. A policy that doesn't cost much, on the other hand, can fool you into thinking that you're getting something for a reasonable or good price. Policies that cost little also cover little — they're priced low because they don't cover large potential losses.

Following are examples of common insurance policies that only cover relatively small potential losses and thus are generally a waste of your hard-earned dollars. As you read through this list, you may find examples of policies that you bought and that you feel paid for themselves. I can hear you saying, "But I collected on that policy you're telling me not to buy!" Sure, getting "reimbursed" for the hassle of having something go wrong is comforting. But consider all such policies that you bought or may buy over the course of your life. You're not going to come out ahead in the aggregate — if you did, insurance companies would lose money! These policies aren't worth the cost relative to the small potential benefit. On average, insurance companies pay out just 60 cents in benefits on every dollar collected. Many of the following policies pay back even less — around 20 cents in benefits (claims) for every insurance premium dollar spent.

Extended warranty and repair plans

Isn't it ironic that right after a salesperson or company persuades you to buy a particular television, computer, high-end smartphone, or car — in part by saying how reliable the product is — they seek to convince you to spend more money to insure against the failure of the item? If the product is so good, why do you need such insurance?

Extended warranty and repair plans are expensive and unnecessary short-term insurance policies. Product manufacturers' warranties typically cover any problems that occur in the first year or even several years. After that, paying for a repair out of your own pocket isn't a financial catastrophe.

Some credit-card issuers automatically double the manufacturer's warranty without additional charge on items purchased with their card. However, the cards that do this typically are higher-cost premium cards, so this is no free lunch — you're paying for this protection in terms of higher fees.

Home warranty plans

If your real-estate agent or the seller of a home wants to pay the cost of a home warranty plan for you, turning down the offer would be ungracious. As Grandma would say, you shouldn't look a gift horse in the mouth. But don't buy this type of plan for yourself. In addition to requiring some sort of fee (around $50 to $100) if you need a service call, home warranty plans limit how much they'll pay for problems.

Your money is best spent hiring a competent inspector to uncover problems and fix them before you purchase the home. If you buy a house, you should expect to spend money on repairs and maintenance; don't waste money purchasing insurance for such expenses.

Dental insurance

If your employer pays for dental insurance, you can take advantage of it. But don't pay for this coverage on your own. Dental insurance generally covers a couple of teeth cleanings each year and limits payments for more expensive work.

You can pay for dental services when needed. Don't be shy about asking upfront what a dentist's fees are. Also know that without insurance, a dentist will generally charge you a higher fee than the negotiated rate that they have with insurance companies. You can ask the office manager if they would charge you a similar rate to those they accept from insurers.

Credit life and credit disability policies

Credit life policies pay a small benefit if you die with an outstanding loan. Credit disability policies pay a small monthly income in the event of a disability. Banks and their credit-card divisions usually sell these policies. Some companies sell insurance to pay off your credit-card bill in the event of your death or disability, or to cover minimum monthly payments for a temporary period during specified life transition events (such as loss of a job, divorce, and so on).

The cost of such insurance seems low, but that's because the potential benefits are relatively small. In fact, given what little insurance you're buying, these policies are expensive. If you need life or disability insurance, purchase it. But get enough coverage, and buy it in a separate, cost-effective policy (see Chapter 15 for more details).

TIP

If you're in poor health and you can buy these insurance policies without a medical evaluation, you may represent an exception to the "don't buy it" rule. In this case, these policies may be the only ones to which you have access — another reason these policies are expensive. The people in good health are paying for the people with poor health who can enroll without a medical examination and who undoubtedly file more claims.

Daily hospitalization insurance

Hospitalization insurance policies that pay a certain amount per day, such as $100, prey on people's fears of running up big hospital bills. Healthcare is expensive — there's no doubt about that.

But what you really need is a comprehensive (major medical) health insurance policy. One day in the hospital can lead to thousands, even tens of thousands, of dollars in charges, so that $100- or $200-per-day policy may pay for just a small portion of a 24-hour hospital day! Daily hospitalization policies don't cover the big-ticket expenses. If you lack a comprehensive health insurance policy, make sure you get one as discussed in Chapter 14.

Cell-phone insurance

I understand that if you just shelled out $800 or more for the latest smartphone, you'd want to protect against the loss or damage of said device. If you can't afford to replace such a costly cell phone, then I would argue don't spend that much on one in the first place.

But if you insist on costly smartphone purchases, the insurance isn't worth it. My review of recent plans shows that the coverage will cost you $150 to $300 just for the first two years. If you do have a loss, you'll also get whacked with a $100 to $200 deductible!

Little stuff riders

Many policies that are worth buying, such as auto and disability insurance, can have all sorts of riders added on. These riders are extra bells and whistles that insurance agents and companies like to sell because of the high profit margin they provide (for them). On auto insurance policies, for example, you can buy a rider for a few bucks per year that pays you $25 each time your car needs to be towed. Having your vehicle towed isn't going to bankrupt you, so it isn't worth insuring against.

Likewise, small insurance policies that are sold as add-ons to bigger insurance policies are usually unnecessary and overpriced. For example, you can buy some disability insurance policies with a small amount of life insurance added on. If you need life insurance, purchasing a sufficient amount in a separate policy is less costly.

5

Your Information Diet

IN THIS PART . . .

Know which Internet, media, and other resources are worth your attention and which you should ignore.

Hire a competent and ethical financial advisor and other professionals when needed.

Chapter **17**

Using Media Resources

Technology and the Internet have changed the way people tap the vast and increasing amount of financial information and advice. Television, radio, magazines, and newspapers continue to attract plenty of eyeballs and listeners, of course, but those media have had to adapt and will continue to evolve because of the pressures of competition.

When I was a teenager and first took notice of the financial world, I was captivated, and so I observed, read, and learned all that I could about it. It's no surprise, then, that I landed in my current profession! What's amazing to me is how much things have changed and how much they haven't changed over the decades.

What has dramatically changed is where and how you can get financial advice and information. In my youth, you could consult lots of newspapers (especially the *Wall Street Journal*), some financial magazines, *Wall Street Week* on PBS television, and investment newsletters. Today, you can still refer to many of these sources for information (although fewer newspapers are around), and in addition, cable TV has seen a sharp increase in financial coverage on its many channels, and the Internet has tremendous numbers of financial websites and blogs.

What has stayed the same are the time-tested and common-sense principles of sound personal financial management and wise investments. Prognosticators who claim that they have a system for beating the system and the ability to produce fat profits are nothing new, and neither are the charlatans who defraud folks out of their hard-earned money.

The challenge with all this financial information, advice, and predictions is to understand what's worth paying attention to and paying for and what you should ignore and perhaps even run away from! In this chapter, I discuss the various sources of financial information, opinions, and advice and how to separate the best from the rest.

Going Online: The Wild West of Advice and Predictions

What has changed the most in recent years about financial advice and information is the enormous growth of the Internet and all the financial "stuff" that is piling up online. As with any medium, however, you need to remember the "buyer beware" mentality when looking for financial information, opinions, and advice online. You can find lots of "free" stuff online, and therein lies one of the great dangers of the online world. I discuss this danger in this section, as well as how to make the most of what's useful on the Internet.

Eyeing the real cost of "free"

Whenever you read a personal finance article online that you don't have to pay for, ask yourself one simple question: How can the website purveyor afford to hire competent personal finance experts to write articles for the website? The answer for many sites is that they hope to make money from advertising. Their desire to make income from advertisers inevitably causes problems for you, dear reader, because it means that the website owner has to be careful to offer content that first and foremost is attractive for advertisers. As a result, websites may shy away from valid criticisms of various financial products, services, and firms. So what you may consider to be "free" content may actually have a hefty cost to you if it offers faulty advice that causes you future headaches and pain.

WARNING

In the worst cases — and unfortunately, this is becoming increasingly common — companies pay websites to post flattering reviews of their products and services. Print publications generally have a tradition of disclosing when an article is paid advertising (known as an *advertorial*), but in the Wild West online, many sites fail to make this important disclosure. I'm not saying that disclosure makes advertorial content okay — but a failure to disclose makes an already bad situation even worse.

Also beware of online links to recommended product and service providers to do business with. More often than not, the referring website gets paid an affiliate fee, sometimes amounting to upwards of 30 percent of the product price. Look for sites that post policies against receiving such referral fees from companies whose products and services they recommend. (As an example, see the disclosure I use on my site, www.erictyson.com.)

AN INSIDE LOOK AT THE LACK OF JOURNALISTIC STANDARDS ONLINE

One day not long ago, I received an email from "John," who said he was interested in promoting my company through his blog and invited me to call him for more information.

Normally, I would simply hit Delete and get on with my workday. However, when I visited the sender's website, I found the following description:

"Our research department goes to great lengths to discover bloggers who possess creative, informative, and entertaining qualities and to then present these bloggers to you, with their respective links, on the . . . blogger platform. We encourage our readers to click on these links to learn more about the blogger and their writings."

Now, I was a bit curious, so I called "John." After the perfunctory greetings, John proceeded to tell me how much he would love to have some of my columns on his company's website and essentially regurgitated the preceding paragraph. He then told me how many hundreds of dollars I would have to pay them to have my articles published on their website! And, he said, that he'd be willing to publish as many of my articles as I'd like. They don't do that for just anyone, he explained, implying that they usually limit how many of an author's articles they will publish. (I guess my track record and credentials are worth something!)

There is a precedent for this type of "advertorial" publishing in the print world. If you've ever gotten those glossy newsletters "featuring" a small company stock you've never heard of before, more often than not, those are paid ads by the company being promoted. In the print world, there's usually a disclosure for such advertorials, albeit too small for my taste in most cases.

What is shameful, extraordinarily misleading, and unethical is the complete lack of disclosure on this well-trafficked website that the "articles" they are publishing are paid advertorials. Sadly, such corrupted content is all too common online, especially and including the financial space about which I write. Alas, increasing numbers of companies are connecting advertisers looking to promote their products with bloggers wanting to earn money by saying flattering things about the companies paying them.

Being aware online

REMEMBER

If you want to best manage your personal finances and find out more, remember that the old expression "you get what you pay for" contains a grain of truth. Free information on the Internet, especially information provided by companies in the financial-services industry, is largely self-serving.

WARNING

You can run into many pitfalls if you rely only on the web for financial advice or if you trust certain information without being certain of its accuracy. Keep the following warnings in mind:

» **Beware of the short-term focus and addictive nature encouraged by many websites.** Many financial websites provide real-time stock quotes as a hook to a site that's cluttered with advertising. My experience in working with individual investors is that the more short term they think, the worse they generally do. And checking your portfolio during the trading day certainly promotes short-term thinking. Another way that sites create an addictive environment for you to return to multiple times daily is to constantly provide news updates and other rapidly changing content.

» **Beware of tips offered around the electronic water cooler.** As in the real world, chatting with strangers and exchanging ideas is sometimes fine. However, if you don't know the identity and competence of online commenters, why would you follow their financial advice or stock tips? Online postings and comments are rife with day traders spreading exaggerations and lies to boost stock prices by a small amount and profit on a quick sale. Getting ideas from various sources is okay, but always verify the info with reliable sources. Educate yourself and do your homework before making personal financial decisions.

» **Stay away from the financial-planning advice offered by financial-services companies that are out to sell you something you don't really need or that doesn't offer good value.** Such companies can't take the necessary objective, holistic view required to render useful advice.

Using the web for gathering information

If you're looking for quality material written by unbiased experts or writers, finding it on the web may seem like searching for the proverbial needle in the haystack, because much of what's online is biased and uninformed. Although I suggest you refer to proven professionals off-line, you can still use the web in your personal financial research.

The following are some important financial tasks you can use the Internet for when gathering information, along with a short list of websites I recommend:

>> **Planning for retirement:** Good retirement-planning online tools can help you plan for retirement by crunching the numbers for you. They can teach you how, for example, changes in your investment returns, the rate of inflation, or your savings rate can affect when and in what style you can retire. T. Rowe Price's website (www.troweprice.com) has several tools that can help you determine where you stand in terms of reaching a given retirement goal. Vanguard's website (www.vanguard.com) can help with figuring savings goals to reach retirement goals.

>> **Researching and trading investments:** You can choose from among many sites for dealing with your investments. The Securities and Exchange Commission (SEC) allows unlimited, free access to its documents at www.sec.gov. All public corporations, as well as mutual funds, file their reports with the agency. Be aware, however, that navigating this site takes patience. If you do your investing homework, trading securities online can save you money and time. Online brokers such as E*TRADE Financial (800-387-2331; www.etrade.com), Charles Schwab, and TD Ameritrade have set a new, lower-cost standard. The major mutual fund companies, such as Fidelity, T. Rowe Price, and Vanguard, also offer competitive online services.

>> **Buying life insurance:** If loved ones are financially dependent on you, you probably know you need some life insurance. The best way to shop for term life insurance online is through one of the quotation services that I discuss in Chapter 15. At each of these sites, you fill in your date of birth, whether you smoke, how much coverage you'd like, and for how long you'd like to lock in the initial premium. When you're done filling in this information, you're provided with a list of low-cost quotes from highly rated insurance companies.

WARNING

Some of the best websites allow you to more efficiently access information that may help you make important investing decisions. However, this doesn't mean your computer allows you to compete at the same level as professional money managers. No, the playing field isn't level. The best pros in money management work at their craft full time and have far more expertise, contacts, and experience than the rest of us. Some nonprofessionals have been fooled into believing that investing online makes them better investors. My experience has been that people who spend time online every day dealing with investments tend to react more to short-term events and have a harder time keeping the bigger picture and their long-term goals and needs in focus.

KEEPING AN EYE OPEN FOR THE AGENDA OF EXPENSE-TRACKING SITES AND APPS

Plenty of folks have trouble saving money and reducing their spending. Thus, it's no surprise that in the increasingly crowded universe of free websites and apps, plenty of sites and apps are devoted to supposedly helping you reduce your spending. These include Mint, Mvelopes, Wally, and Yodlee.

I've reviewed these sites and have mixed-to-negative feelings about them. The biggest problem I have with them is that they're loaded with advertising and/or have affiliate relationships with companies (meaning that the site gets paid if you click on a link to one of its recommended service providers and buy what the provider is selling).

This arrangement, of course, creates an enormous conflict of interest and thoroughly taints any recommendation made by these sites that profit from affiliate referrals. For starters, they have no incentive or reason to recommend companies that don't pay them an affiliate fee. And there's little, if any, screening of companies for quality service levels that are important to you as a consumer.

Also, be forewarned that after registering as a site user, the first thing most of these sites want you to do is connect directly to your financial institutions (banks, brokerages, investment companies, and so on) and download your investment account and spending data. Yes, you should have security concerns, but those pale in comparison to privacy concerns and concerns about the endless pitching to you of products and services.

Another problem I have with these websites is the incredibly simplistic calculators they use. One site that purports to help with retirement planning doesn't allow users to choose a retirement age younger than 62 and has no provisions for part-time work. When this site asks about your assets, it makes no distinction between equity in your home and financial assets (stocks, bonds, mutual funds, and so on).

Getting Financial Perspectives and Advice from the Media

I'm well acquainted with the media. I used to write a regular financial advice column for the Sunday *San Francisco Chronicle* and wrote a syndicated newspaper column and write regularly for my own website (www.erictyson.com). I've done thousands of interviews in various mediums, including radio, television, podcasts, websites and blogs, and print (magazines, newspapers, and many websites). So I've gotten an inside perspective that spans many years. In the following sections, I share what I have observed in my experiences.

Being a smart news consumer

As with any profession, I've seen a range of expertise among the media people I've worked with. Here are some important things for you to keep in mind as a consumer of the media's personal finance coverage and coverage in general:

>> **Remember that most reporters have little — and in some cases no — expertise regarding personal finance.** The best reporters are careful to write only about topics they have sufficient knowledge to tackle or topics for which they're willing and able to interview plenty of experts. Numerous personal finance articles and media pieces have errors and poorly reasoned premises, so beware and be educated in order to separate the best from the rest.

>> **Be aware that the quest for ratings leads to hype.** Most news producers, in their quest for ratings and advertising dollars, try to be alarming to keep you tuned in and coming back for their "breaking news" updates. The more you watch, the more unnerved you get over short-term — especially negative — events. This can cause paralysis and unnecessary trading.

>> **Reduce your exposure to advertising and the messages to spend, spend, and spend.** Coverage of movie stars and other celebrities implicitly and explicitly conveys that your worth as a person is related to your physical appearance (including the quality of clothing and jewelry you wear) and your material possessions — cars, homes, electronics, and other gadgets. Please don't buy into that false message.

>> **Beware the catering to short attention spans.** Producers and network executives believe that if their content goes into too much detail, viewers and listeners will change the channel or turn the page. Many articles include more graphics and pictures than words to keep the reader's interest. Incomplete analysis can cause you to make poorly informed decisions.

>> **Ignore the endless pundits who are interviewed for their predictions about the stock market, interest rates, and anything else that moves in the financial markets.** Prognosticating pundits keep many people tuned in because their advice is constantly changing (and is therefore entertaining and anxiety producing), and they lead investors to believe that investments can be maneuvered in advance to outfox future financial market moves.

REMEMBER

If someone really were good at knowing what was going to happen next, they'd be working full-time at investing money and certainly wouldn't be telling others for free what they expect to happen!

Separating the best from the rest

So should you ignore and shun all the media's personal finance coverage? Of course not — you simply need to distinguish between good and not-so-good financial information and advice. Here's how:

>> **Pay attention to reporters' names and their strengths and weaknesses as you read articles.** As you read a given publication over time, you should begin to make note of the different writers. Get to know who the better writers are so you can spend your limited free time reading the best.

>> **Review older articles and shows.** Although doing so may seem silly and pointless, it can actually be enlightening. By reviewing a number of past issues or shows in one sitting, you can begin to get a flavor for a publication's style, priorities, and philosophies (and you can also see how its past predictions turned out).

>> **Look for solid information and perspective.** Headlines reveal a lot about how a columnist and publication perceive their roles. Sensationalist stories such as "The Next Meltdown Is Coming in 2018" and "These 13 'Tipping Points' Have Us on the Edge of a Depression" are playing into people's fears. Look for articles that seek to educate rather than make short-term predictions and create anxiety.

>> **Keep your big-picture issues in mind.** Have you gotten your overall personal financial plan set? That's an important consideration when contemplating any specific financial advice you may hear or read.

>> **Read the best books for a crash course on a given financial topic.** Good books can go into depth on a topic in a way that simply isn't possible with other resources. Quality books also aren't cluttered with advertising and the conflicts inherent therein. (The worst ones are nothing more than infomercials to send you overpriced seminars, audiotapes, and so on.) For an updated list of my favorites, see my website at www.erictyson.com.

Trusting unnamed "sources" is a bad idea

Over the decades, increasing numbers of articles ("journalism") are being published, especially online, with information and comments from the infamous unnamed sources. This approach is now widely used and can affect the quality of reporting that takes place. A blog named the "Anonymous Source Tracker" on the (now-defunct) website Ink-Stained Wretch made a valiant effort to count the instances of anonymous source usage in the media.

With "breaking news," I see much more use of unnamed sources being cited. Unfortunately, this seems to correlate with a greater incidence of inaccurate information. In the rush to be first or quick with breaking news (especially with all the added pressure from online "news"), journalists and the organizations that they write for are less likely (and frankly able) to fact-check and independently verify what an unnamed source is telling them.

So, why do sources want to remain anonymous? There can be a number of different reasons, including, for example:

>> The source is violating his organization's confidentiality policies and would get fired for divulging said information with his name attached to it as the source.

>> The source wants to harm or damage the reputation of a person she considers an enemy or competitor.

>> The source desires to get attention from fawning media people and wants to feel important and at the center of something exciting.

>> The source fears retribution from a person made to look bad by release of the information.

Now, if you stop and think about each of the preceding scenarios, the first three of the four that I listed don't reflect particularly well on the anonymous source. The last listed reason is the most reasonable of the four, although some may say that you should have the backbone to attach your name to specific criticism rather than doing so anonymously.

Out of curiosity, I checked with the Society of Professional Journalists (SPJ) to see what they say about the use of anonymous sources. Interestingly, the SPJ Code of Ethics contains two specific statements on the subject, which strongly suggest that the American news media overuses anonymous sources. Here's a summary of their advice:

>> Identify sources whenever appropriate. The public expects journalists to be credible, and that expectation is built on the reliability of sources that journalists use. The use of unnamed sources should be minimized. If an unnamed source must be used, the journalist should identify the source as clearly as possible without providing information that would allow the source to be identified.

>> Question a source's motives before agreeing to his request for anonymity. Some sources provide information only when it benefits them. When a journalist receives a request from a source to remain anonymous, the reporter should analyze the reasons for the request, which may include

pushing a personal agenda, advancing a position ahead of a competitor's or a rival's, or attacking an opponent. If the journalist determines that the source has a good reason to be granted anonymity, the journalist should clarify the conditions of anonymity in exchange for the information the reporter is seeking.

My own approach to citing sources largely follows these two major points the SPJ makes. That's why I almost never use unnamed sources in my writing. Sometimes, folks at particular companies are willing to talk to me for background purposes only, and I'm happy to listen to them so long as my research suggests they are trustworthy and credible. However, I always seek to independently verify what an anonymous source tells me.

Be careful reading and accepting journalism that is littered with anonymously sourced comments and content. More often than not, it suggests lazy and rushed journalists and contains errors that the reporter didn't discover due to insufficient fact checking.

Understanding that political partisans are hazardous to your wealth

All networks, publications, and journalists have their biases. I don't have a problem with opinion shows that are clearly labeled as such. The public clearly has an appetite for some of them — how else can you explain the success of MSNBC, CNN, and FOX opinion shows? It's well known and documented that most MSNBC and CNN commentators tilt left politically while FOX shows tilt right. I'm not suggesting that you or anyone else should watch or like such programs.

Now, you may ask what all of this has to do with managing your money.

Political partisans distort the news rather than report the news, and they prevent you from better understanding what's really going on so you can make informed decisions. For example, during the 2008 financial crisis, Keith Olbermann and his liberal partisan pals at MSNBC seemed to take delight in blasting President Bush for the nation's economic problems. In short, they hyped the bad news during 2008 and accused Bush of causing a Depression. I know some liberal folks who panicked and dumped their stocks late in 2008 because they became convinced that the unfolding economic calamity made sense given the supposedly failed policies of President Bush.

Political partisans on the right, such as Glenn Beck and Ann Coulter, can cause bad decision making as well. Both Beck and Coulter continually attacked President Obama and his policies and suggested that the United States was headed for ruin and bankruptcy under his watch. Stock prices rebounded sharply during his presidency, and the economy steadily grew, albeit slowly, during those years.

Stock prices plummeted in March 2020 with the unfolding Covid-19 pandemic and government mandated business closures which led to millions of layoffs. Consuming the daily news during this period was certainly an unsettling experience for most people and included plenty of political sniping and blaming. Those who let their emotions get the best of them and who panicked and sold their stock holdings during or after the steep price decline missed out on one of the best all-time rallies.

REMEMBER

Political partisans overstate the impact that the president and others can have over our economy and financial markets. The financial crisis of 2008 was caused by a multitude of factors and frankly was a bipartisan effort. Blaming it on one party or one politician is absurd. Remember that political partisans distort the news rather than report the news and prevent you from better understanding what's really going on so you can make informed financial decisions. Focus on your goals and working toward them and seek to remain emotionally detached from the political noise around you.

Chapter **18**

Professionals You Hire

O ne of the benefits of living in a country with a relatively high standard of living is that many service providers are available for hire. Professionals can help with an array of services, but at a cost, and they aren't for everyone. When you're young and have a limited income, you probably can't afford to hire a fleet of financial, tax, legal, and other advisors.

Or perhaps you choose not to hire an army of professional advisors because you enjoy doing certain tasks yourself or you simply aren't comfortable delegating a task to someone you hire. Doing certain tasks yourself helps you broaden and enrich your hands-on knowledge, which can pay off down the road.

Whether or not you choose to hire particular professionals, having a solid understanding of a professional's role can help you make a wise choice. In this chapter, I discuss making the decision to hire help and the common advisors you may consider hiring. For each of these professionals, I offer tips on finding competent and ethical advice at a reasonable price.

Seeing the Value of Professional Advice

Making the best personal financial decisions requires knowledge, research, and good judgment. Don't expect perfection — you can do just about everything right, but things may not work the way you hoped for reasons beyond your control.

That doesn't mean, however, that you shouldn't bother working to maximize your chances of making the best decisions given a reasonable input of time and energy on your part.

I was pleasantly surprised when I read Steven Scott's book *The Richest Man Who Ever Lived: King Solomon's Secrets to Success, Wealth, and Happiness* (Crown Business). Books with a title such as this give me cause to pause. But, the book had some practical and powerful information.

In discussing how to make wise decisions, Scott cites the timeless wisdom from Solomon's book of Proverbs. Throughout Proverbs, Scott says, Solomon highlights the value of seeking outside counsel:

> *"Where no counsel is, the people fall. But in a multitude of counselors, there is safety."*

Solomon also discussed the value in finding wise counsel and sidestepping the rest:

> *"He that walks with wise men shall become wise. But a companion of fools shall be destroyed."*

Because I write financial advice books and columns, some people erroneously think that I'm a so-called "do-it-yourself" advocate. I am not. People who read my books and columns are seeking wisdom and information, and I do my best to meet their needs and expectations.

REMEMBER

At critical junctures, hiring competent and ethical help pays off. Too often, though, people fail to hire the right expert and fail to do enough homework before making the hiring decision. I'm all for you doing as much as you're able to do for yourself, but I also aim to help you understand the process for identifying and hiring cost-effective, competent, and ethical help when it makes sense for you to do so.

Considering Financial Advisors

I worked for more than a decade as an hourly based financial advisor. During and since that time, I've fielded many questions from readers about their successes and problems working with financial advisors. The main question you have to ask yourself is whether you even want to use a financial advisor. The following sections help you answer that question, locate quality professionals, and figure out what to ask before you hire.

Preparing to hire a financial advisor

I firmly believe that you're your own best financial advisor. However, some people don't want to make financial decisions without getting assistance. Perhaps you're busy or you simply can't stand making money decisions. And if you shy away from numbers, a good planner can help you.

Because I hear from many readers about problems with hiring incompetent and unethical financial advisors, before you hire a financial advisor, you need to understand the following points:

>> **Educate yourself.** You need to know enough about the topic so you can at least tell whether the financial advisor you may hire knows his stuff. For starters, how can you possibly hope to evaluate the expertise of a particular financial advisor if you're not at least modestly educated on the topic yourself? Most personal financial decisions aren't that complex, so the more you know, the more responsibility you can take for making the best decisions for your situation.

>> **Understand how compensation creates conflicts of interest.** When financial consultants/advisors sell products that earn them sales commissions (for example, investments, insurance, and so on), that arrangement can easily bias their recommendations. Financial planners who perform ongoing money management have a conflict of interest as well, because anything that takes away money for them to manage (for example, paying down debt, buying a home or other real estate, and so on) is of less interest to them.

>> **Ask questions before hiring an advisor.** Take referrals as leads to check on. Never take a referral from anyone as gospel. Do your homework before hiring any advisor.

REMEMBER

A quality financial planner doesn't come cheaply, so make sure you want and need to hire an advisor before searching for a competent one. If you have a specific tax or legal matter, you may be better off hiring a good professional who specializes in that specific field rather than hiring a financial planner.

Recognize that you have a lot at stake when you hire a financial advisor. You're placing a lot of trust in his recommendations. The more you know, the better the advisor you end up working with, and the fewer services you need to buy.

Finding good financial advisors

So where and how can you find the best financial advisors? Here are three places to start searching:

>> **The American Institute of Certified Public Accountants Personal Financial Specialists:** The AICPA (888-777-7077; `www.aicpa.org/forthepublic/financial-planning-resources.html`) is a professional association of CPAs. The organization compiles a list of its members who have completed its Personal Financial Specialist (PFS) program, many of whom provide financial advice on a fee basis. Competent CPAs understand the tax consequences of different choices, which are important components of any financial plan. On the other hand, keeping current in two broad fields can be hard for some professionals.

>> **The National Association of Personal Financial Advisors:** The NAPFA (888-333-6659; `www.napfa.org`) consists of fee-only planners. Its members aren't supposed to earn commissions from products they sell or recommend. However, most planners in this association earn their living by providing money-management services and charging a fee that's a percentage of assets under management. Most have minimums, which can put them out of reach for some people.

>> **Personal referrals:** Getting a personal referral from a satisfied customer you trust is one of the best ways to find a good financial planner. Obtaining a referral from an accountant or attorney whose judgment you've tested can help as well. Remember, though, that regardless of who makes the referral, you should do your own investigation. Ask the planner the questions I list in the next section, "Interviewing advisors." Remember that the person who makes the recommendation is (probably) not a financial expert, and the person may simply be returning the favor of business referrals from the financial advisor.

Interviewing advisors

Take your time to interview any prospective advisor you may hire with the following important questions:

>> **What percentage of your income comes from commissions, hourly client fees, and client money-management fees?** If you want objective and specific financial planning recommendations, give preference to advisors who derive their income from hourly fees. Many counselors and advisors call themselves *fee-based,* which usually means that they make their living managing money for a percentage. If you want a money manager, you can

INVESTIGATE

hire the best quite inexpensively through mutual and exchange-traded funds. If you have substantial assets, you can hire an established money manager.

Advisors who provide investment advice and manage at least $100 million must register with the U.S. Securities and Exchange Commission (SEC). Advisors who manage smaller amounts are often required to register at the state level. You can find out whether the advisor is registered and whether he has a track record of problems by calling the SEC at 800-732-0330 or by visiting its website at adviserinfo.sec.gov/. Otherwise, advisors generally must register with the state in which they make their principal place of business. They must file Form ADV, otherwise known as the *Uniform Application for Investment Adviser Registration.* You can ask the advisor to send you a copy of Form ADV, which includes such juicy details as a breakdown of where the advisor's income comes from, the advisor's relationships and affiliations with other companies, the advisor's education and employment history, and the advisor's fee schedule.

>> **What work and educational experience qualify you to be a financial planner?** A planner should have experience in the business or financial services field and should also be good with numbers, speak in plain English, and have good interpersonal skills. Common designations of educational training among professional money managers are MBA (master of business administration) and CFA (chartered financial analyst). Some tax advisors who work on an hourly basis have the PFS (personal financial specialist) credential. The CFP (certified financial planning) degree is common among those focusing their practice on financial planning.

>> **What is your hourly fee?** The rates for financial advisors typically range from about $100 per hour up to several hundred dollars per hour. Focus on the total cost you can expect to pay for the services you're seeking.

>> **In addition to financial advisory services, what other services do you perform (such as tax or legal services)?** Tread carefully with someone who claims to be an expert beyond one area. The tax, legal, and financial fields are each vast in and of themselves, and they're difficult for even the best and brightest advisor to cover simultaneously. An exception is the tax advisor/ preparer who performs basic financial planning by the hour. Likewise, a good financial advisor should have a solid grounding in the basic tax and legal issues that relate to your personal finances. Large firms may have specialists available in different areas.

>> **Do you carry professional liability insurance?** If the advisor doesn't have liability insurance, she has missed one of the fundamental concepts of planning: Insure against risk. After all, you want an advisor who carries protection in case she makes a major mistake for which she's liable.

>> **Can you provide references from clients with needs similar to mine?** Interview others who've used the planner. Ask what the planner did for them, and find out what the advisor's strengths and weaknesses are. You can find out a bit about the planner's track record and style.

>> **Will you provide specific strategies and product recommendations that I can implement if I choose?** This question is crucial because some advisors may indicate that you can hire them by the hour but provide only generic advice. Ideally, find an advisor who lets you choose whether you want to hire her to help implement her recommendations after she presents them. If you know you're going to follow through on the advice and you can do so without further discussions and questions, don't hire the planner to help you implement her recommendations. On the other hand, if you hire the counselor because you lack the time, desire, and/or expertise to manage your financial life, building implementation into the planning work makes good sense.

Taming Your Taxes with Help

Taxes are likely one of your biggest expenses. No one enjoys paying so much in taxes, complying with seemingly endless tax rules and regulations, and completing federal- and state-mandated tax returns. So it should come as no surprise that an army of tax preparers and advisors is standing ready to help you.

Do you need to use a tax professional? Good tax preparers and advisors can save you money by identifying tax-reduction strategies you may overlook. And they may reduce the likelihood of your being audited, which can be triggered by mistakes. Tax advisors can be of greater use to folks whose financial lives have changed significantly (those who are starting a small business, for instance) and to people who are unwilling to learn tax strategies to reduce their tax burden.

Tax advisors and preparers come with varying backgrounds, training, and credentials. Here are the three main types, with some info that can help you determine which one is right for you:

>> **Preparers:** The appeal of *preparers,* who generally are unlicensed, is that they're comparatively less costly than other tax professionals. Preparers make the most sense for folks who have relatively simple financial lives, who are budget-minded, and who dislike doing their own taxes.

>> **Enrolled agents:** A person must pass IRS licensing requirements to be called an *enrolled agent* (EA), which enables the agent to represent you before the IRS. Continuing education is also required; EAs generally go through more

training than preparers. EAs are best for people who have moderately complex returns and don't necessarily need complicated tax-planning advice throughout the year (although some EAs provide this service as well). You can find contact information for EAs in your area by calling the National Association of Enrolled Agents at 202-822-6232 or visiting its website at www.naea.org/.

>> **Certified public accountants:** CPAs go through significant training and examination before receiving the CPA credential. And to maintain the designation, CPAs also must complete continuing education classes annually. Most CPAs charge $100+ per hour. CPAs at larger firms and in high-cost-of-living areas tend to charge more. CPAs make the most sense for the self-employed and/or for folks who file lots of schedules with their tax returns.

Working with Real-Estate Agents

When you buy or sell a property such as a condominium, town home, or single-family home, if you're like most people, you'll likely work with a real-estate agent who's paid on commission. Although the best real-estate agents can help you find a home that meets your needs, the commission arrangement can create conflicts of interest. Because agents get a percentage of your property's sales price, they want you to complete a deal quickly and at the highest price possible. When you're a seller, the agent's incentives can be good, but when you're a buyer, they can be in conflict with what's best for you.

Some buyers' agents say they can better represent your interests as a property buyer and will sign a contract with you to represent you as a buyer's agent. However, agents working as buyers' brokers to represent you still have conflicts of interest in that they get paid only when you buy and earn a commission as a percentage of the purchase price.

TIP

To find a good real-estate agent, begin by interviewing at least three agents. Ask the agents for references from at least three clients they worked with in the past six months in the geographical area in which you're looking. Look for agents with the following traits:

>> **Local market knowledge:** Investigating communities, school systems, neighborhoods, and financing options can be a huge undertaking. Good agents can help you tap into various information sources as well as share their contacts with you.

>> **Full time and experienced:** Ask how many years the agent has been working full time. The best agents work at their profession full time so they can stay on top of everything. Many of the best agents come into the field from other occupations, such as business or teaching. Some sales, marketing, negotiation, and communication skills can certainly be picked up in other fields, but experience in buying and selling real estate does count.

REDFIN AND DISCOUNT REAL-ESTATE BROKERS

For many years, I have watched as numerous real-estate brokers and companies have sought to undercut what are seen to be high residential real-estate-agent commissions. When a real-estate agent lists a house for sale, the commission is typically 6 percent or so of the sales price (the commission percentage tends to be a little lower for high-priced homes). If the house is sold, that agent who listed the house for sale typically gets half of that commission and the other half is paid to the agent who represented the buyer. (Actually, each agent also splits his commission with the brokerage company he works for.)

Of all the discount real-estate agencies that have been launched over the years, Redfin has been the most successful to date but has only captured a small fraction of the housing transactions in the markets in which it has a presence. Redfin launched its services in Seattle in 2006 and has expanded over the years to now operate in dozens of cities around the country.

Redfin's promise was that through the heavy use of technology (online listings and video tours), reduced commissions, and salary-based agents, house sellers would save money using Redfin and buyers could potentially save time and money too. While the firm has a decent overall reputation, the reality of what Redfin now offers shows far more similarities with traditional real-estate agencies.

Redfin commissions are indeed a bit less and their agents, who generally work in a team approach with clients, are paid a salary. But when it comes to selling your house, working with a commission-based agent more potentially aligns your incentive with theirs — the more the house sells for, the more everyone makes.

In terms of using technology and the Internet to help sell houses, traditional real-estate agencies have largely embraced and matched what Redfin does.

>> **Honesty and patience:** A real-estate purchase or sale is typically a large-dollar transaction from the perspective of your overall personal finances. So you need an agent who always answers your questions truthfully and who always goes out of his way to disclose anything that could affect properties you're considering. You also need a patient agent who's willing to allow you the necessary time to get educated and make your best decision.

>> **Negotiation and interpersonal skills:** Putting a deal together involves lots of negotiation. Ask the agent's references how well the agent negotiated for them. Also, your agent needs to represent your interests and get along with other agents, property sellers, inspectors, mortgage lenders, and so on.

>> **High-quality standards:** Sloppy work can lead to big legal or logistical problems down the road. If an agent neglects to recommend thorough and complete inspections, for example, you may be stuck with undiscovered problems after the deal.

Using Online Resources to Find Service Providers

Finding quality, affordable professional service providers can be a challenge — as can finding the myriad other service providers you may seek, such as an auto repair shop or a plumber. All of us have the battle scars from the school of hard knocks and making bad hiring decisions.

Getting referrals from folks you know often doesn't pan out — and for good reason. Just because your friend or neighbor has had good experiences with a given contractor doesn't mean you will or that you value the same things in a provider.

INVESTIGATE

The Internet has long held the promise of being an information source and exchange for consumers interested in hearing the straight scoop about service providers. Various websites and search providers provide consumers free reviews on companies, but often this is a case where you may well get less than you paid for. On many such venues, most anyone can complete a simple registration by providing an email address, name, and zip code. Due to the anonymity of the reviews and lack of screening, company owners, employees, and friends can easily post puffed-up reviews while competitors can easily criticize their peers.

TIP

There's actually a useful website that enables you to quickly get a handle on the likely authenticity of reviews posted on a particular product or service. Simply go to www.fakespot.com/ and copy and paste the URL for what you'd like assessed.

After reviewing numerous websites that purport to help consumers separate the best service providers from the rest, the sections that follow highlight those that I've found are doing the best job.

On some ratings sites, companies are solicited to buy enhanced listings, and this disguised advertising may make them more appealing to prospective customers.

Angi

Angi (formerly Angie's List) provides to registered users access to data and customer feedback on a wide range of service providers in their local market area. The service, which began operations in 1995, uses proprietary technology to process reports, and every report gets read by an Angi's employee before it gets posted. Reports praising your own business or dissing a competitor's are ferreted out and removed. As happens on eBay, customers and businesses can respond to one another. When Angi receives a report on an unregistered company, that company is allowed to register for free. By registering, the company can then respond by posting to each customer's report. Consumers may not report anonymously, but their identity is only disclosed to the companies they rate. Angi also offers conflict resolution when a customer and company are at odds over their interaction.

Angi says that they have a "zero-tolerance policy" about companies hassling a customer over the posting of negative comments. The report is posted live for all members to see, which obviously offers an incentive for the service company to resolve the issue quickly. If the service company resolves the complaint to the customer's satisfaction, the dispute is considered "resolved" and the negative report is removed from the service company's record. That's the leverage Angi uses to get complaints resolved. The member can then choose to file a new report, but if they do, they must grade the company at a B or above. However, the member is not obligated to file another report.

Angi has not totally forsaken ads. The company offers coupons from highly rated service companies. Companies pay to run coupons and must have an A or B rating. Like a school report card, grades range from A (best) to F (worst). If a company has any unresolved complaints, it can't advertise, regardless of its overall grade.

HomeAdvisor

HomeAdvisor, another large online provider of service-company referrals, is the best firm I reviewed that doesn't rely on member subscriptions. With HomeAdvisor, which is now part of Angi, you register for free and provide personal information, including your home address and details of what you're looking for, and several companies, which have paid HomeAdvisor an annual membership (advertising) fee, will contact you offering their services. HomeAdvisor argues that such fees weed out people who may be operating as a sideline or on a short-term basis and lead to higher-quality, committed contractors being listed on their site.

HomeAdvisor, which is focused on home improvement, repair, and maintenance firms, also has a ratings and review feature where customers can rate the company. To prevent bogus reviews, HomeAdvisor only allows consumers who have found contractors through their service to rate and evaluate those contractors.

Here's how their service works: Suppose you're seeking a contractor to build you a wooden deck. After completing background information on the HomeAdvisor site about your planned project, your information would be sent to three contractors in your area who would contact you, arrange a meeting to discuss your project, and give you a proposal (with some contractors, you can actually schedule these appointments through the HomeAdvisor site).

HomeAdvisor screens all contractors, who must meet numerous criteria including being properly licensed within their state, carrying general liability insurance coverage, and passing a criminal and financial background check (which uncovers negatives such as liens, bankruptcies, and judgments), among other items.

Other resources

Another resource worth checking out is Consumers Checkbook (www.checkbook. org), which compiles service-provider data in the following metro areas: Boston, Chicago, Delaware Valley (Philadelphia area), Puget Sound (Seattle area), San Francisco/Oakland/San Jose, Twin Cities, and Washington, D.C. Checkbook is a nonprofit founded in 1974. Like *Consumer Reports,* it doesn't accept any advertising or money from companies it reviews.

TIP

Another option for checking out service providers is to access the Better Business Bureau (BBB) website in your area, which you can locate through their national website (www.bbb.org). BBB information, which is available without a fee to you, the consumer, may tell you if the company you're considering has any recent black marks but will hardly give you a thorough review of many customers' experiences like those you will find on sites like HomeAdvisor or Angi. BBBs are nonprofits that collect fees from member companies. Thus, they have similar conflicts of interest that Angi and HomeAdvisor have in being "pro" business.

6

The Part of Tens

Get the most from your car without breaking the bank.

Appreciate the people and moments in life that are worth so much more than money.

Make the most of financial apps and sidestep their problems.

Chapter **19**

Ten Ways to Save on a Car

I remember my first car and appreciate the flexibility and joy that having that car provided me. My first car was a generously sized Ford LTD that was effectively a hand-me-down. No longer able to drive, my elderly grandfather had given the car to my parents. After a couple years of additional use, my folks then passed the car along to me when I got my first job and was working in Boston. I didn't have much free time or need to use the car during the workweek, but I was grateful to have it for weekend trips.

In some respects, it was an ideal first car because it was solid and reliable but not overly valuable. It probably didn't get great gas mileage, but I appreciated its safety when a car (a compact) rear-ended my car and barely left a scratch (although the front end of the bad driver's car was totaled).

In this chapter, I highlight some tips and strategies for making the most of your car-driving experiences and doing so in a financially prudent fashion. For more information on other transportation options to help you save money, check out Chapter 5.

Don't Buy a Car in the First Place

My first experience owning a car taught me an important lesson: Car ownership is costly. As a result, I suggest that if you don't need a car, don't buy one — particularly if you live in a city with reliable public transportation or you rarely need a car. Use the subway or bus and save your money. As with renting a home or apartment instead of buying and owning one, sometimes in your life you may be able to do without your own car, and other times you'll feel that having a car is 100 percent necessary. Enjoy the times when you can do without a car because you may save a good deal of money and hassle.

Owning a car requires numerous expenses. In addition to insurance and gas, in my experience with my first car, I faced a seemingly never-ending list of maintenance and repairs, and that list only grew worse the longer I had the car. And having a car in a big city can be a hassle — I had to pay parking tickets from parking my car on the Boston streets and had to deal with not always being available to move the car on designated street-sweeping days. Add the expense of having to pay out of pocket for damages likely caused by a city snowplow that didn't own up to the accident.

When I moved from Boston and over the subsequent decade, many years I chose not to own a car. I was able to do this because I lived either in a city with decent public transit options or in the suburbs close to everything I needed and could manage well with a bike (in a nice year-round climate!). During those years when I didn't have a car, I would rent one on occasion, and that worked out well and was far more economical than owning my own car.

Pay Cash: Shun Leasing and Borrowing

When you do decide to get your own car, do your best to save in advance and pay for the car with your cash savings. For many folks starting out, doing so means setting their sights on a quality used car.

If your parents got you a car, I insist that you stop reading right now and thank them (even if you've done so before) for their generosity and kindness! Texting is fine, but even better is calling to tell them you were thinking of them and wanted to express your gratitude. I'm sure you'll score some bonus points by mentioning that you're reading this book!

Taking out a loan to buy a car or leasing a car are generally much-more-expensive ways to get a car because of the interest you pay (in the case of a loan) or the higher rates (in the case of leasing). Car dealers who are in the business of leasing or originating car loans will, of course, have a different agenda and push these methods because they profit from them. Don't be fooled by zero percent interest loans, either — dealers will sock you with a higher car price to make up for such low-cost financing.

Consider Total Costs

When you compare makes and models of cars, be sure to consider more than the sticker price. Among other cost considerations are fuel, maintenance, repairs, insurance, and how rapidly the car depreciates in value.

TIP

Among the best independent sources that I've found for such information are www.edmunds.com/tco.html and www.motortrend.com/intellichoice.

Compare New with Used

Because a new car depreciates most rapidly in value in the first couple of years, buying a car that's at least a year or two old usually provides you with a better value for your money than buying a new car.

REMEMBER

Don't assume, however, that buying a used car is always a better value. For example, during a severe recession such as the one the United States experienced in 2008–2009, new cars made comparatively better sense than many used cars. The reason for this was a matter of simple economics and supply and demand. More people opted for buying a used car. Fewer folks put theirs on the market, holding off on buying a new one until the economy got better. These two forces squeezed used-car supply and increased used-car prices. At the same time, fewer consumers were buying new cars, forcing dealers to slash new-car prices.

Understand a Car's Real Value Before Negotiating

After you focus in on what make and model of car you want, make sure you do some basic research regarding the pricing of the car type you desire to assist you as you shop around. For new cars, you should know (and can easily find out) what the dealer's cost is for each vehicle. You can find this information at *Consumer Reports* (www.consumerreports.org) as well as the sources I mention in the next paragraph.

TIP

For used cars, a number of sources can assist you with quickly valuing a vehicle based on its condition, features, and mileage. Among the best sources for used-car valuation information are Kelley Blue Book (www.kbb.com) and Edmunds (www.edmunds.com).

Take Care of Your Car

Besides the obvious financial benefit from staying on top of your car's servicing requirements (getting your oil changed regularly, rotating and properly inflating your tires, and so on), you also reap safety benefits as well. That's why you should be proactive about your car's maintenance. (See Chapter 16 for more ideas.)

Of course, not everyone is. I was astonished to see a car with nearly bald tires at the local garage that services my car. I subsequently learned that the woman refused to replace her tires because she "couldn't afford" to do so. (Never mind that she was driving a more costly car than I was!) Clearly, she could afford to do so, but for whatever odd reason (more than likely ignorance about the danger), she wasn't spending her money on new tires. By driving on such old tires, she was causing other problems to her car and, of course, risking a serious accident, which would lead to a large bill and possible injury (or worse) to her and others.

Explore Your Servicing Options

Finding a good auto mechanic — someone who's competent and honest — is no small feat! You're not likely an expert in the various components and operating systems of your car, so you're largely at the mercy of the mechanic telling you that you supposedly need to have something addressed on your car.

The primary advantage of taking your car to an authorized dealer (such as taking your Honda to a Honda dealer) is that the dealer has the proper equipment and technology to test and service your car. The downside to dealers is that they may have higher prices and may push doing packages of significant work at major mileage milestones (for example, 30,000 miles, 60,000 miles, and so on), at least some of which may not need to be done.

Numerous local garages can do the work, and the primary advantage with those can be convenience (choosing one near your home or office) and possibly lower rates. However, an unscrupulous mechanic may push doing work that doesn't need to be done, and you also need to be on the lookout for competence issues, as an independent mechanic may not be able to service the full range of problems on your car's make and model. Auto parts stores, such as Advance Auto Parts, AutoZone, O'Reilly, and Pep Boys, offer free diagnosis when your car struggles to start. They can read the codes on your check engine light, test your battery's voltage, check your alternator and starter, and help you install new wiper blades. They may also be able to recommend trustworthy mechanics in the area.

Drive Safely

Driving faster than 60 miles per hour (70 mph for some car models), accelerating too fast, and having to jam on the brakes wastes gas and adds to the wear and tear on your car over time (and therefore is costly). And what about the people traveling with you? Driving is probably the most dangerous thing you do on a regular basis, so it's not just about your money but also the health and safety of you, your friends, and your family who take trips in your car. See Chapter 16 for details on safe driving and safe cars.

Take a Lean and Mean Insurance Policy

Most states mandate minimum levels of auto insurance. In my experience as a financial counselor reviewing folks' insurance policies, including their auto insurance, people often have the wrong types of coverage — missing things they really need while wasting money on other things they don't need. Be sure to review my auto insurance recommendations in Chapter 16.

Track Tax-Deductible Auto Expenses

You may be able to deduct certain auto expenses related to the use of your car for your job, especially if you're self-employed. Be aware, however, that your expenses for commuting in your car between your home and office aren't deductible.

You can deduct your out-of-pocket expenses (such as gas and oil) that are directly related to the use of your car in charitable work. You can't deduct anything like general repair or maintenance expenses, tires, insurance, depreciation, and so on. If you don't want to track and deduct your actual expenses, the IRS allows you to use a standard rate per mile to figure your contribution.

You can deduct actual expenses for parking fees and tolls. If you must travel away from home to perform a real and substantial service, such as attending a convention for a qualified charitable organization, you can claim a deduction for your unreimbursed travel and transportation expenses, including meals and lodging. Such deductions are only allowed if your travel involves no significant amount of personal pleasure.

Chapter **20**

Ten Things to Value More than Your Money

Throughout this book, I provide information and advice that can help you make the most of your money. Whether you've stuck with me since Chapter 1 or simply skimmed a few chapters, you probably know that I take a holistic approach to money decisions.

Although I hope my financial advice serves you well, I also want to be sure that you remember the many things in life that are far more important than the girth of your investment portfolio or the size of your latest paycheck. I hope this chapter of ten things more valuable than money makes a small contribution to keeping you on the best overall path.

Investing in Your Health

People neglect their health for different reasons. In some cases, as with money management, people simply don't know the keys to good personal health. Getting too caught up in one's career and working endless hours also often lead to neglect of one's health.

Plenty of people suffer from ongoing conditions that damage their body and make them feel worse than need be. Stress, poor diet, lack of exercise, problematic relationships — all these bad habits can harm your health. You only get one body — take care of it and treat it with the respect it deserves!

Staying active and at a healthy weight

Over the years, I have generally been active, but I got lazier as I got older. Over time, I became less active. And my diet wasn't nearly as good as it could be.

I finally got motivated to eat healthier, be more active, and lose weight. I lost 35 pounds over six months and feel and look much better. I weigh now what I did when I was in my 20s! And, I have more energy.

How did I do it? I did some reading and made the following changes:

>> **Hydrating much more:** I always have a large glass of herbal tea nearby, and I find I eat less when I'm better hydrated. Some claim that certain herbal teas speed up your metabolism; I have no proof of that, but maybe I'm getting that benefit too!

>> **Exercising more:** I did find that using a fitness tracker (see the next section) helped me to be accountable and know how active I really was. I also lift weights regularly, which I had done in the past but do more often now.

>> **Eating healthier:** Over the years, I have done various reading about food and nutrition, a field in which thinking and recommendations continue to evolve. I must confess that I found Dr. Mark Hyman's advice to make a lot of sense, and it has worked for me. By eating foods with plenty of good fats and protein, combined with lots of vegetables and Greek yogurt daily, I eat less and feel full longer.

If you have good habits now as a young adult — good for you — keep up the good work! If you don't, please make it a top priority to modify your habits and take care of your health. You'll be glad that you did!

Using fitness trackers to monitor your activity level

With the proliferation of cell phones, few people, especially younger people, wear a wristwatch anymore. But now, more and more people are wearing something that looks like a watch on their wrist but is in fact a fitness tracker first and a watch second. The simplest ones cost less than $100 and track how much activity (for example, the number of steps) you engage in every day.

More sophisticated trackers that typically cost about $100 to $150 can track your heart rate throughout the day as well as your resting heart rate, track many different kinds of exercise, track your sleeping patterns, and even include a GPS device that may be of use, for example, to runners or bikers who want more precise analysis of their exercise patterns and routes.

When I reviewed a number of the better trackers on the market, I was pleasantly surprised and impressed with what they can do. I didn't fully know how active I was on a daily basis before I tried these trackers, but I did know that, like too many of my middle-age peers, I had gradually put on more weight over time and was finally motivated to do something about it.

I enjoyed using the trackers I tried (FitBit and others) which tracked my steps throughout the day and logged specific activities such as when I went for a walk, played a racquet sport, used my rowing machine, and so on. Their online applications, which you can access through the Internet on a computer or through an app on your cell phone, enable you to edit and enter what each specific activity was if the tracker hasn't already correctly identified it.

Just as monitoring your spending and saving can motivate some folks to spend less and save more, I found that tracking my activity definitely encouraged me to be more active and helped with my desired weight loss.

INVESTIGATE

Before buying a fitness tracker, examine the features on each device you're considering and do your best to determine what you really want and are likely to use over time. It's not worth paying for certain features, like GPS tracking, if you're unlikely to use them. Also, be sure to read customer reviews of the devices you're considering to understand what others like and don't like about them.

Making and Keeping Friends

So many items in this consumer-oriented society are disposable, and unfortunately, friends too often fall into that category. These days, it seems like friends aren't really friends as much as they are acquaintances who can further people's careers, and after that function has passed, they're cast aside.

Ask yourself who your true friends are. Do you have friends you can turn to in a time of need who can really listen and be there for you? Take the time to invest in your friendships, both old and new.

When you're in high school and college, it's relatively easy to meet people and make friends. As a young adult in the "real world" going to work daily, many people find it gets harder to make friends. If you enjoy where you work and meet people at work similar to you, you may not experience this "problem" as much as others. (This is, of course, an obvious downside to more people working remotely.) But the point I'd like to make is that most folks find they have to work a bit harder as a working adult to make and maintain friendships. It takes time and effort. Also, consider getting involved in some activities, including playing sports, which is a great way to hang out with others and get some healthy exercise too!

Appreciating What You Have

In my work as a financial counselor and writer, I've had the opportunity to interact with many people from all walks of life. Rich or poor, invariably people focus on what they don't have instead of appreciating the material and nonmaterial things they do have.

TIP

Make a list of at least ten things that you appreciate. Periodically (weekly or monthly) make another list. This exercise helps you focus on what you have instead of dwelling on what you don't. Appreciate your friends and family and your health.

Minding Your Reputation

One of my professors once said, "It can take a lifetime to build a reputation but only moments to lose it." As people chase after more fame, power, money, and possessions, they often devalue and underinvest in relationships and commit illegal and immoral acts along the way.

Your reputation is one of the most important things you have, so don't do anything to taint it.

Think of the people you most admire in your life. Although I'm sure that none of them is perfect, I bet each has a superior reputation in your eyes.

Continuing Education

Education is a lifelong process — it's not about attending a pricey college and perhaps getting an advanced degree. You always have something to discover, whether it's related to your career or a new hobby.

Look for opportunities to master new lessons each and every day. And who knows, maybe someday you'll gain an understanding of the meaning of life. The older people get, the more they have to reflect upon and benefit from.

Having Fun

In the quest to earn and save more, some people get caught up in society's money game, and money becomes the purpose of their existence. They lose sight of what life is really about. Whether you call it an addiction or an obsession, having such a financial focus steers you from life's good things. I've known plenty of people who realize too late in life that sacrificing personal relationships and one's health isn't worth any amount of financial success.

Therapists' offices are filled with unhappy people who spend too much time and energy chasing elusive career goals and money. These same people come to me for financial counseling and worry about having enough money. When I tell them that they have "enough," the conversation usually turns to the personal things lacking in their life. Remember to keep your perspective and live each day to the fullest.

Putting Your Family First

Some employees rightfully fear that their boss may not be sympathetic to their family's needs, especially when those needs get in the way of getting the job done as efficiently as an impatient boss would like. Others put their company first because that's what peers do and because they don't want to rock the boat.

Your spouse, your parents, and your kids, of course, should come first. They're more important than your next promotion, so treat them that way. Balance is key; your actions speak louder than promises and words. Should your boss not respect or value the importance of family, then perhaps it's time to find a new boss.

Knowing Your Neighbors

Your neighbors can be sources of friendship, happiness, and comfort. I often see people caught up in their routine who neglect their neighbors. You live by these people and probably see them on a semiregular basis. Take the time to get to know them even if they will be nothing more than an acquaintance.

You may not want to get to know all your neighbors better, but give them a chance. Don't write them off because they aren't the same age or race, or don't have the same occupation as you. Part of your coherence with greater society comes from where you live, and your neighbors are an important piece of that connection.

Volunteering and Donating

Although the United States has one of the world's highest per-capita incomes, by other, more important measures, the country has room for improvement. Society has some significant problems, such as a relatively high rate of poverty in certain areas, gun violence, divorce, and suicide.

TIP

You can find plenty of causes worthy of your volunteer time or donations. Check out www.volunteermatch.org to discover volunteer opportunities. If you want to donate something as a thank-you to members of the military, visit the National Military Family Association at www.militaryfamily.org. (Military folks can use this site to find out about a wide range of benefits.)

Caring for Kids

The children in society are tomorrow's future. You should care about children even if you don't have any. Why? Do you care about the quality of society? Do you have any concerns about crime? Do you care about the economy? What about your Social Security and Medicare benefits? All these issues depend to a large extent on the nation's children and what kind of teenagers and adults they someday become.

Investing in your children and other children is absolutely one of the best investments you can make. Understanding how to relate to and care for kids can help make you a better and more fulfilled person. (And I think that understanding kids can help you better understand what makes grown-ups tick, too!)

Chapter **21**

Nearly Ten Things to Know about Apps

At the risk of starting with the very basics, apps are to smartphones what software is to personal computers. As we spend more time on smartphones, more programs — known as apps — are being developed to run on our phones.

Most apps are offered by large companies as another option for their customers to be in touch with and interact with what they offer. The financial institutions that you do business with — banks, mutual fund companies, brokerage firms, and so on — are a common example. For sure, some start-ups focus on apps because they can provide the company with a potentially lower-cost way to get new customers.

In this chapter, I provide advice for how to make the most out of apps and sidestep common app pitfalls and problems, and I highlight the best financial apps that I have reviewed.

You May Well Get What You Paid for with "Free" Apps

Though they haven't gotten the attention that computer viruses, computer malware, and computer ransomware attacks have garnered, similar problems have arisen with smartphone apps. The worst of the lot can end up tracking and spying on you. The worst ones are a scam and/or some sort of virus or malware.

In addition to those issues, you should also check out the background and agenda of any company offering a financial app and how it may be making money from the app. Most apps are nothing more than glorified advertising from the company behind the app. Sure, they may dangle something seemingly helpful (for example, offering a free credit score, stock quotes, and so on), but ultimately you should uncover what their agenda and reputation are. Many free credit score apps, for example, make money from affiliate fees from credit cards they pitch you.

INVESTIGATE

Do your homework and research an app before downloading and beginning to use it. Check with more than one independent source and read independent reviews, especially those that are critical and less than flattering. And stay far far away from the many apps that claim they can show you how to make big bucks doing little from the comfort of your own home.

Conduct and Manage Financial Tasks

You can use apps to do more and more tasks that previously needed to be done online and through a regular computer. The dizzying pace of technological change continues as many smartphones function as mini-computers in your hand.

The best apps can help you perform common financial tasks such as

>> Getting better value when shopping for a specific product or service

>> Tracking where you're spending money weekly and monthly

>> Checking your banking account balance

>> Doing basic investment research

Although some apps are provided free of charge by companies that are seeking to promote their own services, others charge modest fees (like a software company does) because the app is all they are selling.

Use Apps Only from Legitimate Companies with Lengthy Track Records

You will notice that most of the apps recommended in this chapter are from companies with noteworthy track records of success. For sure, technology is disrupting and changing many industries and companies. But that doesn't mean that you should only do business with new firms that exist solely online, in the cloud, and so on.

TIP

Research the history of companies that you are considering doing business with. When seeking the link for a mobile app, get that link and download the app from the company's website so you're sure you are getting their actual app rather than a knock-off or a fraudulent one.

Consider the Alternatives to an App

Before downloading and using an app, you should question the need for it and consider the alternatives. Remember that the company behind the app wants to tie you to it so you'll buy more and spend more with them. Is that your goal?

You likely have your phone with you all the time. Do you really want this app running, sending you notifications and in your face all the time? Maybe, maybe not — think about it and examine the alternatives. One of my colleague tells me the following: "I learned this the hard way. A Google representative came to campus and shared AppAdvice and encouraged us to try out free apps. I did and found myself paying extra for storage for apps I didn't need."

Keep Focused on Your Spending

Some folks need and want extra help and hand-holding when it comes to licking the problem of overspending or simply feeling on top of where their money goes and doing something constructive about it. As I detail in Chapter 17, many websites and related apps purport to address this problem but in reality have massive conflicts of interest through the kickbacks (affiliate relationships) they have with companies that they direct business to. Advertising is also a common problem.

There are some apps that to date have overcome these problems, but things can change, so don't take my current recommendation in this space as a forever endorsement. That said, I like the Goodbudget app for its simplicity and practicality. The basic version provides you with up to one year of expense-tracking history in ten main categories (envelopes). There is also a paid or premium version ($60 per year), which provides up to seven years of expense tracking with unlimited categories as well as email support. I suggest starting with the free version and then deciding in the future whether an upgrade is worth your while.

Also, I'm not a fan of apps that have you store your credit-card information in the app (for example, games, iTunes, and so on) so you can automatically charge purchases. For some folks, this can quickly lead to overspending.

Settle up with Friends But Beware Fees

Going out with friends or doing other activities often involves spending money. So long as you can afford these outings and you're hitting your savings targets and goals, great! Regardless, though, make sure everyone is paying her share. Sometimes you may have to cover for someone who is low on cash or left his wallet at home. Other times, one of your friends can help you out. Apps like Venmo, Square Cash, Gmail/Google Wallet, and PayPal can help you get paid and allow you to pay others to whom you may owe money.

Pay close attention to possible fees, especially when using a credit card. Venmo, for example, hits you with a 3 percent fee on credit-card transactions but doesn't charge a fee for other transactions, including usage of debit cards. PayPal has no fees on direct money transfers but does charge 2.9 percent plus $0.30 for debit and credit-card transactions.

Save Money on Commonly Purchased Items

Some apps are simply designed to save you money. GasBuddy, for example, will show you the price for gasoline at various service stations in a local area (see Figure 21-1). It's free for consumers to use.

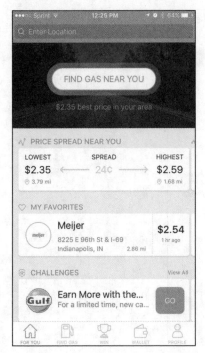

Source: GasBuddy

FIGURE 21-1:
GasBuddy can
help you save
money on gas.

Especially when going on lengthy car trips, car tolls can add up quickly. Tollsmart Toll Calculator is a low-cost app that enables you to compare toll costs for alternative routes. The Waze app can help with navigating traffic.

ShopSavvy enables you to shop across online and in-store retailers for specific products you enter or for which you scan a barcode.

Tap into the Latest Economic and Financial Data

The St. Louis Fed's signature economic database — FRED, which stands for Federal Reserve Economic Database — is accessible through an app (see Figure 21-2). Here's a rare case where you can have a wealth of data on the economy and financial markets at your fingertips and never be bombarded with ads or plugs to buy things.

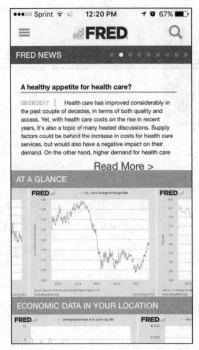

Source: FRED

FIGURE 21-2:
The FRED app puts financial data at your fingertips.

Invest with Confidence

Of course, many banks, investment companies, brokers, and so on have apps. So if you have a favorite investment firm or bank, check out what it offers. For its broad array of cost-effective funds with solid long-term performance, I use Vanguard's app.

REMEMBER

Just because you have an app that gives you 24/7 access to your accounts and financial market data doesn't mean you should obsessively follow these things. Doing so will likely make you a worse investor.

Index

A

accessories, minimizing to cut costs, 76

accounts. *See* bank accounts; retirement accounts

acquisition debt, 111

activity level, monitoring, 282–283

addictions
  financial websites as encouraging, 252
  kicking to reduce healthcare costs, 82
  spending, 50

adjustable-rate mortgages (ARMs), 109–110, 111

adjusted gross income (AGI), 87

advertising
  on Angi, 270
  on online financial sites, 250
  reducing exposure to, 255

advertorials, 250, 251

advisors, financial
  finding good, 264
  interviewing, 264–266
  overview, 17, 262
  preparing to hire, 263

affiliate fees/links, 79, 251, 254

Affordable Care Act (Obamacare), 211, 213–215, 218–219

affordable home, purchasing, 71

agents
  disability insurance, 227
  health insurance, 217, 218, 220
  real-estate, 108, 204, 267–269

AGI (adjusted gross income), 87

alternative medicine, 82

American Institute of Certified Public Accountants (AICPA), 264

American Opportunity (AO) credit, 38, 94

amortization, negative, 110–111

amount owed, role in credit score, 54

Angi, 270

AnnualCreditReport.com, 56–57

anonymous source usage in media, 256–258

applications, rental, 99–100

appraisers, 204

appreciation
  potential for in real estate investments, 198
  for what you have, 284

apprenticeships, 135

apps
  expense-tracking, 254, 289–290
  financial, tips regarding, 287–292

ARMs (adjustable-rate mortgages), 109–110, 111

asset allocation, 162, 179–180, 182, 183–185

asset management accounts, 43, 175

assets
  defined, 8
  in net worth, 8–9
  protected by bankruptcy, 47–48

ATM networks, 170–171

attitudes toward money, exploring, 122–123

auto insurance
  collision and comprehensive, 241
  getting best value, 242
  liability protection, 240–241
  overview, 238, 240
  riders to bypass, 241–242
  saving money on, 279

auto ownership
  buying new versus used, 277
  cheaper options, 75
  considering insurance costs before, 242
  maintenance, 278
  overview, 275
  paying cash for, 276–277
  real value, understanding, 277–278

employers
  benefit plans through, 82, 119
  disability insurance through, 225
  group health plans offered through, 214, 215, 221
  retirement plans through, 183–185
employment
  career counseling, deductible costs related to, 39
  changing, 141–142
  entrepreneurial options, 138–141
  getting career started, 131–132
  investing in career, 138
  overview, 131
  relation to education and training, 133
  requirements for Medicaid coverage, 215
  second jobs, 139
  seeking value for education dollars, 133–137
  unemployment, 142–144
employment income
  calculating to determine savings rate, 11
  of child, paying for education with, 191
  low, saving despite, 31
  taxable, 83–84
  working around to get mortgage, 112
enrolled agents (EAs), 95, 266–267
entrepreneurial options
  investing in small business, 140–141
  overview, 138
  purchasing small business, 140
  starting small business, 138–140
environment, effect on money beliefs and practices, 124
equity
  and cost of renting versus buying home, 99
  defined, 70
  as investment, 154
  paying for education with, 190, 191
  tapping into, 98
errors
  common in young adulthood, 18–20
  on credit reports, fixing, 14–15, 16, 58–59, 112
escrow charges, 113
estimated tax payments, 90

excess liability insurance, 243
exchange-traded funds (ETFs)
  advantages of, 153
  leveraged and inverse, 158–159
exemptions, elimination of, 86
exercise, maintaining health through, 144, 282
expenses, in living-together contracts, 117. *See also specific expense types*; spending
expense-tracking sites and apps, 254, 289–290
experience
  financial advisor, 265
  real-estate agent, 268
experts
  evaluating, 164–165, 200
  ignoring, 255
extended warranty and repair plans, 244

F

FAFSA (Free Application for Federal Student Aid), 187
family
  financial goals related to, 29
  focusing on, 285
  living with, 70
fashion spending, 76
Federal Deposit Insurance Corporation (FDIC), 172
Federal Emergency Management Agency (FEMA), 237
Federal Reserve Economic Database (FRED) app, 291–292
federal student loans, 36, 37, 40
federal tax breaks for education, 38. *See also* taxes
fee-based financial advisors, 264
fees
  banking, assessing, 173
  credit counseling agency, 47
  for payment app use, 290
FICO scores, 13, 53, 54, 57
Fidelity Investments, 186
finances. *See also* financial checkup; *specific related topics*
  common mistakes, 18–20
  during young adult years, 1–3

total costs
  of car ownership, 277
  of credit card purchases, 50
towing provisions, car insurance, 241–242
town homes, 106
trade schools, 135–136
training, relation to successful career, 133. *See also* education
transaction accounts, 169–170
transportation expenses, 75
Treasury bonds, 180–181
"True Cost to Own" calculator (Edmunds), 240
Trump, Donald, 211
Truth in Savings Disclosure, 173

U

umbrella insurance, 243
unemployment, 142–144, 201
Uniform Application for Investment Adviser Registration (Form ADV), 265
uninsured or underinsured motorist liability, 241
university. *See* education; student loans
unnamed sources, trusting, 256–258
unneeded products, buying, 77
used cars, buying, 277
utility costs, containing, 72

V

vacancy rates, researching, 202
vacation (second) homes, 200
vacation spending, 78
valuation
  car, 277–278
  property, 203–205
Vanguard, 182, 185–186
vehicles. *See* car insurance; car ownership
vocational schools, 135–136
volunteering, 286

W

waiting periods, disability insurance, 226
WalletHub, 58

warranties, 244
websites
  for credit scores, 56–58
  expense-tracking, 254
  for financial information and advice, 250–253
  resources to find financial professionals, 269–271
weight, healthy, 282
Why People Buy Things They Don't Need (Danziger), 77
wills, 119, 120, 232
withdrawal penalties, retirement accounts, 31, 89
work
  career counseling, deductible costs related to, 39
  changing, 141–142
  entrepreneurial options, 138–141
  getting career started, 131–132
  investing in career, 138
  overview, 131
  relation to education and training, 133
  requirements for Medicaid coverage, 215
  second jobs, 139
  seeking value for education dollars, 133–137
  unemployment, 142–144
Workers' compensation, 225
worth, net
  assessing change in to find savings rate, 11–12
  calculating, 10
  defined, 8
  financial assets, 8–9
  financial liabilities, 9–10
  overview, 8

Y

young adult years, finances during. *See also* financial checkup; *specific related topics*
  common mistakes, 18–20
  overview, 1–3

Z

zero-based budgeting, 27
zoning of property, 154, 207

About the Author

Eric Tyson is an internationally acclaimed and bestselling personal finance author and speaker. He has worked with and taught people from all financial situations, so he knows the financial concerns and questions of real folks. Despite having an MBA from the Stanford Graduate School of Business and a BS in economics and biology from Yale University, Eric remains a master of "keeping it simple."

He figured out how to pursue his dream after working as a management consultant to Fortune 500 financial-service firms. Eric took his inside knowledge of the banking, investment, and insurance industries and committed himself to making personal financial management accessible to all.

He is the author of five national bestselling financial books in Wiley's *For Dummies* series, including books on personal finance, investing, mutual funds, home buying (coauthor), and real estate investing (coauthor). His *Personal Finance For Dummies* won the Benjamin Franklin Award for best business book of the year. An accomplished personal finance writer, his syndicated column is read by millions nationally, and he was an award-winning columnist for the *San Francisco Examiner*.

Eric's work has been featured and quoted in hundreds of local and national publications, including *Newsweek*, the *Wall Street Journal*, *Los Angeles Times*, *Chicago Tribune*, *Forbes*, *Kiplinger's Personal Finance*, *Parenting*, *Money*, and *Bottom Line/ Personal*; on NBC's *Today Show*, ABC, CNBC, Fox Business, PBS's *Nightly Business Report*, CNN, and FOX; and on CBS national radio, NPR's *Marketplace Money*, and Bloomberg Radio.

Eric's website is www.erictyson.com.

Author's Acknowledgments

I hold many people accountable for my perverse and maniacal interest in figuring out money matters and the financial-services industry, but most of the blame falls on my loving parents who taught me most of what I know that's been of use in the real world.

Many thanks to all the people who provided insightful comments on this book, especially and including Mary Ann Campbell.

And thanks to all the wonderful people on the front line and behind the scenes at my publisher, Wiley, especially Linda Brandon, Tracy Boggier, and Christy Pingleton.

Publisher's Acknowledgments

Senior Acquisitions Editor: Tracy Boggier
Development Editor: Linda Brandon
Copy Editor: Christine Pingleton
Proofreader: Debbye Butler

Technical Editor: Dr. Mary Ann Campbell, CFP
Production Editor: Mohammed Zafar Ali
Cover Image: ©Drazen_/Getty Images

Leverage the power

Dummies is the global leader in the reference category and one of the most trusted and highly regarded brands in the world. No longer just focused on books, customers now have access to the dummies content they need in the format they want. Together we'll craft a solution that engages your customers, stands out from the competition, and helps you meet your goals.

Advertising & Sponsorships

Connect with an engaged audience on a powerful multimedia site, and position your message alongside expert how-to content. Dummies.com is a one-stop shop for free, online information and know-how curated by a team of experts.

- Targeted ads
- Video
- Email Marketing
- Microsites
- Sweepstakes sponsorship

20 MILLION PAGE VIEWS **EVERY SINGLE MONTH**

15 MILLION UNIQUE VISITORS PER MONTH

43% OF ALL VISITORS ACCESS THE SITE **VIA THEIR MOBILE DEVICES**

700,000 NEWSLETTER SUBSCRIPTIONS TO THE INBOXES OF **300,000** UNIQUE **INDIVIDUALS EVERY WEEK**

# of dummies

Custom Publishing

Reach a global audience in any language by creating a solution that will differentiate you from competitors, amplify your message, and encourage customers to make a buying decision.

- Apps
- Books
- eBooks
- Video
- Audio
- Webinars

Brand Licensing & Content

Leverage the strength of the world's most popular reference brand to reach new audiences and channels of distribution.

For more information, visit dummies.com/biz

PERSONAL ENRICHMENT

Staying Sharp
9781119187790
USA $26.00
CAN $31.99
UK £19.99

Facebook
9781119179030
USA $21.99
CAN $25.99
UK £16.99

Guitar
9781119293354
USA $24.99
CAN $29.99
UK £17.99

Investing
9781119293347
USA $22.99
CAN $27.99
UK £16.99

Beekeeping
9781119310068
USA $22.99
CAN $27.99
UK £16.99

Digital Photography
9781119235606
USA $24.99
CAN $29.99
UK £17.99

Meditation
9781119251163
USA $24.99
CAN $29.99
UK £17.99

Pregnancy
9781119235491
USA $26.99
CAN $31.99
UK £19.99

Samsung Galaxy S7
9781119279952
USA $24.99
CAN $29.99
UK £17.99

iPhone
9781119283133
USA $24.99
CAN $29.99
UK £17.99

Crocheting
9781119287117
USA $24.99
CAN $29.99
UK £16.99

Nutrition
9781119130246
USA $22.99
CAN $27.99
UK £16.99

PROFESSIONAL DEVELOPMENT

Windows 10
9781119311041
USA $24.99
CAN $29.99
UK £17.99

AutoCAD
9781119255796
USA $39.99
CAN $47.99
UK £27.99

Excel 2016
9781119293439
USA $26.99
CAN $31.99
UK £19.99

QuickBooks 2017
9781119281467
USA $26.99
CAN $31.99
UK £19.99

macOS Sierra
9781119280651
USA $29.99
CAN $35.99
UK £21.99

LinkedIn
9781119251132
USA $24.99
CAN $29.99
UK £17.99

Windows 10
9781119310563
USA $34.00
CAN $41.99
UK £24.99

SharePoint 2016
9781119181705
USA $29.99
CAN $35.99
UK £21.99

Fundamental Analysis
9781119263593
USA $26.99
CAN $31.99
UK £19.99

Networking
9781119257769
USA $29.99
CAN $35.99
UK £21.99

Office 2016
9781119293477
USA $26.99
CAN $31.99
UK £19.99

Office 365
9781119265313
USA $24.99
CAN $29.99
UK £17.99

Salesforce.com
9781119239314
USA $29.99
CAN $35.99
UK £21.99

Coding
9781119293323
USA $29.99
CAN $35.99
UK £21.99

dummies.com

dummies
A Wiley Brand

Learning Made Easy

ACADEMIC

9781119293576
USA $19.99
CAN $23.99
UK £15.99

9781119293637
USA $19.99
CAN $23.99
UK £15.99

9781119293491
USA $19.99
CAN $23.99
UK £15.99

9781119293460
USA $19.99
CAN $23.99
UK £15.99

9781119293590
USA $19.99
CAN $23.99
UK £15.99

9781119215844
USA $26.99
CAN $31.99
UK £19.99

9781119293378
USA $22.99
CAN $27.99
UK £16.99

9781119293521
USA $19.99
CAN $23.99
UK £15.99

9781119239178
USA $18.99
CAN $22.99
UK £14.99

9781119263883
USA $26.99
CAN $31.99
UK £19.99

Available Everywhere Books Are Sold

dummies.com

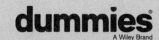

Small books for big imaginations

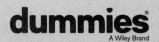